SCOTTISH INDUSTRIAL POLICY

SERIES: 1

Editors: Neil Hood and Stephen Young

MULTINATIONALS IN RETREAT

THE SCOTTISH EXPERIENCE

by Neil Hood and Stephen Young
for the University Press

EDINBURGH

© Neil Hood and
Stephen Young 1982
Edinburgh University Press
22 George Square Edinburgh

Set in Linotron Times Roman
and printed in Great Britain at
The Camelot Press Ltd
Southampton

British Library Cataloguing
in Publication Data

Hood, Neil
Multinationals in Retreat: the Scottish experience
1. International business enterprises
2. Scotland – Economic conditions
I. Title II. Young, Stephen
338.8′8′09411 HD69.17

ISBN 0-85224-428-2

CONTENTS

TABLES AND FIGURES

Tables and Figures

Tables and Figures

PREFACE

This book represents a further stage in the development of the authors' work on multinational enterprises, with the focus in the present study on multinational divestment and the implications of rundown strategies for the Scottish economy and policy makers in Scotland. Most of the present authors' previous work on multinationals in Scotland has been based on fairly large sample studies. This is a different, case-study approach to the subject, an approach which is aided by the concentration of closures and of job losses in a small number of large and often long-established operations in Scotland. There is no doubt that the cases of Singer, Chrysler/Peugeot, NCR, Hoover, Honeywell and Goodyear require to be documented. Some of these cases will and should remain as landmarks in industrial history in Scotland: they should act as a reminder of the longer-term problems that may result from the short-term pursuit of jobs; of the difficulties that can arise from large-scale employment build-ups at particular locations; of the fact that regional incentives cannot override basic economic logic, and that decisions made on political grounds may remain to haunt those involved.

Special thanks are due to Christine Reid of the Business Information Centre at Strathclyde Business School for her continued assistance, suggestions and patience during our preparation of the case studies. We are also grateful to the staff of the Mitchell Library and the Glasgow Herald Library. For help with the Singer case we would like to thank Michael McDermott, a student at Glasgow University, whose undergraduate thesis, 'Singer Clydebank: the Anatomy of Closure', was a source of useful information. Eddie McAvoy, the shop stewards' convener at Hoover Cambuslang provided interesting insights into the activities of the company. Aside from the case studies, the book presents aggregate data on closures and openings of overseas-owned units in Scotland in the recent past and on recent trends in foreign direct investment. Much of this data was supplied by the Scottish Economic Planning Department and our thanks are due to the members of the Department, especially those who may have had their work delayed by our own requests. Finally, we would like to thank our secretaries Margaret Murray, Sandra Cranston and particularly Betty McFarlane for struggling successfully with our writing yet again, even if with the aid of a magnifying glass.

INTRODUCTION

'Analysis suggests that the failure of the Scottish economy to produce growth as rapidly as that of Great Britain as a whole has been due primarily to weak representation within Scotland of these industries that expanded at a rapid pace over the period', Toothill Report, 1961.[1]

Much has happened in the Scottish economy since that conclusion was drawn in 1961. For example, acceleration of direct investment interest by dynamic foreign-owned multinational enterprises in the 1960s, combined with the strongly positive oil effect of the 1970s redressed the balance in a number of sectors. This in turn was reflected by the 1970s in an improvement of the Scottish–UK relative position on a number of indicators including income, employment and industrial structure. Looking back from the early 1980s, the relevance of the Toothill analysis for this book lies in the apparent shortfall on expectations which were associated with foreign direct investment (fdi) in the Scottish economy. An inflow of foreign corporations with a strong commitment to Europe was undoubtedly seen at that time as vital in changing the character of industrial expansion and giving Scotland a stronger representation in high growth sectors. Against a catalogue of recent large-scale closures by many of these same companies, the reality appears somewhat different. Not surprisingly, there is confusion and bewilderment in some quarters as to the merits of the original strategy. Much of the comment is ill-informed and there is a strong case for some considered analysis before reaching wider policy conclusions.

The motive for embarking upon this book was that some fundamental changes were occurring within long established foreign-owned manufacturing companies in Scotland. Given the increased rate of decline in total manufacturing employment since the late 1970s it may seem wholly unsurprising that the affiliates of multinational corporations suffer equal misery. On the other hand, it has been fairly well established that such firms exhibit greater employment robustness than indigenous firms in times of recession and, at best, go solidly against the trend displayed by older, declining industries. In such instances, for Scotland, the witnessing of large numbers of closures among long established multinational enterprise (MNE)

1

plants is a totally new experience and one not readily understood. The aim of this study is, therefore, to find explanations for this process of multinational retreat, and to consider the policy implications. It should be stressed that there are no grounds for regarding these events as indicative either of the unsuitability of the Scottish economy for foreign investment or for concluding that such investment will not play an important part in the economic development of Scotland in the future. At the same time the central thesis is that some processes of significance have been working themselves out in this sector and that their significance should be fully assessed and the policy implications evaluated.

The period of considerable employment reduction within parts of the foreign-owned sector in Scotland has gathered momentum since the mid-1970s. While full details of the many aspects of this are provided later in this chapter, one set of information is necessary at this preliminary stage. Between 1976 and 1981, a number of foreign-owned units closed which at their maximum employment provided nearly 45,000 jobs in Scotland. In order to provide some perspective on the scale of this decline, the job loss is roughly equivalent to all the employment offered in US plants in Scotland in 1960. Put another way, it is comparable to the total employment in shipbuilding and ship repairing (but excluding marine engineering) in Scotland in 1960, the demise of which attracted so much attention in the subsequent decade. Of course, in the MNE case these jobs were not all lost since 1976, since as later tables show much labour shedding had occurred prior to closure.

Estimating the effects of regional policy is a difficult exercise. One respected estimate would place the positive employment effects of regional measures in Scotland at around 66,000 over the period 1960–76.[2] Set against this, the loss of 45,000 jobs (in gross terms) in the MNE sector is substantial. This is especially so when perhaps 75 per cent of these jobs have been lost since the mid-1960s. About half of the jobs created from regional assistance in Scotland have thus been lost through MNE closures. This in no way negates the case for regional policy; it rather strengthens it, given that such decay has existed in what was formerly a very dynamic group of affiliates. The creation of employment related to oil provides a final basis for comparison. Even if the figures referring only to employment in established companies, wholly related to the North Sea oil industry, are considered, the progression in Scotland from around 5,000 jobs in 1973 to just under 50,000 in 1981 is startling and correctly attracts attention. While these oil jobs were building up over this period, Scotland was probably losing half of that employment benefit from the decline of the MNE affiliates under discussion. The only reasonable conclusion to be drawn from these figures is that changes of this order of magnitude require further investigation, hence the intention of this book.

There are obviously many different ways in which to examine an issue such as this. The approach taken here attempts to combine a balanced review of the evidence of the impact of the MNE on the Scottish economy, with an explanation of the processes underlying the retreat of a particular group of multinational companies from their Scottish bases. These then are the themes which dominate chapter 1. A careful examination of this phenomenon suggested the necessity to combine aggregate statistical method with deeper consideration of the individual circumstances of a selection of the major corporate actors in the Scottish scene over recent years. It was for this reason that chapter 2 consists of a study of six cases of multinationals, where the emphasis is placed on establishing the policies pursued in Europe and relating these to the Scottish affiliate. The book concludes with a review of the policy implications in chapter 3.

NOTES AND REFERENCES
1. *Inquiry into the Scottish Economy, 1960–61 (Toothill Report)*, Scottish Council (Development and Industry) (Edinburgh) 1962.
2. J. Marquand, *Measuring the Effects and Costs of Regional Incentives*, Government Economic Service, Working Paper 32, p.49, Table 12 (Moore & Rhodes data) 1980.

1

MULTINATIONALS
AND THE SCOTTISH
ECONOMY

Trends and Characteristics of MNE Investment in Scotland

The Development of Foreign Direct Investment in Scotland. Scotland was an early base for US-owned foreign direct investment – North British Rubber Company (subsequently Uniroyal) in Edinburgh in 1856 and Singer in Glasgow in 1867 being amongst the first US-owned companies in Britain. From that period until 1939 the growth in US units in Scotland was almost negligible. While there are no accurate employment data for either the UK or Scotland before World War II, it is estimated that there were around 9,000 jobs in US plants in the UK in 1939.[1] In terms of relative distribution, Scotland was substantially underrepresented at that time, with only 5 units operating as against an estimated 227 in the UK as a whole. The postwar period saw a significant build-up of US-owned companies in Scotland, although the growth was more gradual than in other parts of the UK until the early 1960s.

Because there are reliable estimates for only a limited number of years, it is difficult to obtain an accurate view of these developments. Table 1 provides a series of estimates for American direct investment since 1945, but these must be treated cautiously in view of the variety of sources and definitions employed. The period 1965–75 was by far the most important as far as new openings by US corporations in Scotland were concerned. As table 1 suggests a very substantial change has occurred in the US employment position since the mid-1970s, but since this is the main theme of the book it will be considered in detail later in the chapter. In essence thus a period of slow growth in US investment was followed by a sharp rise over a ten-year period, only to be superseded by an even more rapid rate of employment decline.

Foreign direct investment in Scotland has been dominated by the US as a source country. At its peak employment in 1975, US-owned manufacturing companies accounted for some 14 per cent of total manufacturing employment in Scotland – with an additional 3 per cent of manufacturing employment being in plants from other foreign sources. There has been a substantial expansion in the number of units owned by Continental European companies during the 1970s. These were estimated to have risen

4

Table 1. Growth of United States* Direct Investment in Manufacturing
Industry in Scotland

	1945	1954	1964	1972	1975	1981
No. of units	6	28	73	n.a.	169	170
Employment						
% of total	n.a.	29,700	52,000	81–85,000	86,366	59,000
manufacturing						
employment	n.a.	4.0	7.2	12.6–13.2	13.6	12.4

*No figures were available on non-us direct investment prior to 1975. But in 1975 there were
108,200 people employed in 280 foreign-owned units; the comparable figure for 1981 was
80,457 people in 288 units.

SOURCES:
1. Data on number of units 1945–64: D.J.C. Forsyth, *US Investment in Scotland*, Praeger
(New York) 1972, p.38.
2. 1954 employment data: J.H. Dunning, *The Role of American Investment in the British
Economy*, PEP Broadsheet 507, PEP (London) 1969, p.85.
3. Data on employment 1964: Scottish Council Research Institute, *US Investment in
Scotland*, Scottish Council (Edinburgh) 1974.
4. 1975 and 1981 data and estimates of employment for 1968 and 1972: Scottish
Manufacturing Establishments Record (SCOMER).

from 30 in 1973 to 73 by 1981, many being established through the
acquisition of indigenous companies.[2] The units formed have on the whole
been very small and total employment in these Continental European
companies has remained stable at around 14,000 (after taking into account
the Talbot closure in May 1981). As at 1981, there were, in addition, 33
Canadian-owned units, belonging, interestingly, to only 13 enterprises. The
two most important Canadian companies were Hiram Walker and Seagrams

Table 2. Overseas-owned Units and Associated Employment by
Country of Ownership (1981)

Country	No. of units	% of units	Employment (000)	% of employment
USA	170	59	59	73
Canada	33	11	6	7
Netherlands	23	8	4	5
Other Europe	50	17	10	13
Other	12	4	2	2
Total	288	100	81	100

SOURCE: SCOMER

Ltd, both with 9 manufacturing units. Finally, it is worth noting that there
were three Japanese firms engaged in manufacturing in Scotland in 1981. In
total, there were 108,200 people employed in 280 foreign-owned units in
1975, a figure which had declined to 80,457 in 288 units by 1981.

Before examining a number of the characteristics of MNE investment in Scotland, it is important to note the Scottish/UK relative position in the ten expansionist years up until 1975. Between 1966 and 1971 Scotland attracted about 20 per cent of the foreign openings in the UK, a figure which rose to over 25 per cent between 1972 and 1975.[3] In this latter period, greatly aided by the impact of oil development, the plants attracted to Scotland accounted for around 50 per cent of the employment achieved in the UK by all incomers from abroad, thus emphasising the relative advantage enjoyed by Scotland in that period. As events have developed this advantage was shortlived, although it may well have served to alleviate an already serious effect post-1975. In any case, it is worth observing that between 1950 and 1975 overseas-owned units contributed just over one-quarter of the 230,000 jobs emerging from all openings in Scotland – a substantial figure by UK standards.

Overseas-Owned Units in Scotland and Other UK Regions. In order to set the foreign ownership position in Scotland into perspective, table 3 presents data on the distribution of overseas-owned manufacturing units in all Assisted Areas and the Southeast of England. At the outset, the definitional differences between the Department of Industry and Scottish Manufacturing Establishments Record (SCOMER) should be noted as accounting for the differences in the numbers of units in this and preceding tables.[4] While Scotland has a considerably higher number of foreign units than other major Assisted Areas of the UK, the overall proportion is close to that which might be anticipated on the basis of shares of manufacturing employment. Where Scotland differs from other Assisted Areas is in the importance of Canada as a source country. There is also some concentration of Dutch-owned units in Scotland, although in general the Scottish share of units of Continental European ownership is low, despite the expansion during the 1970s.

Sectoral Distribution. The sectoral distribution of foreign direct investment is shown in table 4. The concentration in the mechanical, electrical and instrument engineering sectors is very marked, with these three accounting for some 58 per cent of the employment in foreign-owned units. This broad pattern has remained relatively consistent since the early 1960s, although two factors have operated to reduce the degree of concentration. These are the volume of closures in the US-owned mechanical engineering sector and the greater degree of industrial diversity associated with the growth of Continental European ownership. Another important dimension of table 4 relates to the figures for electrical engineering. While always of significance, the employment mix has changed in this sector with the decline or demise of a number of the original heavy electrical engineering companies and the expansion of electronics companies in terms both of units operating and employment. As a result over 50 per cent of employment in the Scottish electronics industry is in foreign-owned companies.

Regional Distribution. Table 5 introduces the regional distribution of foreign-owned units. As is to be expected, these are heavily concentrated in the Central Belt, reflecting the overall distribution of economic activity. The

Table 3. Distribution of Overseas-owned Manufacturing Units by Region and Country of Origin (1979)

Country of origin	U.K.* Total no. of units	S.E. England No.	% of UK	N.W. England No.	% of UK	N. England No.	% of UK	Wales No.	% of UK	Scotland No.	% of UK	N. Ireland No.	% of UK
USA	2,091	741	35.4	247	11.8	109	5.2	114	5.5	210	10.0	45	2.2
Canada	241	73	30.3	24	10.0	22	9.1	8	3.3	46	19.1	2	0.8
North America total	2,332	814	34.9	271	11.6	131	5.6	122	5.2	256	11.0	47	2.0
Denmark	59	21	35.6	13	22.0	3	5.1	1	1.7	3	5.4	—	—
Germany	194	54	27.8	23	11.9	9	4.6	19	9.8	12	6.2	9	4.6
France	118	54	45.7	10	8.5	3	2.5	6	5.1	6	5.1	2	1.7
Netherlands	251	99	39.4	35	13.9	11	4.4	5	2.0	26	10.4	7	2.8
Rep. of Ireland	70	12	17.1	22	31.4	1	1.4	2	2.9	2	2.9	5	7.1
Other EEC	42	16	38.1	14	33.3	4	9.5	—	—	4	9.5	—	—
EEC total	734	256	34.9	117	15.9	31	4.2	33	4.5	53	7.2	23	3.1
Austria	184	52	28.3	25	13.6	10	5.4	17	9.2	14	7.6	4	2.2
Sweden	125	45	36.0	13	10.4	5	4.0	6	4.8	12	9.6	1	0.8
Switzerland	178	60	33.7	21	11.8	6	3.4	5	2.8	17	9.6	1	0.6
Japan	9	1	11.1	1	11.1	1	11.1	4	44.4	1	11.1	—	—
All other countries	89	28	31.5	9	10.1	7	7.9	8	9.0	9	10.1	4	4.5
Rest of world total	585	186	31.8	69	11.8	29	5.0	40	6.8	53	9.1	10	1.7
World total	3,651	1,256	34.4	457	12.5	191	5.2	195	5.3	362	9.9	80	2.2

* Row items will not sum to 100 per cent or to UK total because only Assisted Areas and the Southeast of England are included in the table.

SOURCE: Department of Industry, 1980 (unpublished data).

Table 4. Overseas-owned Units Live in Scotland: Breakdown by Industry (1981)

Industry	Overseas-owned units				Employment in overseas-owned units as % of total industry employment
	Units		Employment		
	No.	% of total	No.	% of total	
Mechanical engineering	57	20	18,381	23	31
Electrical engineering	43	15	18,454	23	43
Instrument engineering	16	6	9,468	12	65
Food, drink, tobacco	46	16	7,923	10	10
Chemicals, coal and petroleum products	26	9	7,913	10	28
Paper, printing and publishing	23	8	4,443	6	12
Other manufacturing	14	5	4,384	5	38
Textiles, leather, clothing	21	7	3,853	5	5
Shipbuilding, vehicles, metal goods not elsewhere specified	23	8	3,309	4	4
Bricks, pottery, glass, timber, furniture	12	4	1,129	1	4
Metal manufacture	7	2	1,200	1	5
Total	288	100	80,457	100	17

SOURCE: SCOMER.

data in table 5 draw attention to some important changes in the share of foreign units which has occurred since the mid-1970s. The decline in employment in foreign-owned units has not been equally shared by the regions, and as the table indicates the volume of job loss borne by Strathclyde has been disproportionately high. In contrast to the sharp decline in both units and employment in that region, several others have experienced either small-scale growth or have maintained employment against the national trend. To some degree the pattern emerging in table 5 reflects the relative distribution of economic prosperity in Scotland since the mid-1970s, and particularly the relative stability of the economies of the West and East of the country.

Size of Overseas-Owned Units. Turning to the question of the size of overseas-owned units, the data in table 6 is of particular relevance to this study. The overseas-owned units are shown to be on average very much larger than the indigenous group. Thus overseas-owned units, which account for 7 per cent of the total number of units in manufacturing industry in Scotland, are responsible for 17 per cent of employment. At the upper end of the size scale, employment in foreign-owned companies has been and is still heavily concentrated in a small number of very large plants employing

Table 5. Regional Distribution of Overseas-owned Units in Scotland (1975 and 1981)

Region	Overseas-owned units				Employment in overseas units			
	1975		1981		% of total manufacturing employment in each region		% of total overseas employment by region	
	No. of units	Employ-ment (000)	No. of units	Employ-ment (000)	1975	1981	1975	1981
Borders	9	1.5	13	2.0	13	16	1	3
Central	10	2.3	11	2.2	7	7	2	3
Dumfries & Galloway	10	1.9	8	1.9	18	18	2	2
Fife	33	6.0	31	5.5	15	15	5	7
Grampian	20	4.5	27	4.5	12	15	4	6
Highlands & Islands	12	4.6	14	4.7	36	36	4	6
Lothian	25	6.9	29	7.1	10	12	6	9
Strathclyde	140	66.7	131	41.7	19	17	62	52
Tayside	21	13.9	24	10.8	30	28	13	13
Total	280	108.2	288	80.5	17 17		100	100

SOURCE: SCOMER.

Table 6. Size of Overseas-owned Units in Scotland (1981)

No. of employees		Overseas-owned		UK-owned		Overseas-owned as % of total
		No.	%	No.	%	
11–24	Units	43	15	1,285	33	3
	Employment	723	1	n.a.	n.a.	3
25–49	Units	49	17	979	25	5
	Employment	1,755	2	n.a.	n.a.	5
50–99	Units	41	14	623	16	6
	Employment	3,007	4	n.a.	n.a.	6
100–199	Units	50	17	418	11	11
	Employment	6,689	8	n.a.	n.a.	10
200+	Units	101	35	385	10	20
	Employment	68,267	85	n.a.	n.a.	22
Total	Units	288	100	3,840	100	7
	Employment	80,457	100	n.a.	n.a.	17
Average size of unit (No. of employees)		326		103		

SOURCE: SCOMER

several thousand people. A number of companies in this category are the focus of attention in the next chapter, since the employment consequences of decline in such units has been highly pertinent in the Scottish case. Even after the closures of a number of these large units, employment in establishments of 200 or more people still account for 85 per cent of jobs in the overseas-owned sector compared with about 60 per cent in the UK-owned sector. As earlier work by the present authors revealed, at least among US firms the growth and performance of the smaller companies was much more satisfactory than that of the larger affiliates in the years up to the mid-1970s.

Age Distribution of Overseas-Owned Units. A general view of the vintage of overseas-owned units is provided by table 7. Around three-quarters of the units operating in 1981 had opened since 1950, and these accounted for 60 per cent of employment. Between 1955 and 1970, the openings within each of the five-year periods averaged around 2,000 jobs per annum. As the table shows, 1970–4 saw a substantial improvement on that figure, only to be followed by a sharp decline in employment generation thereafter. The last period should be regarded cautiously, however, in that while there is evidence to suggest that the new openings are smaller employers of labour than those in the past, at least some expansion has still to come from the recent entrants.

Overall Performance. Before undertaking a more detailed evaluation of the empirical evidence on the behaviour of foreign-owned companies in

Table 7. Overseas-owned Units in Operation in Scotland by Year of Opening (to 1981)

| Period of opening | Overseas-owned units | | | | Employment of live overseas-owned units as % of all live units |
| | Units | | Employment | | |
	No.	% of total	No. (000)	% of total	
Pre-1950	80	27	30.1	38	11
1950–54	8	3	3.9	5	17
1955–59	22	8	10.7	13	36
1960–64	21	7	5.7	7	17
1965–69	46	16	8.9	11	17
1970–74	61	21	15.7	20	32
1975–79	42	15	4.7	6	25
1980 or later	8	3	0.7	1	30
Total	288	100	80.5	100	17

SOURCE: SCOMER.

Scotland and assessing their impact, it is desirable to summarise the limited information on the overall performance of the foreign sector. As regards net output per head, the foreign-owned units have recorded consistently higher figures than the Scottish average (table 8). The higher net output partially reflects industrial structure and age of plants. From the UK perspective, net output per head in overseas-owned units in Scotland is lower than the UK average for foreign-owned units. This may again be a partial reflection of

Table 8. Net Output per Head: Overseas Units in Scotland (£)

	1973	1975	1977
(a) Overseas-owned	4,448	5,775	7,873
(b) All units in Scotland	3,557	4,814	6,908
(c) Ratio of overseas-owned to all units in Scotland	1.25	1.20	1.14

SOURCE: Annual Census of Production.

structure, but probably is more closely related to the role played by Scottish units in the parents' corporate network.

Some more detailed performance data, derived from the 1977 Annual Census of Production, are shown in tables 9 and 10. As the first of these tables indicates, the overseas-owned establishments achieved higher gross value added (GVA) per employee than all Scottish manufacturing establishments. In that year, however, the net capital expenditure per employee was marginally less. But both in terms of GVA and capital expenditure per employee, there is a substantial disparity between overseas-owned establishments in Scotland and in the United Kingdom as a whole. These differences are not readily explained, although industrial structure, ownership mix, technology and corporate policies all play some part. Some further analysis of the industrial pattern of overseas ownership is possible from table 10. Because the whisky industry is such a large part of the overseas-owned food, drink and tobacco sector probably explains the difference in that area. Similarly the Scottish electronics sector compares very favourably with the UK. The overall Scotland/UK relative in both GVA and net capital expenditure per employee is influenced by the 'other manufacturing industry' figures. Structure may therefore play some part in explaining the differences, but as implied much more work is needed to understand these patterns.

A final issue of interest concerns the volume of Government assistance going to foreign firms. The data on offers of Selective Financial Assistance (SFA) to foreign and indigenous companies since 1972 is shown in table 11. The greater average size of offers to foreign firms (nearly three times as great as those to UK-owned companies) arises because of the larger scale of

Table 9. Contribution of Overseas-owned Establishments in Scotland and the UK (1977)

	SCOTLAND			UNITED KINGDOM		
	Overseas–owned establish-ments	All establish-ments	Contribution of overseas–owned establish-ments %	Overseas–owned establish-ments	All establish-ments	Contribution of overseas–owned establish-ments %
Employment (000)						
— Total	102.5	616.9	16.6	1,006.5	7,280.4	13.8
— ATC*	28.5	150.0	19.0	329.3	2,007.1	16.4
Net capital expenditure (£m)	80.4	489.4	16.4	880.4	4,774.7	18.4
Gross value added (£m)	690.3	3,707.3	18.6	8,238.1	43,991.6	18.7
Per employee						
— Net capital expenditure (£)	785.0	793.0	0.99†	875.0	656.0	1.33†
— GVA (£)	6,735.0	6,010.0	1.12†	8,185.0	6,042.0	1.35†

* Administrative, technical and clerical staff
† Ratio of overseas-owned to all establishments
SOURCE: Annual Census of Production

foreign units and consequently of projects. It also reflects degrees of capital intensity and levels of technology, as well as the higher incentive loading in the offers for new inward direct investment projects, where Scotland is in competition with other areas. In this regard, it is worth noting that the annual number of SFA offers to foreign firms has risen very substantially since 1979, in part due to the increased efforts to attract new investment to Scotland and in part due to a change in the guidelines for eligible projects.

The Impact of Foreign Direct Investment on the Scottish Economy: A Review of the Evidence

The intention in this section is to move to the next level of analysis and examine the evidence on the impact of foreign direct investment in Scotland. To do this requires a frame of reference. A search of the now extensive literature on multinationals immediately highlights the difficulty faced in this exercise. The theoretical work on the assessment of gains and losses from foreign investment is largely undeveloped, remains at rather high levels of abstraction and is ambiguous in its predictions.[5] Most of the work in recent years which has been concerned with the assessment of MNE impact has therefore concentrated on the designation of broad areas within which gains and losses might occur, thereafter weighing the evidence in the specific case; this is essentially the approach adopted here, with the impact of foreign direct investment being assessed under four broad headings, resource

Table 10. Net Capital Expenditure and Gross Value Added per Employee, by Industry Group (1977)

	SCOTLAND				UNITED KINGDOM			
	Overseas-owned establishments		All establishments		Overseas-owned establishments		All establishments	
Industry grouping	Net capital expen- diture	Gross value added	Net capital expen- diture	Gross value added	Net capital expen- diture	Gross value added	Net capital expen- diture	Gross value added
					(£ per employee)			
Food, drink and tobacco	2,316	14,785	931	8,273	1,229	9,326	923	7,337
Chemical and allied industries	1,579	10,608	1,811	11,674	2,084	10,394	1,940	10,593
Mechanical engineering	715	6,147	589	5,645	527	6,919	501	6,108
Instrument and electrical engin- eering – of which	572	6,638	475	5,423	562	6,266	437	5,489
Electronics	724	8,190	545	6,248	579	6,870	447	5,745
Textiles, leather and clothing	330	5,144	240	3,872	393	5,101	251	3,789
Other manufacturing industries	581	4,522	986	5,465	804	8,933	652	5,953
Total manufacturing	785	6,735	793	6,010	875	8,185	656	6,042

SOURCE: Annual Census of Production.

Table 11. Offers of Section 7 Assistance in Scotland* (to 31 October 1981)

	Number of offers	Total offer value (£m)	Average offer value (£000)
To UK-owned companies	1,239	136.2	110
To overseas-owned companies	251	101.6	405
Total	1,490	237.8	160
Overseas-owned as % of total	17	43	

* Under the 1972 Industry Act. The data in this Table exclude shipbuilding.
SOURCE: SEPD

transfer effects, trade and balance of payments effects, competitive and anti-competitive effects, and sovereignty and autonomy effects.[6]

Before proceeding to this discussion, a number of important problems should be noted. By whatever framework the benefits and costs of foreign investment in an economy are analysed, one of the central issues is the postulation as to what might have happened in the economy in the absence of that investment. In effect such benefit/cost exercises require a bench-mark, although in an application to foreign direct investment they can scarcely ever be given one. For example, the weighting given to benefits and costs in employment creation in Scotland would differ substantially if it were to be assumed that most of the 85,000 jobs in multinationals in 1981 were supplementary to these which would have been generated in the absence of foreign investment. In reality it is very difficult to determine whether they are supplementary to, or a substitute for, indigenous employment creation – whether generated by Scottish or UK companies. While many of the jobs are in sectors with low indigenous company involvement, it is reasonable to assume that unemployment would not have been tolerated at the levels implied by the complete absence of foreign investment. The measure against which costs and benefits are to be standardised is thus not readily determined in such cases.

A second problem surrounds the time and distance horizon over which benefits and costs are to be considered. For instance, the effects of export-oriented multinationals in Scotland are to be measured far beyond the Scottish or even the British economy. In such circumstances a much more modest cut-off point is essential, in order to confine the consideration of the relevant effects. Many assessments of impact make a valid distinction between the short-run and long-run effects of foreign direct investment. The former might include the balance of payments and employment effects, while the latter relate to issues such as the level and distribution of real income and the impact on the competitiveness of the host economy. In these and other areas, short-run costs can be offset by long-run benefits and vice versa. The third and crucial problem emerges directly from the nature of the variables. The determination of the impact of foreign direct investment involves considering variables that are often both economic and political, neither of which are always readily quantified. Finally, there remains the problem that the potential effects identified below as a framework for analysis are not *a priori* gains or losses, but could be either depending on the project, circumstances surrounding the investment, policy of the investor and so on.

In order to set the scene for the review of the effects of multinationals in Scotland, there are two important contextual considerations concerning foreign direct investment which require brief comment.

Entry Methods and Motivations. When examining these questions, it is immediately necessary in Scotland to distinguish between US and Continental European companies. For US corporations, the establishment of new facilities in greenfield sites has been by far the most common method of entry. This contrasts with the evidence for the UK as a whole where the larger US multinationals have shown a bias towards acquisition entry. So 58 per cent of the US manufacturing facilities set up in the UK between 1951 and 1975 took the form of acquisitions.[7] In the Scottish case, part of the difference in emphasis may be a reflection of the fact that as many as one-third of the US affiliates were owned by parents who had no direct manufacturing overseas before the Scottish plant was set up.[8]

While the available data are not directly comparable, there is evidence to indicate that the later and smaller volume of Continental European investment into Scotland has been based more on acquisition than on greenfield entry. This may be partially accounted for by the changed circumstances of the 1970s, where industrial decline and restructuring has increased the opportunities for low-cost entry through takeovers. Again this risk-minimising strategy appears to have been attractive to a number of small European companies in the early stage of internationalisation. Of course, where entry by acquisition is predominant, the location of the manufacturing facilities may be incidental and thus many of the motivational forces difficult to explore.

Turning more specifically to motivational questions, a distinction by ownership group has again to be employed. There is clear evidence that US parent companies have generally specified an area of market operations for the Scottish plants, and that these have become progressively more oriented towards European markets.[9] The mechanisms of market widening appear to have varied considerably. For example, some American plants in Scotland set up to supply important customers within the domestic (US) market have had their responsibilities widened in the interests of security: while others, by far the largest group, have changed from supplying the UK only (or principally), to supplying all or parts of Europe, often with a designated part of the corporation's product range. While much less is known about the motivation of European investment, some recent evidence has contradicted the view that European affiliates in Scotland are likely to be established in order to supply the UK market rather than act as an export base for Europe or beyond.[10] It would appear that around half of output is exported, with more recent European entrants having a somewhat higher propensity to export. Perhaps equally important, the level of exporting does not seem to depend on whether entry was by acquisition or by a *de novo* subsidiary.

As a backcloth to the subsequent examination of adjustments in the European corporate strategies of US multinationals with Scottish affiliates, it is necessary not only to look at entry but also to consider the progressive establishment of plants throughout Europe. The importance of Scotland as a European 'port of entry' for US investment has already been noted. Two separate studies in recent years have drawn attention to the geographical expansion of US firms with Scottish plants.[11] Both point to the sequence of subsidiary development after Scotland as being predominantly to West Germany and France, and emphasise the initial importance of a plant-by-market strategy. The emergence of these networks, the subsequent relative growth rates within the markets concerned, and the performance of the respective plants within the networks are factors which have proved to be of crucial importance to Scotland. A number of centre–periphery questions immediately emerge from this, although to date no substantial evidence has emerged pointing to either a change in the nature or a decline in the scale of Scottish operations as a result.

Changing Role of the Scottish Operations. One of the difficulties faced in evaluating the impact of multinationals is that by their very nature both the parent and the affiliates are undergoing constant change. There is ample evidence of this occurring in Scotland. The previous section observed the broad direction of change in respect of market motivations. It remains therefore to examine the allied changes in product roles and organisation which have accompanied these – especially in us affiliates.

Almost all the us corporations established their European affiliates first to assemble and then manufacture selected parts of their us product range. The expected progression thereafter was to decrease the intake of us-sourced components or parts of the range by increasing the scope of European manufacture. The next stage for some was the development of products designed within Europe specifically for European markets. Often concomitant with such moves was the development of integrated production for the European market, utilising all group plants in a variety of sourcing roles. As has been amply illustrated, the process is not always as clear cut as implied here, but the direction of change is well established.[12] The integration of product ranges on a Europe-wide or sometimes a world-wide basis has been one of the causes of rationalisation in us affiliates since the mid-1970s and is a theme which is developed further within the case studies in chapter 2. As the bulk of European investment is more recent, it is difficult to detect a dominant pattern in product policy. The later entry of many of these affiliates and the geographical proximity of the parent may result in their being more integrated as a group from an earlier stage of development; although the acquisition emphasis and parents' international inexperience might work in the opposite direction. In any event, the scale of employment change and the impact of any rationalisation thrust would be generally less severe in this sector.

Reflecting the changes in both product and market roles, the organisational framework within which many of the us affiliates operate changed substantially within the 1970s. Many corporations have experienced considerable difficulty in arriving at a stable policy for controlling and monitoring their European operations. Two sets of factors appear to have influenced this. Environmental dimensions including the rate of change in the market, the development and enlargement of the European Economic Community (eec), macro-economic conditions of the 1970s, competition from European-owned corporations and some loss of original technological advantage, have all played a part in inducing change. A further set of influences is internal, in that us corporate attitudes to centralisation and decentralisation have been seen to vary considerably. The late 1970s evidenced an apparent shift towards more centralised policies within US corporations with Scottish affiliates.[13] This is largely a consequence of adopting strategies of an integrative nature. A number of the consequences of this reduction in the relative degree of organisational autonomy will be examined later, especially as it affects performance measurement at affiliate level. Of course, it has to be borne in mind that in terms of the existence of key functions, such as Marketing and Research and Development, most MNE affiliates in Scotland have consistently displayed branch plant charac- teristics and thus little functional autonomy. For example, data suggest that around 40 per cent of the US plants in Scotland undertake no R&D work and that, where present, only about one-half of the R&D undertaken could ever be regarded as contributing anything to fundamental product and process development.[14] There is no suggestion that greater centralisation will in itself lead to a diminution of the role of Scottish operations, and a more important factor is the product franchise. There is some limited evidence to suggest that as some plants are given a more specialist product role, more responsibility for R&D and Marketing will follow. Since many of the organisational changes in European-owned firms are of relatively recent date, it is not easy to determine how these have or will affect affiliates in Scotland.

From the discussions above, it will be immediately obvious that assessing the evidence on impact to date is a hazardous procedure. It is essential, even so, since it is necessary to establish a base to which future developments can be related, and one within which the consequences of the adjustment process of recent years can be assessed.

Resource Transfer Effects. Within this group of effects, the potential gains emerge through the transfer of capital, technology and management to the host economy. In regard to technology, the low-cost access to the R&D of the parent company and the potential diffusion of technology through detailed and tough specifications to indigenous subcontractors, may both be of real benefit. As regards management, the spin-off effects from people occupying managerial, financial or technical posts in the MNE and subse- quently moving into indigenous companies, could be substantial. Similarly, local competitors and suppliers might both gain from observing the operation of more efficient managerial control systems. Against all of these items has to be set a series of potential losses. For instance, the investment projects of multinationals may consistently prove to be more attractive to domestic lending institutions than those of indigenous firms. The diversion- ary effect of the latter may be fairly serious in some instances, although possibly less so in an economy such as Scotland with a well developed financial infrastructure. There are also potential offsetting influences on the technology side relating to the development of technological dependence and other issues.

Very little formal work has been done on the volume of foreign capital inflow into the Scottish economy which has been associated with direct investment. The general evidence would suggest that many projects were initially funded by the parent on a limited scale, utilising policies of minimising asset exposure by renting premises and benefiting from governmental assistance. Competition for internationally mobile projects has largely preserved the level of parent capital inflow at a low level. The process of development thereafter has chiefly been financed by either affiliate profit retention or locally initiated borrowing, whether from UK or international sources. There is ample evidence in Scotland of an inflow of home country banks designed to support MNE affiliates, although the extent to which these have channelled indigenous as distinct from international funds to the companies is not known. Neither is there evidence one way or the other to support allegations that MNE affiliates, by invariably being more attractive lending propositions, have actually reduced the funds available to indigenous companies in Scotland.

Turning to the technology component of the MNE package in Scotland, some more substantial evidence does exist. It is clear that the US-owned sector has been validly regarded as more technologically advanced than the indigenous sector both in terms of the research intensity of the activities which they undertake and in their technological sophistication.[15] But two allied questions arise before it is possible to comment on the benefit accruing. The first surrounds the existence and effectiveness of diffusion from this sector. Concern has been long expressed in Scotland about the limited level of local subcontracting which has been associated with MNE affiliates. In the electronics area it has been shown that almost half of the direct contacts established by multinational firms regarding sources of inputs were with overseas sources, whereas over two-thirds of the sales linkages were directed towards customers within the UK.[16] The desire to rectify this in electronics was reflected in a recent Scottish Development Agency commissioned study.[17] Among the deficiencies identified in Scottish subcontracting was the absence of companies sufficiently large to serve volume feeder plants, a lack of willingness to engage in speculative effort to demonstrate their ability as potential suppliers and a lack of both technical specialisation and marketing effort. Subcontracting connections are obviously only one aspect of diffusion; others may be equally important if somewhat less tangible. It has proved difficult to measure the extent and impact of the migration of senior staff to indigenous firms. Similarly, the strength of commercial relations of all types with multinationals is regarded as having brought benefit to a number of Scottish companies, although little formal work has been done on this.

The second area of technology which has attracted much attention is the nature of the local R&D activity within the MNE affiliate. For the parent corporation the principal determinants of affiliate R&D in US companies are known to include a minimum economic scale factor, relative costs and unit productivity, the requirements of foreign markets and a variety of 'negative inducements'.[18] From the viewpoint of Scotland as a host country, the economy has long suffered from the outflow of skilled personnel in professional specialisms such as are employed in R&D laboratories, while the existence of such labs could be expected to produce a number of important externalities. Information on R & D activities in us affiliates is hard to come by. Estimates for 1969 put the expenditure on in-house and purchased R & D at 1.4 per cent of sales in us affiliates in Scotland; this was rather similar to the figure for American firms in the uk as a whole. During the 1960s it seemed that us affiliates were more research intensive than their uk counterparts, but by 1975 the gap appeared to have been more or less closed.[19] Recent research has shown the R & D/sales ratio to range from 6 to 12 per cent in a number of the research intensive us electronics firms in Scotland; it is difficult to interpret this without comparable information for indigenous companies.[20] As regards the actual R & D activity, data collected in 1976 indicated that some 50 per cent of us-owned plants undertook no R & D.[21] There was a greater tendency for longer established and larger plants to have some R & D. This suggests that as production facilities grow the requirement for research and development to support the facility increased. But in reality the explanation is rarely as simple as that, and subsequent evidence has suggested that a progression to higher levels of R & D activity follows revisions in corporate product charters. From the Scottish perspective, the basic presumption has generally been that more R & D and higher order R & D would not only provide employment for highly qualified manpower but would also be a reflection of greater local plant autonomy and (implicitly) offer greater future security for that operation. While the former is true by definition, there is no necessary relationship between R & D and plant autonomy, especially in highly integrated and specialised production systems, and in multinational systems where R & D programmes are centrally planned and coordinated. The status of the affiliate should be enhanced nevertheless, and this may be important when any decisions are being made on rationalisation (see the Honeywell case in chapter 2).

A final point should be made on the transfer of managerial skill. At local level, management of mne affiliates in Scotland has almost exclusively been in the hands of uk nationals, except sometimes at start-up or when problems are being experienced by the subsidiary concerned. In that sense there have been notable benefits in developing a cadre of trained managers, a considerable number of whom have subsequently moved overseas within the corporate network. The question whether the degree of autonomy under which they have operated, and hence their ability to develop entre-preneurially, is significantly different from what it would have been in the absence of foreign direct investment is an impossible one to answer. Almost all other alternative industrial strategies for Scotland would have involved a high degree of external control and perhaps, historically, less advanced technology. Nor is there any clear evidence that managerial skills have been diverted from indigenous companies, considering the persistent volume of exports of Scottish graduates.

By far the most outstanding benefit to emerge from the transfer of this package of resources is the creation of employment. In the Scottish case the availability of a large volume of unused resources obviously facilitated expansion in the foreign-owned sector at minimum cost to indigenous industry. Allied to this is the benefit accruing to Scotland from the expansion of output and relative growth rates of foreign firms. Yet the employment creation aspect has to be tempered by a number of considerations. For example, the low rates of employment creation both of highly skilled and managerial jobs have been a cause for some concern, as has the female bias in employment creation, especially in the electronics expansions of the last few years. Given the economic experience of Scotland, most of these issues are lost in the scale of the direct employment contribution.

Trade and Balance of Payments Effects. It is important when examining this group of effects to distinguish between those associated with different phases of an MNE affiliate's development and those with different corporate policies. There may be a favourable balance of payments effect associated with the initial capital inflow as a subsidiary is established. This might well be offset by higher import propensities in the early years of operation. In a more mature subsidiary, the gain or loss will be determined by a variety of corporate policies such as the market area designated to be sourced from the plant and other policies pertaining to transfer pricing, dividend repatriation, management charges, local borrowing and local sourcing. In all of these areas, there is potential for either positive or negative effects on the balance of payments.

Although the absence of data has meant that little comprehensive work has been undertaken on the topic, it has generally been accepted that the balance of payments effect of foreign investment is favourable. The Forsyth study concluded that, for US investment, this was so by a wide margin in the late 1960s and that it was likely to remain so while the US-owned sector was growing by both the continued inflow of new firms and the ploughing-back of profits.[22] No equivalent study has been undertaken since then, although it is necessary to weigh the effect of developments in knowledge about inward investment since that date.

On the exports side, MNE affiliates have been shown to be consistently more export-orientated than indigenous firms. Evidence emerging over recent years has confirmed this. It should be noted that even although the commitment to European markets on the part of US affiliates is high, it has been shown that some 40 per cent still depend on the UK for half of their sales.[23] Additionally, while around 50 per cent of European affiliate volume appears to be exported, the limited number and small size of the companies concerned limits the contribution being made to the balance of payments.[24] These qualifications apart, the export contribution remains substantial. As regards the trends on the import side, evidence is very thin and tentative. The proposition that direct imports from the parent company tend to diminish over time is broadly confirmed, although company practice varies widely.[25] A more complex issue is how imports (and exports) are affected by the process of network integration which has taken place since the early 1970s. Adjustments in sales configurations are often slow and there is as yet no Scottish evidence on this question. However, some tentative work for the UK as a whole, has shown that although the sectors of UK industry in which international participation is high still tend to have relatively more favourable trade balances than the rest of industry, it is in these sectors that the largest deterioration in trade performance occurred during the 1970s.[26] While there are several possible explanations of this, the effect of international corporate integration ranks among them. There is no reason to believe that Scotland would be either exempt from that effect or more seriously affected by it than the rest of the UK.

Returning to the two caveats sounded by Forsyth in his predictions of a continued favourable balance of payments position, the inflow of new US firms has clearly reduced considerably. Taken together with the effect of closures this will have changed the absolute growth in export volume in some sectors. Moreover, many of the newer entrants in electronics are smaller and globally integrated before arriving and may well make a relatively smaller contribution than some of those which have closed. The European propensity to acquire in Scotland is again relevant, as in the short term this will not lead to substantially increased exports.[27] Taking the second prediction, namely the continued ploughing back of profits, evidence is very slender. Capital expenditure relative to all Scottish manufacturing has remained high and the effective marginal rates of tax for MNE affiliates remained low.[28] While this is apparently largely being financed from profits and local borrowing, the exact patterns remain unknown. Nor is there evidence to indicate that policies on dividend repatriation and management charges have changed to the detriment of Scotland.

In summary, there are a number of forces at work influencing the balance-of-payments contribution. Taken together they may be judged to be capable of reducing the margin by which this effect is favourable in Scotland, without showing any signs of adjusting the overall position of gain. Much more work is needed on this issue before an authoritative evaluation would be possible.

Competitive and Anti-Competitive Effects. There is ample evidence from the theory of industrial organisation to show that the efficiency of resource allocation and the distribution of economic welfare are much influenced by the structure of markets in which firms operate. In the specific context of exploring the impact of foreign direct investment on host country markets, the economic power of the MNE as against that of the indigenous company is an important factor. Although the MNE affiliate may be small locally, its market power is derived from the resources of the group and from the international nature of its parent's operations which generally allow greater flexibility in product, production, promotion and pricing than that enjoyed by domestic companies. In addition, multinationals do influence the competitive environment through their labour relations practices. These extend from the effects of higher productivity/higher wage-earning plants on local labour markets to the impact of large international companies on established management-union negotiating practices.

Taking first the question of the effect of the economic power of multinationals on the Scottish economy, a major difficulty recurs. As has been illustrated earlier in this chapter, the US affiliates are concentrated in specific sectors not all of which had, at the time of foreign entry, a strong indigenous presence. The effects of an MNE presence on the structure, conduct and performance of these markets is therefore difficult to determine. This is complicated by the fact that in some sectors, for example, computing and electronics, much of the competition is inter-MNE affiliate. Such oligopoly situations have posed barriers to indigenous entry at one level, while creating substantial subcontracting markets at another. It is highly improbable that the Scottish electronics industry would be anything close to its present scale without foreign investment, and these intermediate goods markets would not exist in their present form. Having said that, the strength of the incoming companies has been such that 'despite the growth of electronics employment in Scotland, neither ownership nor linkage characteristics suggest the emergence of a distinctly Scottish industry or regionally-based complex'.[29] Looking at another sector a considerable volume of the mechanical engineering investment in the 1960s was in consumer products which were being introduced to European markets and for which no indigenous technology or manufacturing capacity existed. So relatively few local firms were directly affected in terms of their products and markets. In short, the aggregate competitive effect is indeterminate, and no-one has attempted to assess it for Scotland. But there are dimensions of the larger question which are more manageable and it is to these that most attention should be directed.

The emergence of a bias towards acquisition in European investment is one such dimension. It is not known whether Scotland is typical in this regard. Other UK work points to foreign acquisition activity being of larger indigenous companies, generally concentrated in high technology and capital intensive sectors, with the more concentrated industries recording higher acquisition rates.[30] Too little is known about this in Scotland to comment on the Scottish pattern in detail, but it seems to have involved some quite small companies and to be somewhat more diversified than other foreign investment. The more important questions surround its effects, especially the impact on technological progressiveness, product range, competition and efficiency. While there are no a priori reasons to conclude that loss will ensue from foreign takeover, there is as yet little evidence of the infusion of new management, technology or products into Scottish companies acquired by Continental European parents.[31] In fairness, this is a relatively recent phenomenon, but it is one on which an open verdict would have to be returned as there is all still to prove in terms of Scottish benefit.

Another important and wide-ranging question surrounds the performance of MNE affiliates. It has been widely believed that they make very effective use of local resources by operating at higher levels of productivity, efficiency and profitability than comparable indigenous companies. This in turn is regarded as having desirable demonstration effects which filter through into the local economy. Certainly, there is evidence to point to higher levels of investment in US firms in Scotland and, as was noted earlier when broad trends were being studied, higher levels of net output in overseas units compared to all Scottish manufacturing units.[32] But two questions remain, namely whether the differences are more apparent than real, and whether the spin-off implied actually happens. Regarding the former, a UK study using 1971/2 data is important. Examining the performance of the mechanical engineering industry it was shown that comparisons between the performance of MNE affiliates and indigenous companies were significantly biased by a failure to take into account both the industrial and the regional distribution of foreign direct investment. When removed, indigenous firms were found to have higher labour productivity and to export more. It would be unwise to generalise from this one piece of evidence, in terms of the data, methodology or the timing, but it does draw attention to the need to temper these comparisons and compare like with like. The difficulty of such an exercise is apparent, even when one aspect such as profitability is examined. The most recent work in Scotland on US affiliates draws attention to the marked disparity in profit performance both within the foreign sector and between it and the indigenous sector depending on a variety of corporate development considerations.[33] No consistent relationship was, for example, shown to exist between Standard Industrial Classification (SIC) group, growth and performance.

On the question of spin-off from MNE affiliates, the less than adequate receptiveness of the local environment to opportunities has already been noted. This should not detract from the measurable employment contribution which is made by MNE investment, estimated as generating at least another 40 jobs outside the affiliate for every 100 within it.[34] However approximate this estimate there is clearly potential to increase it, although it is just possible that in some established industries the major local opportunity is past, as affiliates become more dependent on intra-group sourcing.

As has been implied the primary consideration in this context is MNE performance relative to that of indigenous companies. There is another dimension which is of very considerable significance in determining the impact of foreign direct investment, namely the relative performance of Scottish-based affiliates when compared with other units in the parent's network. It has to be recognised that from the parent corporation's viewpoint the conformity of an affiliate to external performance norms such as profitability is only one part of performance achievement. At least of equal significance are a series of internal measures of efficiency employed to monitor the relative performance within the network. From the perspective of the host country it is through this mechanism that some of the international dimensions of resource allocation affect the economy concerned. Until recently this was a real gap in our knowledge within Scotland and while it remains a difficult area to research, the underlying processes are now better understood.[35] The distinction between profit-centre and cost-centre control mechanisms was shown to be important, the former being judged largely by rates of return measures; while in the latter greater stress was placed on budget achievement and a complex of intra-group perform-ance norms. The trend towards adopting the cost-centre approach in US companies was associated with integration and the tentative evidence suggested that Scottish affiliates performed less adequately against group targets in such systems compared with other European affiliates. Should this be subsequently verified it has potentially very serious implications for Scotland in the longer term.

Certain labour market issues are relevant to the discussion on competitive and anti-competitive effects on the Scottish economy. Regrettably, most of the limited evidence that exists in Scotland regarding MNE affiliates and labour concentrates on strikes, and pays little attention to the equally important issues surrounding competitive bidding for skilled labour, attitudes to unionisation, general effects of multinationals on negotiating procedures, conditions of work and so on. The earliest work attempting to cover many of these aspects, pointed to a worse strike record in US-owned firms in Scotland between 1960 and 1969 than was true either for industry in general or for most of the comparable indigenous firms.[36] It was further concluded that the impact on labour relations in Scotland was largely confined to the US sector itself, with only marginal spillover elsewhere.

A number of more recent studies has led to some modification of these views. One covering the period 1970–7 for the chemical, mechanical and electrical engineering sectors in Scotland has concluded that MNE affiliates are neither more nor less strike prone than indigenous firms (as regards the total number of strikes) but are significantly more strike prone in terms of both size of strikes (numbers involved) and working days lost (strike duration).[37] A substantial part of the differences in this and earlier studies is explained by the larger average size of foreign units rather than by ownership or any other variable.

The only recent evidence to address wider labour issues is rather restricted since it covers only 1978–9 and was largely undertaken for publicity purposes.[38] It records around 30 per cent non-union plants in the US sector, but, while noting the lower union involvement in smaller and medium-sized plants, does not analyse the consequences. No signs emerged of generally unacceptable levels of absenteeism or labour turnover, but experience is known to vary here substantially. Finally, most companies appeared to regard labour productivity in Scotland as comparing favourably with comparable plants elsewhere; in this respect, the results conflict with a number of other findings. One of the most thorough Scottish Development Agency (SDA) sectoral studies covering the electronics industry again pointed to mixed labour experience.[39] Absenteeism records, for example, were not shown to be significantly different in foreign firms, although levels above 5 per cent were deemed unacceptable. The incidence of labour disputes in the electronics industry in Scotland was shown to be low with one of the major labour problems being the inability to recruit technicians in adequate numbers.

More generally, MNE affiliates do dominate labour markets in some sectors and in some geographical areas on account of the salaries offered and the conditions of work. In these circumstances multinationals have probably been responsible for a general improvement in both, while at the same time posing some problems for indigenous firms. Some specifically multinational dimensions do arise in labour relations in Scotland, as no doubt elsewhere, particularly the use of withdrawal threats as a bargaining weapon. As the cases will later illustrate, this has on occasions led to a very hostile management–labour environment. A number of open questions remain on the labour side. For instance, the trend to plant integration has clear implications for labour relations. One view is that the pressures to introduce home-country labour-relations practices might grow in order to raise productivity or to reduce the incidence of industrial unrest. The results to date do not suggest that such introduced practices (e.g. union non-recognition, more highly structured payment systems and more generous employee fringe benefits) have been beneficial in differentiating foreign and indigenous company experience. The pressures to improve plant productivity are likely to remain strong, nevertheless, and will prove testing for labour relations in MNE affiliates in Scotland.

Sovereignty and Autonomy Effects. There is a basic paradox in evaluating the impact in this area. While the involvement of multinationals in the development of a host economy invariably involves a loss of economic independence, and is therefore to be regarded as a cost, the exact nature of the loss depends on what would have happened in the absence of foreign direct investment. The level of UK interdependence is such that much of the alternative employment creation would probably have been externally controlled in any event. Many of the concerns surrounding the closures discussed later are related to sovereignty and autonomy issues and it is an open question whether the employment in these plants would have been more robust had greater local autonomy existed. On a wider canvas, it is arguable that given the limited feasible alternatives for the Scottish economy, some of the costs outlined in this section should be willingly paid as they are offset by substantial benefits in other directions.

The issue is clearly an important one, but it has often attracted more passion than rigour, partly at least because the questions posed are difficult to address formally. At its root is the balance between centralisation and autonomy in decision-making at branch plant level. Put at its strongest, 'the major problem with a regional economy that is dominated by externally controlled enterprises is probably that of the changing balance between innovative, entrepreneurial-type decision making and routine management-type supervision'.[40] There are obviously many possible determinants of that balance, including plant size, number of affiliates in the parent corporation's network, plant performance, and organisational and product strategy.

Many of these factors exert an influence in any multi-plant firm, independent of ownership, although in the case of the international firm the distance of the locus of strategic decision making is frequently viewed as in itself potentially detrimental to the branch plant. The particular balance which characterises the MNE sector in Scotland could be regarded as leading to a loss of autonomy of two different forms, both of which are considered below.

The first surrounds the relationship between external control and a variety of dependency measures. Potential losses identified here emerge from the view that high degrees of external control will lead to a very open regional economy in Scotland, and specifically that the large US component in Scottish manufacturing has been a focal point for externally generated economic fluctuations. There is in fact little concrete evidence to support this contention, and it could be argued the other way, namely, that higher export earnings and a smaller emphasis on the slow growth UK market reduces volatility. The issue which has been most widely debated relates to the possibility of technological dependence in branch factory operations of international companies and the subsequent reduction of the Scottish economy's potential for future self-generating growth. As has been noted earlier it is now well established that the majority of foreign units undertake no R&D or Marketing in Scotland, and that on the whole where these functions are delegated, the activity involved is not very substantial.[41] Whether other UK Assisted Areas exhibit similar patterns is not known, but preliminary evidence points that way.[42] There is, however, little evidence to suggest that external ownership involving firms based in other parts of the UK leads to a markedly different distribution pattern of decision-making authority in Scottish plants than where a multinational corporation is involved. In short, foreign ownership *per se* may not have created higher rates of 'dependency' in Scotland than would have existed in any event; although the fact that multinationals may only have reinforced these patterns is in itself a cause for concern.

The second broad area where sovereignty and autonomy issues exist concerns the responsiveness of the MNE to the economic policy measures adopted by the host government. Among the more important aspects of this in a Scottish context is whether or not regional policy measures designed to strengthen designated areas, make any material difference to the policies of internationally mobile companies. While many attempts have been made to examine this question, the results are at best inconclusive;[43] there are admittedly grounds for believing, for the UK at least, that 'positive regional policies have had a positive effect'.[44] With respect to the initial locational decisions of US multinationals, it has been fairly widely accepted that the dominant reason for investing abroad was either UK or European market growth, whereas the specific decision to choose Scotland was related to high levels of regional financial assistance. It is more difficult to determine the effect of regional aids in an on-going operation. Recent Scottish evidence has drawn attention to the importance of incentives within MNE affiliates 'at particular key times and in certain key decision areas, namely at start up; in major decisions involving both capacity extension and retooling; and in marginal decisions where the regional incentives could prove to be an important balancing factor'.[45]

A much larger question is whether such policy measures exert any measurable influence on the nature of the activity within an MNE in an Assisted Area. A recurring theme is whether financial assistance can influence the level of technical capability within an MNE affiliate. In a recent detailed study of research and development within the affiliates of US-owned electronics companies in Scotland, it was concluded that the effect of regional incentives on technical facilities and technology was minor, although the role attributed to incentives was slightly higher in R&D-intensive affiliates.[46] For the same industry, the SDA sector study concluded that multinationals will need encouragement to transfer technical capability into their Scottish operations, but it was readily acknowledged that financial incentives could not be the overriding consideration for a multinational's decision in this field. There are in short few grounds for believing that an MNE is more or less responsive to regional measures in its technology policy than an indigenous firm.

Before leaving the regional policy and sovereignty issue, it is worth noting that a broader debate has been raging in recent years over the extent to which multinationals do or do not concentrate their activities in more developed regions in the UK and over the contribution which multinationals might make to regional disequilibria.[47] Some comments were made on the Scottish/UK pattern earlier in this chapter (see pp.6–7). The most recent data indicate that the tendency for Assisted Areas in the UK to receive an above average share of inward manufacturing investment has apparently halted.[48] This has given rise to a number of fears that areas like Scotland might, by definition, suffer in some reallocation of MNE-owned economic activity. This is a difficult area to evaluate and no empirical work has been done on the topic since early 1978. The most recent study on US affiliates in Scotland did not lend support to the view that Scotland was losing key functions on a large scale, in spite of an acceleration of inter-plant integration. Despite this, continuous monitoring is required to stay in touch with corporate policies.

Within the last few years in Scotland, the sovereignty and autonomy question has come together with the other evaluative dimensions to focus attention upon particularly contentious acquisition proposals involving foreign companies. Before concluding this section it is therefore worth noting the principal strands of these debates, since the trends in foreign direct investment throughout Europe do point to such bids becoming more frequent in the future. In the Hiram Walker (HW) and Highland Distillers (HD) case for example, there was a strong regional dimension in some of the evidence given to the Monopolies and Mergers Commission (MMC).[49] Against a background of already high foreign ownership in the whisky industry, it was argued *inter alia* that 'foreign ownership would not bring any compensating advantages in the form of a new technology or additional employment to this traditional Scottish industry'.[50] That could certainly be said of a number of similar acquisitions, many of which never reached the MMC. In that sense, the MMC at least provides a forum where the arguments can be formally rehearsed, and some qualitative judgement made about the net impact. In this case the MMC, in finding against the takeover, formally concluded that the merger would deprive Highland Distillers' top management of the opportunity to take strategic decisions. In this case considerable weight appears to have been attributed to some autonomy questions, although many of the other impact variables discussed within this section of the chapter were also featured.

By far the most controversial foreign merger proposal in recent years was the competitive bidding by the Standard Chartered Bank and the Hong Kong & Shanghai Banking Corporation for the Royal Bank of Scotland. The plethora of evidence given to the MMC on this case merely emphasised that it was a classic case of an indigenous company short on strategy and managerial vision, and hence open to a change of ownership.[51] The debate raged round almost all of the questions considered previously in this chapter. Among them was the issue of precisely what skill the new owner was transferring to Scotland; and what would be the consequences for employment, executive development and the UK balance of payments of the predicted centralisation of decision making? These two cases may be harbingers of a new trend in attitudes towards foreign direct investment in Scotland, where articulate voices are heard in favour of a more considered attitude to external ownership. The fact that they have attracted such attention is not unrelated to the context within which this whole book is written. The authors believe that a careful approach is required and that the subject needs to be considered on a broader front where attraction and monitoring are linked. This, however, is an issue which will be developed fully in the concluding chapter.

Interim Observations on Scottish Impact. Reviewing the evidence as a whole, there is little doubt that foreign direct investment has continued to bring substantial net benefit to the Scottish economy. At the same time there are grounds for believing that the processes of change outlined at the beginning of this section carry with them the potential to alter substantially the balance of benefits and costs in a considerable number of projects. For example, a system of integration of branch plant operations in Scotland which diminished local added value, accelerated imports and reduced export franchises may offer relatively little more than employment. Welcome though this is, employment is a necessary, but should not be a sufficient, condition for encouraging foreign direct investment in a sophisticated economy. Fortunately there are few MNE affiliates in Scotland which operate at this primitive end of the spectrum, but changes can and will go in either direction. Taking the more positive view, the net benefit could be increased in many cases by indigenous rather than foreign corporate initiative. The recent evidence in electronics has yet again drawn attention to the substantial unsatisfied subcontracting demand for intermediate products arising from the agglomeration of foreign (and UK-owned) companies in Scotland.[52] Resolution of such deficiencies is not easy, but the opportunity for some further local employment creation exists in these areas.

This summary is, nevertheless, an interim one, in that the serious employment rundown within the MNE sector during the second half of the 1970s has yet to be considered. This process of multinational retreat – the extent, causes and consequences – forms the basis for most of the remainder of the book.

Multinationals in Retreat

Closures of Overseas-Owned Units in Scotland. 'The 1970s . . . has seen not only a further contraction of employment in Scotland's "traditional" industries but also a collapse of employment in a number of newer firms who came in bringing with them modern industry in the post-war period. Companies such as Timex, NCR, Massey–Ferguson, Goodyear, . . . Talbot, Monsanto, SKF, . . . and Hoover have all shed jobs and in some cases closed completely in the recent past. The question which is on many people's lips is – if we are losing jobs at this rate in the so-called modern, advanced sectors of industry, where are the new jobs going to come from in the future?" (STUC Annual Report, 1980).[53]

Employment in foreign firms changed strikingly in the recent past and with this change has come a different, almost despairing, view of prospects in the multinational sector, as the above comment from the Scottish Trades Union Congress (STUC) reveals. In part the comment reflects the fact that expectations from foreign-owned companies had been unreasonably high. It has been widely assumed that the early competitive advantages of US corporations in particular were durable, almost by definition. To many observers in Scotland it has thus come as something of a shock that many of these corporations have been vulnerable at both parent and affiliate level. To some degree this is surprising given the volume of sectoral decline experienced in Scotland since World War II, but it would appear that the general perceptions of externally owned firms were different from those associated with certain sectors of indigenous industry. Of course, for many years foreign ownership was almost exclusively associated with expansion, growth and job creation in Scotland. Indeed, it has to be acknowledged again that the complex environmental changes which have engendered more negative developments are all recent in origin and their final outcome is still not totally understood.

The harsh reality of the present situation is brought sharply into focus in table 12, which presents data on closures of foreign-owned units during the period 1976 to 1981. As indicated, 61 units, which at peak had employed over 44,000 people in Scotland, were closed in these years. Before commenting on the data further, it is necessary to make a few remarks concerning the derivation of the figures. The information is based on

Table 12. Overseas-owned Closures in Scotland (1976–81)

	No.	Maximum employment	Latest employment
By Year			
1976	8	2,654	2,049
1977	9	3,473	1,358
1978	9	2,814	441
1979	11	4,030	2,610
1980	14	19,976	1,946
1981	10	11,531	5,504
	61	44,478	13,908
By Region			
Strathclyde	40	39,675	11,536
Borders	1		
Central	2		
Dumfries & Galloway	1		
Fife	6		
Grampian	2	4,803	2,372
Highland	1		
Lothian	7		
Tayside	1		
	61	44,478	13,908
By SIC			
Food, drink and tobacco	3		
Chemicals & allied industries	5	1,474	1,006
Mechanical engineering	9		
Vehicles	2	31,777	6,807
Metal goods not elsewhere specified	5		
Instrument engineering	5		
Electrical engineering	13	6,336	2,657
Textiles	5		
Leather, leather goods & fur	1	3,432	2,444
Clothing & footwear	3		
Timber, furniture	3		
Paper, printing & publishing	4	1,499	994
Other manufacturing	3		
	61	44,478	13,908
By Country of Ownership			
USA	35	27,575	5,785
Netherlands	6	4,630	2,017
Canada	7		
Denmark	2		
Sweden	2		
Switzerland	2	12,273	6,106
W. Germany	3		
Other	4		
	61	44,478	13,908

Table 12 (contd.)

	No.	Peak employment
By Peak Employment		
Under 20	4 ⎫	311
20–49	7 ⎭	
50–99	14	991
100–199	10	1,480
200 and over	26	41,696
	61	44,478
By Last Known Employment		
Under 20	7 ⎫	692
20–49	17 ⎭	
50–99	12	769
100–199	11	1,488
200 and over	14	10,959
	61	13,908

SOURCE: SCOMER.

manufacturing units, that is factories in separate geographical locations. So if an MNE has several factories in different towns in Scotland, closure of any one of these will be recorded in the data. On the other hand, if a multinational company has several plants in the same town or city, closure will not be recorded until all these factories are shut. The data thus underestimate the extent of plant closure. The figures in the table draw a distinction between the maximum employment during the lifetime of the unit and the latest employment data available prior to divestment. Both sets of figures inevitably pose some difficulties: the former tends to exaggerate the current employment impact of closures, while the latter often underestimates it substantially, in that unit employment invariably declines both prior to closure announcements and prior to closure. What is important is that closure was preceded by a period, sometimes a fairly lengthy period, of job attrition, representing, for the workers concerned, a time of considerable anxiety and uncertainty. For a good number of companies in this category peak employment occurred in the late 1960s or early 1970s with conditions of booming demand, although employment at Singer declined almost continuously for two decades prior to closure in 1980.

As the data show, the closures have been concentrated by year – in 1980 and 1981; by region – in Strathclyde; and by sector – in electrical and mechanical engineering. Divestments were concentrated at the end of the period covered, and this indicates that there were factors specific to the years 1980 and 1981, such as the recession and strength of sterling. The severe impact on Strathclyde Region where some 60 per cent of employment was in

31

overseas-owned units in 1975 (see table 5), is worth re-emphasising, since Strathclyde has suffered around 90 per cent of the job loss through closures. Overriding all these issues is the fact that divestments have been highly concentrated in terms of plant size. Table 12 indicates that around 94 per cent of jobs lost have been in units employing over 200 people, but even this substantially underestimates the position. Most of the job loss has occurred with the closure of a small number of large and sometimes long-established companies, with serious, indeed devastating effects on dependent communities. The most important of these divestments are discussed fully in the case section, including Singer, Talbot, Goodyear, Honeywell and Hoover; and there are others such as Burroughs, Monsanto, Massey–Ferguson and Standard Telephones & Cables (STC).

Massey–Ferguson, the Canadian-based manufacturer of farm machinery (although employment in the UK was three times as great as that in Canada) opened its Kilmarnock factory in 1949.[54] A wide range of farm machinery was produced until the mid-1960s, when, following a plant/product specialisation programme in Europe, manufacture in Scotland was concentrated on the medium-sized range of combine harvesters. Employment at Kilmarnock rose to a maximum of over 2,000 at the end of the 1960s. During the late 1970s, the company experienced severe problems at the international level; there was a decline in demand for combines and there were difficulties with an attempted diversification programme. In November 1978 the decision was taken to transfer combine harvester production from Scotland to France as part of a major rationalisation effort. This was to leave the Kilmarnock plant with about 500 workers to build a new range of farm balers; but as events turned out the announcement of large-scale redundancies in 1978 was merely the precursor to closure of the Scottish factory which took place in 1979 in the face of continued market decline.

The closure of Monsanto's nylon plants at Dundonald and Cumnock in Ayrshire in 1979 with the loss of 900 jobs, was part of this American corporation's complete withdrawal first from the polystyrene and then the nylon business in Europe.[55] Divestment of Monsanto's nylon activities took place against a background of steadily declining demand for the product because of competition by other synthetics and a general policy by most manufacturers of rationalisation and the closure of small, inefficient nylon production units. For Monsanto, the withdrawal from the nylon industry in Europe meant the closure of plants in Germany, Luxembourg and England as well as Scotland, and the loss of 2,300 jobs overall.

Another important MNE closure in Scotland took place in 1977, when STC, the British subsidiary of the giant ITT conglomerate, shut its plant in East Kilbride. At peak in 1974 STC had employed about 1,200 people, a figure which had fallen to 550–600 by time of closure. The GPO was almost the sole customer of the East Kilbride facility, accounting for about 90 per cent of its output of mechanical and electrical telephone exchange equipment. A successful scheme of tariff changes by the GPO led to a smoothing of daily peaks and troughs and to a large reduction in demand for equipment. With alternative markets at home and overseas restricted by the specialised nature of the equipment and no new products coming on-stream, the East Kilbride factory was closed.

Yet a further example of multinational retreat concerns Burroughs, where the changeover from electro-mechanical to electronic technology led to large-scale job losses in Scotland and elsewhere within the corporation's international network. What is clear from even these few examples is that the causes of closure are complex and require detailed examination of the corporation's circumstances at both parent company and affiliate levels. Before completing these introductory comments on multinational retreat, it is worth pointing out that among the 61 units which closed between 1976 and 1981 were a number of quite small operations. Some of these were owned by parent corporations who had little experience of international production and it is perhaps here that the exclusive recessionary effect was most severely felt.

Openings of Overseas-Owned Units in Scotland. In order to take a balanced view of multinational closures in Scotland, table 13 presents equivalent data on openings of overseas-owned units in Scotland during the 1976–81 period. Among this group are companies such as Devro Ltd, a spin-off from an existing, successful Johnson & Johnson subsidiary in Scotland, Gray Tool Co., Tannoy Products and the clothing manufacturers

Table 13. Overseas-owned Openings in Scotland (1976–81)

	No.	2nd Year Employment
By Year		
1976	7	682
1977	10	1,082
1978	5	519
1979	3	
1980	5	517
1981	3	264
	33	3,064
By Region		
Strathclyde	18	1,591
Lothian	6	971
Central	2	
Grampian	1	
Tayside	1	
Borders	1	502
Highlands	1	
Dumfries & Galloway	2	
Fife	1	
	33	3,064

33

Table 13 (contd.)

	No.	2nd Year Employment
By SIC Order		
Food, drink & tobacco	4	
Chemical & allied industries	4	1,254
Metal manufacture	1	
Mechanical engineering	4	
Electrical engineering	8	
Shipbuilding & marine engineering	1	1,052
Metal goods not elsewhere specified	2	
Textiles	2	
Clothing & footwear	5	758
Other manufacturing industries	1	
	33	3,064
By Second Year Employment		
Under 20	7	91
20–99	13	643
100 and over	13	2,330
	33	3,064
By Country of Ownership		
USA	23	2,359
Canada	2	
France	1	
Japan	1	
Netherlands	3	705
Norway	1	
Sweden	1	
Other	1	
	33	3,064

SOURCE: SCOMER

Levi Strauss and Blue Bell Apparel. Again care has to be taken in interpreting this table and comparing it with the figures on divestments. Employment build-up in new entrant units is invariably slow and there are doubtless many good long-term prospects within the openings. On the other hand, the units opening earlier in the period are still relatively small and have offered relatively little employment expansion. At the same time, the reduced number of openings between 1978 and 1981 is of concern. This is a consequence of a reduced rate of growth of foreign direct investment, intensified competition from Assisted Areas in Europe for internationally mobile projects, recessionary conditions and so on. The only other issues to stress in table 13 are the perhaps surprising sectoral diversity of the openings, given the publicity focused on the electronics industry, and the fact that the u s has remained by far the dominant source.

Expansion and Contraction in Overseas-Owned Units in Scotland. To complete the balance on job rundown and job creation, it is necessary to look at the effects of expansions and contractions within existing foreign units over a comparable time period. As table 14 indicates, the growth of established multinational affiliates has provided a much more significant source of additional employment than of openings. Included within these figures are a number of corporations where the reshaped European strategy has been of positive benefit to Scotland. Unfortunately, however, and here the data difficulties in table 14 are important, these expansions have been more than offset by contractions within the foreign-owned sector.

Table 14. Expansions and Contractions in Existing Overseas-owned Units in Scotland (1976–81)

	Employment in 1976	Employment change 1976–81*
Expansions	24,641	+ 7,116
Contractions	53,671	− 15,035
Other†	27,765	n.a.

* To avoid double counting with figures in Tables 12 and 13, the Table excludes all units which opened and closed since the beginning of 1976. Employment change is compared between mid-1976 and mid-1981.

† 'Other' includes units which showed no employment change; units which closed/opened since the beginning of 1976; and units for which complete information up to 1980/81 was not available.

SOURCE: SCOMER

The net effect of all these developments is not readily determined from tables 12–14, particularly because of lack of data relating to the years in which 'maximum employment' occurred. Referring back to the aggregate figures presented earlier in the chapter, nevertheless, it is apparent that employment in the overseas-owned sector declined by 28,000 in the period under consideration. By any criteria this is of major significance.

Forecasting Employment Change in Overseas-Owned Units. In concluding this discussion on employment change, and particularly employment rundown, it is interesting to consider the extent to which these were predicted by the corporations. In the Scottish context, the present authors did compile a series of company estimates of employment change over the five-year period up to 1982 for a sample of u s affiliates in Scotland, based on interviews undertaken in 1977 and 1978. These forecasts have been compared with the actual employment experience in the companies concerned up to 1981, and the results are presented in tables 15 and 16. Taking table 15 first, it is clear that the forecasts were rather optimistic, both

Table 15. Employment Change 1977–81/2 for Sample US Firms in Scotland – Comparison of SCOMER Employment Change with Hood & Young Forecast Change*

INDUSTRY	Number of establishments	SCOMER					HOOD & YOUNG				
		1977† employment	1977–81† Gross increases	Gross decreases	Net change	1981 Employment	1977† Employment	1977–82 Gross increases	Gross decreases	Net change	1982 Forecast employment
VII, XII Mechanical engineering, metal goods not elsewhere specified	18	18,291	+355	−8,397	−8,042	10,249	16,974	+2,327	−2,910	−583	16,391
VIII, IX Instrument and electrical engineering	19	19,575	+2,297	−4,284	−1,987	17,588	19,370	+2,945	−1,930	+1,015	20,385
III, V, XIII to XIX Other manufacturing	11	7,436	+457	−2,885	−2,428	5,340	7,340	+793	−175	+618	7,958
Total	48	45,302	+3,109	−15,566	−12,457	32,845	43,684	+6,065	−5,015	+1,050	44,734

* The forecasts referred to in Tables 15 and 16 were these made on the basis of expectations for the future obtained from interviews with companies during 1977/78, as published in N. Hood & S. Young, *European Development Strategies of US Owned Manufacturing Companies Located in Scotland*, HMSO (Edinburgh) 1980.

† SCOMER employment in 1977 and 1981. The employment in the latest available year was used if the data for these years were not available.

‡ 1977 Employment. The Hood & Young employment (based on company data) was compared with SCOMER. Small units with significant differences between the two sources were excluded from the analysis and this is the principal reason for this table being based on 48 affiliates and not the original 55.

SOURCE: SEPD

Table 16. Percentage Employment Change 1977–81/2 for Sample US Firms in
Scotland – Comparison of SCOMER Employment Change with Hood &
Young Forecast Change

		% Employment change	
INDUSTRY		SCOMER 1977–81 Actual	Hood & Young 1977–82 Forecast
VII, XII	Mechanical engineering, metal good not elsewhere specified	− 44.0	− 3.4
VIII, IX	Instrument and electrical engineering	− 10.2	+ 5.2
III, V, XIII to XIX	Other manufacturing	− 28.2	+ 8.4
	Total	− 27.5	+ 2.4

SOURCE: SEPD

in terms of the gross increases and gross decreases in employment which
were expected. As the table shows, however, the differences varied
substantially by sector. For example, net expansion was expected in
instrument and electrical engineering, but the gross increases were offset by
much larger losses than were expected. Conversely, in the first industrial
group in table 15 (mechanical engineering, metal goods not elsewhere
specified) while net job losses were expected by 1982, in the event the
redundancies in mechanical engineering were far greater than anticipated by
the companies. The results have been influenced by changes in a number of
large companies.

Inevitably, forecasts of employment obtained from company interviews
(especially at plant level) are likely to be over-optimistic. But there is little
doubt that allowing for this initial optimism and for the large closures, there
has been a degree of rapidity in the reduction of employment which was not
anticipated by anyone in 1977. While this could be interpreted variously, it
was already clear when the initial study was undertaken that many of the
companies were in transition and it is reasonable to hypothesise that the
recession has accelerated their speed of movement in directions which they
had planned to take at a more considered pace. In addition, the large
differences between forecast and actual employment suggest that some of
the American companies with plants in Scotland were caught out by the
intensity of competition at the end of the 1970s, by the spread of automation
in the production process and by the speed of introduction of new product
technology. All of such issues emerge clearly in the case studies which
follow.

NOTES AND REFERENCES

1. J.H. Dunning, *American Investment in British Manufacturing Industry*, Allen & Unwin (London) 1958.
2. N. Hood, A. Reeves & S. Young, 'Foreign direct investment in Scotland: the European dimension', *Scottish Journal of Political Economy*, vol.28, no.2, 1981.
3. 'Overseas investment in Scottish manufacturing industry', *Scottish Economic Bulletin*, no.20, Spring 1980.
4. A number of these are considered, for example, in *Overseas Ownership in Scottish Manufacturing Industry, A Statistical Note*, SEPD, ESU1/5, March 1981.
5. See, for example, papers by MacDougall, Jasay & Kemp on this topic in J.H. Dunning (ed.), *International Investment*, Penguin Books (Harmondsworth, Middlesex) 1972.
6. A summary of which is provided in N. Hood & S. Young, *The Economics of Multinational Enterprise*, Longman (London) 1979, chapter 5.
7. J.P. Curhan, W.H. Davidson & R. Suri, *Tracing the Multinationals: A Source book on US-Based Enterprises*, Ballinger Publishing Company (Cambridge, Mass.) 1977.
8. N. Hood & S. Young, 'US investment in Scotland: aspects of the branch factory syndrome', *Scottish Journal of Political Economy*, vol.23, no.3, 1976.
9. ibid., p.290; N. Hood & S. Young, *European Development Strategies of US Owned Manufacturing Companies located in Scotland*, HMSO (Edinburgh) 1980, p.61.
10. Hood, Reeves & Young, 1981 (n.2), p.177, table 6. These findings should be compared with *European Manufacturing Investment in Scotland*, Scottish Council (Development & Industry) (Edinburgh) 1979.
11. S. Young & N. Hood, 'The geographical expansion of US firms in Western Europe: some survey evidence', *Journal of Common Market Studies*, vol.XIV, no.3, 1976; Hood & Young, 1980 (n.9), table 4.14.
12. Hood & Young, 1980 (n.9), table 6, pp.60–1.
13. ibid., section 3.3 et seq.
14. Hood & Young, 1976 (n.8), p.285; Hood & Young, 1980 (n.9), chapter 4.
15. D.J.C. Forsyth, *US Investment in Scotland*, Praeger (New York) 1972, chapter 6.
16. P.J. McDermott, 'Multinational manufacturing firms and regional development: external control in Scottish electronics industry', *Scottish Journal of Political Economy*, vol.26, no.3, 1979, p.302.
   For earlier work arriving at similar conclusions see W.F. Lever, *Migrant Industry, Demand Linkages: Some Paradoxes in Regional Development*, Urban & Regional Studies Discussion Paper no.12, University of Glasgow, 1974.
17. *Scottish Electronics Subcontracting and Components Manufacturing Industries*, study undertaken by Makrotest (London) for the Scottish Development Agency, February 1981, section 6, pp.67 et seq.
18. N. Hood & S. Young, *The R&D Activities of US Multinational Enterprises: A Survey of the Literature*, study undertaken for the Department of Industry (London) June 1981.
19. ibid., chapter 10.
20. P. Haug, *R&D Intensity in the Affiliates of US-owned Electronics Companies Manufacturing in Scotland*, M.Phil. Thesis (unpublished), University of Edinburgh, 1981.

21. Hood & Young, 1976 (n.8), pp.285–6.
22. Forsyth, 1972 (n.15), pp.251–2.
23. Hood & Young, 1980 (n.9), p.60.
24. Hood, Reeves & Young, 1981 (n.2), table 6.
25. Hood & Young, 1980 (n.9), p.56.
26. M. Panić & P.L. Joyce, 'U.K. manufacturing industry: international integration and trade performance', *Bank of England Quarterly Bulletin*, vol.20, no.1, 1980.
27. Hood, Reeves & Young, 1981 (n.2).
28. This is illustrated, for example, in Hood & Young, 1980 (n.9), p.57.
29. P.J. McDermott, 'Organisation, ownership and regional dependence in the Scottish electronics industry', *Regional Studies*, vol.10, 1976, p.334.
30. I. Smith, *Some Aspects of Direct Inward Investment in the United Kingdom, with particular reference to the Northern Region*, Discussion Paper no.31, Centre for Urban & Regional Development Studies, University of Newcastle-upon-Tyne, 1980.
31. Hood, Reeves & Young, 1981 (n.2).
32. As illustrated in data quoted in Hood & Young, 1980 (n.9), p.57.
33. Hood & Young, 1980. For earlier work on this topic see Forsyth, 1972 (n.15), pp.64 et seq.
34. Forsyth, 1972 (n.15), p.104.
35. Hood & Young, 1980 (n.9), pp.68–74 discusses these processes.
36. Forsyth, 1972 (n.15), chapter 7. Also, D.J.C. Forsyth, 'Foreign-owned firms & labour relations: a regional perspective', *British Journal of Industrial Relations*, vol.11, no.1, 1973.
37. J. Hamill, *Labour Relations in Foreign-Owned Firms in the UK*, Ph.D. Thesis (unpublished), Paisley College of Technology, 1982.
38. *Labour Performance of US-Owned Plants in Scotland*, study undertaken by P A International Management Consultants for the Scottish Development Agency, September 1979.
39. *The Electronics Industry in Scotland: A Proposed Strategy*, study undertaken by Booz, Allen & Hamilton for the Scottish Development Agency, April 1979.
40. J. Firn, 'External control & regional policy', in G. Brown (ed.), *The Red Paper on Scotland*, EUSPB, 1972, p.164.
41. Hood & Young, 1976 (n.8), especially tables II, IV and VI.
42. As emerging from a study undertaken by the authors on behalf of the Department of Industry, Scottish & Welsh Offices and Department of Commerce, Northern Ireland, entitled 'A comparative study of corporate strategies of manufacturing MNEs operating in areas of high levels of regional assistance in UK and Eire'. The study ran from April 1980 to March 1982.
43. See, for example, *The Effects of Investment Incentives and Disincentives in the International Investment Process*, Working Group on International Investment Policies, OECD (Paris) 1981.
44. J. Marquand, *Measuring the Effects and Costs of Regional Incentives*, Government Economic Service, Working Paper 32, 1980.
45. Hood & Young, 1980 (n.9), p.97. This type of evidence has occasionally emerged in specific cases as, for example, in the evidence of Honeywell to an Expenditure Committee: Second Report from the Expenditure Committee, *Regional Development Incentives*, HMSO (London) 1973.
46. Haug, 1981 (n.20), chapter 11.
47. This debate is summarised in H.D. Watts, 'Large firms, multinationals and

regional development: some new evidence from the United Kingdom', *Environment & Planning A*, vol.11, 1979.

48. N. Hood & S. Young, *Foreign Ownership in UK Regions*, Working Paper 1(1), March 1981. Paper prepared as part of Department of Industry sponsored study 'A comparative study of corporate strategies of manufacturing MNEs operating in areas of high levels of regional assistance in UK and Eire'.

49. *Hiram Walker – Gooderham & Worts Ltd and the Highland Distillers Company Ltd*, Monopolies & Mergers Commission, HC 743, HMSO (London) 1980.

50. ibid., para. 7.3.

51. For a rehearsal of one set of arguments in this vein see *Quarterly Economic Commentary*, Fraser of Allander Institute, University of Strathclyde, vol.7, no.1, July 1981.

52. Makrotest study for SDA, 1981 (n.17).

53. Scottish Trades Union Congress, *Annual Report, 1980* (Glasgow) 1980.

54. M. Brownrigg, 'An application of the regional multiplier to industrial contraction', *Town Planning Review*, April 1980.

55. *The Engineer*, 17 May 1979.

2

CASE STUDIES
OF MULTINATIONALS
IN RETREAT

In this, the major section of the book, six company case studies are presented, with the aim of improving understanding of the complex processes underlying multinational retreat. The cases presented are those of Singer in Clydebank, Chrysler & Peugeot in Linwood, Hoover in Cambuslang, NCR in Dundee, Honeywell in Lanarkshire and Goodyear in Drumchapel. Their significance lies in the fact that they include nearly all the major cases of divestment and job rundown; indeed, the job loss in these six firms alone in Scotland has totalled a massive 39,500 people (based on peak employment figures). Again, included within the group are companies which have completely shut down in Scotland (Singer, Talbot and Goodyear), others which have largely come through the most painful rationalisation period (NCR & Honeywell, especially the Information Systems Division) and others which are still in the process of reorganisation and job rundown (Hoover). The fact that the multinationals studied are at different stages in the rationalisation process is partly a result of the differential timing of technological change and loss of competitiveness and partly due to variations in the timing of corporate response. All except Talbot (itself formerly owned by Chrysler) are American multinationals, reflecting the historical growth pattern of foreign direct investment in Scotland. On the other hand, although all the corporations are long-established in Europe, not all have been in Scotland for a long period of time. Singer was established in Scotland in the nineteenth century; NCR, Hoover, Honeywell in 1946–8; Goodyear in 1957 and Rootes (subsequently Chrysler & Peugeot) in 1963.

The basis on which these cases were prepared is that of considering developments in Scotland within the context of the MNE's European or sometimes global strategies. So each case begins with a brief review of the development of the corporation concerned, the internationalisation process and recent corporate performance. Corporate developments, particularly in Europe, are described and analysed; and the influences upon, and objectives and consequences of, European strategy assessed. Within this framework, developments in Scotland are considered, and most attention is given to recent events, where closure or job loss resulted. Finally, each case ends with some brief comments on the lessons for policy makers.

SINGER IN CLYDEBANK

The Early Years

I.M. Singer and Company was established in 1851 as the world's first manufacturer of practical sewing machines. The company was not the first American foreign direct investor in Europe.[1] This distinction belongs to Samuel Colt who built a factory in London in 1852 to manufacture revolvers, while in 1856 a New Jersey based firm, J. Ford and Company established a plant for the production of vulcanised rubber in Edinburgh.[2] But both of these operations proved unsuccessful and were sold out to British interests by the second half of the 1860s. If not the first US direct investor in Europe, Singer was certainly the first American international business. From 1855, when the company sold its French patent for a single thread machine to a French merchant, Singer expanded rapidly and widely overseas. Generally the company's foreign business was handled through independent franchised agents, although in Britain, Singer operated with salaried representatives, initially in Glasgow and by 1861 in London. From a European base in Britain, branch offices were then established in Germany and Sweden, while in Britain itself the branch network was gradually expanded.

Singer did not have either the domestic or foreign markets to itself in its formative years. Its main rival and market leader until the late 1860s was another American firm, Wheeler & Wilson.[3] In January 1867, the then British manager wrote to the parent company complaining that Wheeler & Wilson were 'certainly whipping us bad in Glasgow',[4] partly because of a shortage of supplies from the US. It was perhaps not coincidental then that in the spring of 1867 the directors of the Singer company took the decision to manufacture in the United Kingdom. Company correspondence does not indicate specifically why Singer embarked upon foreign production, but a number of factors seem to have had a bearing on the decision. During the American Civil War, the company could sell in Britain at prices lower than those in the US because of the premium on foreign exchange; after the Civil War, US currency was restored to its normal specie value and premiums on foreign exchange were cut; and freight and duty charges were further barriers to exports. At the same time wages in the US were rising and public demand for sewing machines was outstripping production capacity.

The reasons for the choice of Glasgow as a site are somewhat difficult to ascertain. The person who handled the site investigation was Vice-President George R. McKenzie, a Scot who had emigrated to the US and joined the Singer company some years previously. Although the Scottish connection may have been significant, Glasgow offered economic advantages such as an iron smelting industry, cotton thread companies and an active shipbuilding and steamship business with world-wide links. McKenzie himself indicated that shipping facilities and low labour costs were the main criteria. In conversation seventeen years later he remarked that 'it was the cheapness and docility of labor that was perhaps the most important consideration'.[5]

The initial plant was located at no. 1 Love Loan, High John Street, and commenced assembly, using imported parts, in the autumn of 1867. This factory was a small, experimental affair but, from a production of 30 machines a week at the end of 1867, output increased to 300 machines a week in 1869 with machine tools being sent to Glasgow to facilitate local manufacture. The Love Loan plant was abandoned for a factory in Bridgeton in 1873 and by 1881 Singer had three separate Glasgow factories. The company became convinced that freight, production and labour costs could be substantially reduced with a new plant, and in May 1882 construction began at a site in the then district of Kilbowie. On completion in 1885, this was the largest sewing machine factory in the world, employing over 5,000 people and with a manufacturing capability of 10,000 machines a week; from the plant, output was distributed world-wide through the vast and formidable Singer sales organisation. From these early beginnings further foreign manufacturing plants followed to reinforce Singer's stranglehold on the world sewing machine market. By the end of the nineteenth century the company was well along the road towards its goal of 'peacefully working to conquer the world'.[6]

The Singer Company[7] Post-World War II

Until the late 1940s the Singer Company sold two out of every three sewing machines in the world, its position as one of the first truly multinational companies being strengthened by production from Canada, France, Germany and Italy as well as Scotland. On the other hand, in 1958 the company was selling sewing machines designed in the nineteenth century, and 94 per cent of its sales were still in that basic product area. The heavy reliance on traditionally designed sewing machines, and particularly machines manufactured in developed countries, began to pose problems with the emergence of competition. This came first from European firms and producers in India and Communist China, but then, more importantly, from Japanese companies. Japan produced virtually no sewing machines prior to 1945, whereas (following the granting of a Singer patent at the end of the war) in 1957 300 companies were producing 2.3 million machines compared with Singer's output of 1.9 million. Singer's market share fell to about 30 per cent in the US and 35 per cent in most foreign markets, while profits fell 25 per cent between 1951 and 1957.

The company's response was to establish a joint venture operation in

Japan in 1955 and thereafter to set up manufacturing and assembly plants in a number of low-cost locations throughout the developing world. Existing plants were modernised, the company's service and distribution networks were improved and an aggressive promotional campaign was started to market the company's new, and expensive 'zig-zag' model.[8] By 1962, Singer's market share in the US was back to 40 per cent.

Despite these measures, the prospects for expanding sales of sewing machines were limited because of near saturation in major developed countries and an increase in the proportion of working women with the attendant decline in the attractiveness of home sewing. Therefore, under chief executive Donald P. Kircher, Singer embarked upon an ambitious, wide-ranging diversification programme, which resulted in the acquisition of 22 companies between 1962 and 1973. The firms purchased were in such diverse fields as heating and air conditioning, business machines, furniture, housing, banking, aerospace and tufted and knitting machinery. Some of these investments were, as it turned out, distinctly unsound. For example, in 1968 General Precision Instrument Corp., a producer of aviation electronics equipment was acquired, just prior to the collapse of the aerospace boom. Earlier in 1963 Singer had entered the business machine market by buying Friden Inc.; this company manufactured electro-mechanical calculators and accounting machines but the market was soon to be revolutionised by the advent of electronics. This latter business segment was to prove a continuing drain on corporate resources. In 1974 the company had to borrow $150 million mainly to finance its business machine operations; in the same year it was decided to liquidate the remaining electro-mechanical parts of the business (including a factory in the Netherlands), writing-off $30 million in the process. For the whole year a loss of $10 million was announced (Appendix, table 1).

The period of major transition for Singer did not really commence until the following year. Thus 1975 marked the end of the era of expansion and wide diversification and the beginning of one of retrenchment, cutbacks and consolidation. The ritual management changes followed the 1975 losses and a new chief executive, Joseph B. Flavin, was appointed to take Singer out of low-return diversification and back into three main areas of business – sewing, consumer and government products. During 1975 and 1976 actions were taken to withdraw from businesses which were unprofitable or peripheral to the main areas of activity. Therefore Tele-Signal products, photo-typesetting equipment, upholstered furniture and other minor product lines were disposed of or discontinued in 1975. Furthermore the Water Resources Division and German mail order business were sold. Write-offs in the 1975 accounts totalled $325 million and Singer made a staggering loss of $452 million for the year as a whole. Withdrawal from peripheral lines of activity continued into 1976, the most important decision being to withdraw from business machines: the international operations of Singer Business Machines were sold to the British computer firm, ICL in 1976 and the US side was sold to TRW Inc., after a $162 million write-off. By the end of that year, employment in the Singer group was 50,000 lower than at the peak in 1968. While Flavin was able to sort out these non-sewing activities the deep-rooted problems in Singer's core business-sewing machines were left unresolved. These returned dramatically to the forefront of attention as another huge loss was announced in 1979.

The Role of Sewing Products in the Singer Company

As pointed out, sewing machines accounted for 94 per cent of the company's sales in the late 1950s. The diversification programme meant that the relative importance of sewing machines declined substantially into the early 1970s (Appendix, table 2). Thereafter, as Singer rapidly relinquished their interests in a variety of fields, the importance of consumer sewing machines, at least, rose again to account for almost half of corporate turnover in 1977. The total market for home sewing machines is very flat or even declining in Europe and the USA, and although there is a large untapped market in the developing countries, competition from Japan, Korea, Taiwan and latterly East Europe remained a serious threat to Singer. Japan alone was estimated to control 50 per cent of the world market.[9] The company response was to stress consumer education in the poorer countries so as to increase the acceptance of home sewing and knitting, and to utilise electronics technology in sewing machines for the industrialised states.

The industrial sewing and textile machinery sector proved the immediate problem in the 1970s as the data in Appendix, table 2 and figure 1 reveal. This product group includes industrial sewing machines for the clothing industry, knitting machinery and carpet tufting equipment. These sectors suffered greatly in the aftermath of the 1974 recession, owing, for example, to the large number of closures of clothing manufacturers in the developed world and the low level of capacity utilisation among others. But once again the major problems emanated from Japanese competition. Industrial sewing machine output worldwide totalled 400,000 units in 1957, of which Singer accounted for 175,000 units (44 per cent). Over the next twenty years, global output rose to 1.2 million units, but Singer contributed only a little over 100,000 units of this and the company's market share was nearly halved. For the future, forecasts indicate slow growth in the sector, with world-wide sales rising to perhaps only 1.3 million units by 1984.[10] In response to these actual and projected developments, Singer in 1976 introduced an industrial sewing machine line using the electronics technology developed for consumer machines, with the hope that the progressive application of this technology across the product range would enable the company to resist further encroachment upon its market position.

In truth, in both consumer and industrial sewing machines, the response was 'too little and too late'. Until the very end of the 1970s the company patently failed to appreciate the nature of market changes and of the competitive threat. Moreover, costs and efficiency in the crucial European and American plants were out of control, capital investment in the sewing machine sector had been neglected and Singer's rambling multinational

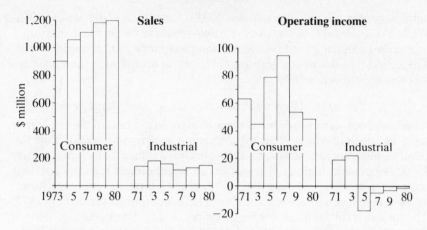

Figure 1. Sales and operating income for sewing products. Note difference in scale for sales and operating income. Source: Corporation accounts.

empire was in drastic need of reorganisation and central control and planning.[11] Only four years after one period of restructuring, Singer was forced to embark upon an even more fundamental rationalisation programme in its central business area, with ominous implications for Clydebank.

The European Operations of the Singer Company

In the early years of the company, manufacture was concentrated in two major operations: Elizabeth, New Jersey and Clydebank. With the expansion of European markets and the introduction of tariff barriers to protect indigenous firms, Singer established further European plants in France, Germany and Italy prior to World War II. Clydebank remained by far the biggest facility and was, in fact, the largest operation in the Singer group. The massive facility occupied 88 acres in three separate manufacturing units, being about twice the size of any other Singer works. The plant accounted for around twenty per cent of Singer output in some years and, as such, was a major source point for world markets; between 80 and 90 per cent of output was exported in total, with the US becoming the biggest single export market. Unlike the other European operations, the Scottish facility was nearly completely self-sufficient (compare NCR) with every step in the production process from metal casting to painting taking place in-house. Trains brought the cast-iron or aluminium straight into the factory, and finished sewing machines came out at the other end.

In the post-war period the European operations were modernised and reorganised to improve their competitiveness. The effect of this was particularly striking at Clydebank, where a steady reduction in manpower took place from the late 1950s. The operation, producing middle-of-the-range consumer machines, industrial machines and needles (although it had

46

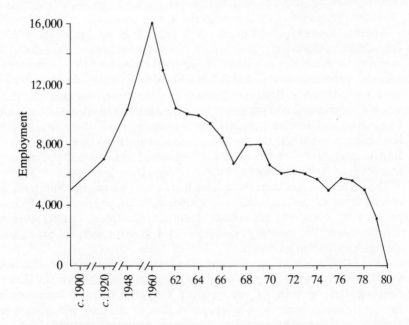

Figure 2. Employment at Singer, Clydebank. Figures obtained from a variety of sources. From 1960 onwards, data relate to end year employment.

once also briefly produced electric cookers) had employed about 10,000 immediately after the war: this rose to a maximum of 16,005 in 1960 before a gradual rundown to approximately 7,000 in 1970 (see figure 2). This rundown was partly related to modernisation, and the introduction of new labour saving designs and new materials, particularly the replacement of sheet or cast iron by plastics. But other factors also played a part. Some activities at Clydebank were moved to lower-cost locations abroad: the woodworking division, responsible for the production of cabinets, tables and benches, was closed in 1966 with the loss of 1,200 jobs for this reason. The failure of volume to rise as fast as anticipated (because of foreign competition) had an impact on labour requirement, while there may, in addition, have been a deliberate attempt to reduce the importance of Clydebank. Poor performance and the impact of labour disputes were part of the reason for this: in the first half of 1965 alone, for example, there were 76 separate work stoppages.[12]

Singer was still committed to Europe and as evidence of this a new plant was built in Monza, Italy in 1968. The plant specialised in bottom-of-the-line consumer sewing machines. High-volume production produced substantial economies of scale, so that although labour costs were 50 per cent higher than in Japan at the time, the overall operating costs in Singer's Italian and Japanese plants were essentially similar. The latter operation was handicap-

47

ped by a wide product line which encompassed die-cast and cast-iron consumer products as well as industrial sewing machines.[13]

Another new greenfield plant was built in Europe during the 1960s at Blankenloch (Germany). This facility was designed to produce industrial as opposed to consumer machines. Prior to the decision to manufacture in Europe, production of industrial machines was concentrated at Singer's factories in the USA. Because of trends in wage costs, production in the US was not competitive and the assets were transferred chiefly to the company's Clydebank and Karlsruhe plants. Subsequently, most of the machinery at Karlsruhe was shifted to the nearby Blankenloch factory. This move to Europe was started in 1958 but not completed until 1966, by which time, arguably, Europe itself was no longer a competitive location.

The European assets of the Singer Company also expanded rapidly as a consequence of the acquisition and diversification programme which was pursued vigorously in the 1960s. Business machines, refrigerators and washing machines, military equipment and so forth were all produced at various locations in Europe.

As at 1973, therefore, the European operations of Singer were as shown in table 1. With respect to consumer sewing machines, the various factories concentrated on part of the product range: Karlsruhe manufactured top-of-the-line machines, Clydebank middle-of-the-line and Monza bottom-of-the-line machines, while Bonnieres produced portable consumer sewing machines. The Continental European plants were much more closely integrated than the UK operation, with motors for the Italian machine being manufactured in France and castings for the French machines being produced in Germany. Needle manufacture was also centralised at Wurselen. Thus by the early 1970s, Singer had progressed a considerable way towards product and component specialisation within its plants in mainland Europe. The high degree of in-sourcing at Clydebank was obviously a serious anomaly, but closer integration may have been uneconomic while Britain was outside the Common Market. The manufacturing pattern within Europe was, nevertheless, geared to electro-mechanical products. Locations, degrees of integration, levels of capacity etc. could be expected to be different with a new (electronics) technology. Because the products manufactured in the various European factories were basically different, the consumer machines were sold in many of the same markets: Europe, Canada and the United States were major markets with some sales to Latin America and Asia. As table 1 indicates, industrial machines were produced in two locations, Blankenloch and Clydebank, although by reason of the enormous growth in Japanese production both plants were operating at a low level of capacity utilisation. The Singer retail sewing centres were another major employer of labour in Europe, as elsewhere in the world.

Excluding sewing machines, the major manufacturing facilities were at Leini, Nijmegen and at various locations in the UK. Reference has already been made to the upheavals within the corporation which followed the decision to remove Singer from many of the diversified areas of business

Table 1. The European Operations of Singer (1973)

		Employment
France	Bonnieres – portable consumer sewing machines, motors, plastics	1,019
Germany	Karlsruhe – top-of-the-line consumer sewing machines, castings	1,225
	Blankenloch – industrial sewing machines and parts	935
	Wurselen – needles for felling, tufting and sewing machines	630
Italy	Leini – refrigerators and washing machines	1,920
	Monza – bottom-of-the-line consumer sewing machines	1,600
Netherlands	Nijmegen – business machines	900
United Kingdom*	Clydebank – middle-of-the-line consumer sewing machines, castings, motors, industrial sewing machines, needles	6,500
	Stevenage – Business Machines Division and sales organisation for office products and retail information systems	666
	Blackburn – Tufting Machinery Division for tufting and textile equipment	630
	Other UK – Link-Miles Division, builder of commercial and military simulation equipment	698
	– retail outlets	1,736
		18,459

* Performance data for the Singer Company (UK) Ltd. are given in Appendix, Tables 3 and 4.
SOURCE: Singer News Service.

which the company had entered from 1963 onwards. At the European level, the company's involvement in the manufacturing of washing machines and refrigerators was terminated and the production of electro-mechanical billing and accounting products also ceased, leading to the closure of the factories in Italy and Holland. The withdrawal operation commenced in 1974 and continued through the following year.

Singer Sewing Machine Operations in Europe and the Role of Clydebank post-1974

By the mid-1970s, Clydebank still had a crucial role in the manufacture of sewing machines for the Singer group. The success or failure of Clydebank and of Singer were thus intimately related as they had been for nearly a century. From the early days, Clydebank occupied a curious position within the Singer corporation: in 1905 Singer had organised a wholly owned subsidiary, Singer Manufacturing Company Ltd for the purpose of acquiring and operating the Clydebank facility. However in 1917, three-quarters of the stock held in the British facility was distributed to shareholders as a dividend, perhaps for tax reasons. So until the late 1950s, Singer Manufacturing Company held only a minority interest in its British affiliate.[14] This probably meant a substantial degree of autonomy for the factory, while it was turning in adequate profits. The factory had the reputation of being 'run on rather feudal lines: the management kept themselves to themselves, having as little contact with the outside world (even with the local community) as possible . . .'.[15]

This comfortable situation was changed with the arrival on the scene of low-priced, sophisticated machines from Japan and elsewhere. At once, more attention began to be paid to manufacturing costs, productivity levels, restrictive practices and so on within the factory. A whole host of claims were made from the management side: the company asserted that productivity was grossly below that of comparable Singer plants abroad because of restrictive labour practices; on a related point, there were complaints of overmanning and a complex and rigid union structure involving 151 different unions; worker resistance to outside sub-contracting was criticised, and so on – all, apparently, the familiar ingredients of the British disease. As one commentator observed: 'What has been happening in this factory over the past fifteen years encapsulates virtually all the well-known weaknesses of British industry – weak management, fragmented trade unions, inefficient working practices leading to high costs . . .'.[16] It may have been true, to quote one Singer executive, that, 'There is no plant quite like Clydebank. It has such an entrenched system. There are more than 40 people, for example, doing nothing all week but count out cash because the workers like their money in envelopes . . . That's not 1979, that is 1884.'[17] Yet this has to be set alongside the equally valid comment that: 'The nearly century old plant is appallingly antiquated with manufacturing operations on several floors and a casting operation that would be out of date in Chungking.'[18] It was within this context that the traumatic events leading to the eventual closure of the Clydebank factory must be interpreted. (See Appendix, table 3 for data relating to the Clydebank facility in the late 1970s.)

The Reorganisation of Industrial Machine and Needle Manufacture Operations. The problems facing Singer in the mid-1970s were particularly acute in the industrial sewing machine sector (see figure 1). In Europe, the decision was taken in 1976 to close Blankenloch with the loss of 600 jobs. From the start output had been in excess of demand, and because of stock build-up, the factory was operating only one day per week by 1975. It was decided to concentrate the European production of industrial machines at Clydebank and the machinery and inventories were transferred accordingly. This move did nothing to aid Singer's fortunes, and only compounded the difficulties which were being experienced at Clydebank (with both industrial and consumer machines). The facts are illuminating:[19]

> The industrial sewing unit of the plant had not known a profitable year in the 1970s, either before or after the Blankenloch transfer. As the 1977 Annual Report stated: 'Production problems in another industrial

sewing product line (Clydebank) severely affected results.'[20] Clydebank also accounted for a large part of the company's world-wide loss of $3.4 million on industrial machines during the first six months of 1978.

The purchase by Singer UK of machinery and inventories from Blankenloch for £1.3 million was one factor contributing to these financial troubles of Clydebank.

In 1978, Singer was operating at only 34 per cent capacity worldwide and 35 per cent at Clydebank in industrial sewing machine manufacture. As at Blankenloch earlier, machines were being built for stock.

Major training problems were experienced after the transfer of industrial machines, substantially increasing start-up costs at Clydebank.

A large number of components were required to be purchased from outside firms in the UK and there were reports of difficulties with suppliers.

The failure of the Blankenloch transfer operation was heavily criticised by Clydebank management. It was felt that the move was badly planned and that inadequate time was allowed for the transfer, and major legal difficulties emerged out of the failure of the machinery to comply with UK safety standards. The move, moreover, was being undertaken in a situation with a rapidly deteriorating market. The transfer was barely complete, therefore, when in 1978 the corporation proposed to implement a further series of changes in its industrial machine and needle operations in Europe. The plans were as follows:

Industrial machine manufacture would be phased out from Clydebank, and therefore from Europe as a whole, by 1981. Production would be concentrated at the US factory in Elizabeth, where electronic industrial machines were being produced.

Industrial needle manufacture would be ended at Clydebank and European output concentrated at Wurselen. Both factories had previously been running at less than half their capacity. It was decided to concentrate industrial needle production in Germany because Wurselen was the centre of world needle production and because the Wurselen plant, employing 611 in 1978, had no other products; all R&D was, in addition, based in Wurselen. Clydebank in turn would concentrate more heavily on household needles.

As a consequence of restructuring, jobs would be gained in the US and at Wurselen. At Clydebank conversely, the 1978 employment level of 4,800 was to be reduced to 2,000 over a four-year period (although the change in employment was partly associated with reorganisation of the consumer machine operation).[21]

The Reorganisation of Consumer Sewing Machine Operations. The plans for the consumer machine business in Europe were less far-reaching. What was required was greater component specialisation and therefore greater inter-plant links within Europe to maximise economies of scale. Proposals to integrate the European manufacture of consumer machines were aimed most obviously at Clydebank. As part of the restructuring of this facility, it was proposed to invest £8 million to modernise the plant and introduce a new line of lightweight sewing machines which would be assembled using components supplied by the Singer plants on mainland Europe.[22] This proposal maintained the position of Clydebank as the European production centre for middle price range sewing machines, with Bonnieres, Monza and Karlsruhe also retaining their respective parts of the product range. For the time being at least Karlsruhe was to be the only factory utilising new electronics technology. The argument was that because of the high cost involved, micro-processor equipment, at the time, was only suitable for expensive, top-of-the-range machines which contributed about 10 per cent of Singer's sales.

Alternative Proposals for Clydebank. When the restructuring programme was announced in June 1978, the unions were given three months to respond to the management's plans. Their reaction was to commission a study to analyse the company's world-wide restructuring and to investigate alternative strategies for Clydebank. This feasibility study was undertaken by PA Management Consultants at a cost of £75,000, financed by a levy from the workers and by a grant from the Scottish Development Agency.[23] The company, for their part, agreed to cooperate fully with the consultants' investigation.

Meetings to discuss the consultants' proposals were held in the early autumn of 1978. The workforce were decidedly unhappy at the consultants' recommendations, which would still have entailed substantial job losses, but in November the report and its proposals were passed to Singer management. The fundamental premise of the report was that there was still a market for certain of the industrial sewing machines produced at Clydebank. The report therefore proposed the retention of five industrial machines from the existing range of 40 models, with the saving of 750 jobs.[24] Concentration on these most competitive models, it was argued, would provide a base from which to develop and launch new machines capable of regaining market share for Singer. It was also recommended that the manufacture of industrial needles should be retained at Clydebank. In order to restore the plant to profitability, however, it was accepted that additional investment would be required, and, equally importantly, changes would be required to increase productivity substantially. The consultants were strongly critical of the lack of investment at Clydebank in former years: Singer UK had been consistently adding less to fixed assets than it had written off in the form of depreciation, and in spite of the impact of inflation had committed little new finance to working capital. Moreover in 1975, for instance, Singer UK paid out £2.4 million in dividends although it only made a net profit of £0.3 million.

The report emphasised the 'industrial museum' nature of the Clydebank factory: of the machine tools in use, more than 10 per cent were over 50 years old, of which nearly 2 per cent were over 75 years old, and incredibly, seven items were over 100 years old. The particular problem was the industrial machine division where most of the output was produced in a seventy-year-old six-storey building. Much of the machinery was more than 50 years old, with the foundry having been built in 1894. Low investment was claimed to have led to several major problems including high maintenance and operating costs, high scrap levels and high transportation costs when moving materials between floors. The resulting low productivity was aggravated by a wage structure which provided insufficient incentives to the workforce.[25] New payment systems were proposed and it was recommended in addition that the limitations placed on the use of outside subcontractors by the unions should be lifted.

The Singer Company responded fairly positively to these proposals. Following further negotiations a revised offer was made in respect of industrial machine manufacture at Clydebank which would have retained 500 jobs (compared with the consultants' recommendation of 750 jobs). The conditions attached to this offer were that there would be a new pay structure, improved flexibility and the introduction of outside contractors to do some jobs. Moreover, the British Government should provide some of the additional capital, estimated at between £2 million and £4 million to pay for new buildings and equipment and subsidise the machines made at Clydebank for a temporary period to enable Singer to match the price of competing models made in Taiwan.

In mid-December 1978 the workers voted to reject cooperation with the management in implementing the reorganisation programme and associated redundancies, and Singer, in turn, announced that the factory would be closed in the early 1980s. A massive campaign involving the Government, local authorities, community leaders and the Church was mounted to persuade the workforce to reverse their decision. Ultimately in January 1979 the joint union–management plan was accepted by the workforce, but only after a stormy meeting in which union officials were heckled and jeered.[26] Employment at the plant was to be reduced to 2,350 over a period with phased redundancies beginning immediately.

Detailed negotiations had still to take place on the methods of implementing the plan. Realisation that this was to be no easy task came only a month later when assembly workers refused to agree to cuts in overtime, and a week-long strike followed. In June 1979, short-time working was introduced because of a world-wide drop in orders. On 8 October, it was announced that Singer was reviewing its European operations with a view to closing one of the principal plants. Finally, on 12 October the closure of Clydebank became official. In announcing the news the Vice President of Corporate Relations stated that: 'Singer just cannot continue in Clydebank. We are going to withdraw by June 1980. The plant will close. The bottom has fallen out of the market. As from today investment at Clydebank will cease. We are losing more here than at any other location in the world.'[27]

Soon after, further job cuts were announced in other European plants, and the facility at Elizabeth, New Jersey (opened even earlier than

Clydebank, in 1873), was closed as the company began to concentrate on strengthening its sewing-machine production in Third World locations. Restructuring was planned to continue through to 1981, with severe cutbacks in the number of company-owned outlets, which historically had been a key feature in Singer's marketing system. It was truly the end of an era.

The Singer Closure and the Clydebank Economy

By the late 1970s, the Singer operation at Clydebank was a mere shadow of its former self. The halcyon days when the company had a station named after it and the sewing machine was represented on the Clydebank coat-of-arms were gone. It is still true, nevertheless, that Singer Clydebank was almost regarded as an institution and closure came as a hammer blow to the local economy, following as it did the substantial job losses at shipyards on the upper Clyde, the closure of nearby Goodyear as well as the plants of Beatties Biscuits and scws Biscuits and other factory rundowns. A study undertaken in 1978[28] indicated that if Singer had closed at that time, when it employed 5,100 people, the consequences would have been very severe. Between 8,200 and 8,400 persons in the UK would not have had a job who otherwise would have done. Job losses of this magnitude would have meant an 80 per cent increase in unemployment in the Clydebank Employment Exchange Area, annual income losses of £17–20 million (at 1978 prices) in Strathclyde Region and fiscal costs to the State (lost tax revenue and increased benefit expenditure) of between £19 and £21 million per annum (at 1978 prices). At time of closure, employment at Singers was well below the 1978 figure, but this once-for-all job loss has to be seen against a backcloth of 20 years of job attrition. During this period the unemployment rate in Clydebank rose steadily to a figure of 15.1 per cent in 1981 (table 2).

The decision to close Clydebank as opposed to other European factories, in the face of substantial overcapacity, was related primarily to relative

Table 2. Unemployment in Clydebank

June	Clydebank No.	%	Strathclyde Region No.	%	Scotland No.	%
1971	2,650	6.5	n.a.	n.a.	115,523	5.6
1972	3,390	7.7	n.a.	n.a.	126,603	6.1
1973	2,538	5.8	n.a.	n.a.	92,287	4.3
1974	2,104	4.7	n.a.	n.a.	77,940	3.6
1975	2,302	5.5	60,390	5.6	101,590	4.7
1976	3,027	7.6	85,318	7.9	144,134	6.7
1977	3,725	9.8	109,873	10.2	186,218	8.6
1978	3,793	9.5	111,218	10.2	187,150	8.4
1979	3,618	9.1	106,631	9.8	182,796	8.1
1980	4,852	11.4	133,694	12.3	223,150	9.9
1981	5,721	15.1	177,835	16.1	305,801	13.5

SOURCE: Manpower Services Commission, Glasgow.

performance, which in turn was a function of factors such as the product mix, capital investment, labour productivity and so forth. Clydebank suffered because of its role in the manufacture of industrial sewing machines, a major product problem for the corporation over a number of years. Aspects of the 'British disease' loom large and problems over cooperation in implementing the reorganisation programme probably sealed the fate of the factory.

Some Implications of the Singer Case

One important issue concerning the Singer case relates to the successive switching of locations for the manufacture of industrial sewing machines. In a little over 20 years production was switched from the USA to Germany and the UK, then to the UK alone and finally back to America. This would seem to confirm many of the criticisms made of 'runaway' multinational firms, which are alleged to shift production around the globe to exploit low labour costs, take advantage of host government incentives, stable political regimes and so forth. While such considerations were obviously relevant in the Singer case, the extent of the production transfer was related chiefly to planning problems and an underestimation of the speed of market decline. Even so this does not diminish the importance of the issue from a policy viewpoint.

One interesting feature of the case concerns the role of national and international unions in questioning and subsequently changing Singer's strategy for Europe. When a large multinational corporation, such as Singer, reappraises world-wide strategy, there must inevitably be a tendency to take a 'broad brush' approach. This may lead, for example, to divestment decisions because – on balance – the operation does not meet corporate objectives. Yet there could be parts of any such operation which were worth saving, when viewed from a narrower and more localised perspective. This certainly appeared to be the case with Singer Clydebank, where the management consultants were able to identify particular areas of activity which could have been viable.

A related issue concerns the attitudes of Singer management to the consultants' investigation. For 18 months prior to the company's announcement of its reorganisation plans, the local unions claimed that Singer refused to provide them with any information (and the case was brought up before the Organisation for Economic Cooperation and Development (OECD) committee on multinationals as a result). On the other hand, the company seem to have cooperated fully with the consultants' study. Any attempt to formulate an alternative strategy clearly requires full access to information and cooperation from the company concerned.

One less than satisfactory feature of Singer's agreement to alter its plans in respect of industrial sewing machines was its insistence that the UK Government cooperate in providing finance. If the plan to retain manufacture in Europe was not viable then the company should have gone ahead with its original intention to locate all industrial machine production in the USA; if it was viable and Singer would benefit in future, then Government finance was unnecessary.

APPENDIX

Table 1. Performance Data for The Singer Company

Year	Sales ($000)	Assets ($000)	Net income* ($000)	Shareholders equity ($000)	Employees	Net income as % of shareholders		Rank (by sales) in Fortune Directory
						Sales	Equity	
1980	2,786,600	1,529,300	38,100	427,400	71,000	1.4	8.9	140
1979	2,598,100	1,482,400	(92,300)†	396,300	77,000	–	–	132
1978	2,469,200	1,435,400	62,800	502,300	81,000	2.5	12.5	113
1977	2,294,300	1,461,900	94,200	457,400	86,000	4.1	20.6	109
1976	2,125,500	1,589,000	74,200	373,300	85,000	3.5	19.9	105
1975	2,568,000	1,797,100	(451,900)†	306,200	98,000	–	–	73
1974	2,661,700	2,016,000	(10,100)†	768,900	111,000	–	–	66
1973	2,527,600	1,897,200	94,500	817,800	122,000	3.7	11.6	52
1972	2,217,500	1,608,900	87,500	763,200	117,000	3.9	11.5	47
1971	2,099,454	1,669,716	70,812	774,480	120,000	3.4	9.1	41
1970	2,125,059	1,635,034	75,123	774,489	133,000	3.5	10.1	43
1969	1,902,144	1,438,615	77,721	680,914	133,000	4.1	11.4	45
1968	1,754,553	1,408,917	69,392	620,305	135,000	4.0	11.2	43
1967	1,137,653	1,049,173	50,154	466,294	105,000	4.4	10.8	69
1966	1,049,227	983,332	47,280	435,050	107,700	4.5	10.9	71

* After debiting $7,700,000 loss from discontinued operations in 1973, $39,100,000 in 1974, $410,600,000 in 1975 and crediting $900,000 in 1976 and $3,300,000 in 1977. 1976 net income figure also includes an extraordinary credit of $14,000,000, while 1977 net income includes extraordinary credits of $16,400,000.

† Bracketed figures indicate losses.

SOURCE: 'The Fortune Directory of the 500 Largest US Industrial Corporations', *Fortune*, various editions; corporations accounts.

Table 2. Percentage of Sales by Major Product Areas

Product Area	1971	1973	1975	1977	1979	1980
Consumer sewing machines and related products	42.7	42.3	48.4	48.7	46.0	43.5
Industrial sewing and textile machinery	8.2	8.7	7.5	5.4	5.5	5.3
Aerospace systems	18.2	15.5	16.3	16.6	20.0	23.7
Housing	5.9	7.2	6.8	7.4†	6.3†	6.1†
Metering and controls equipment	6.3	6.8	6.3	8.6	8.0	8.2
Furniture	3.9	7.7	4.6	6.2	5.8	5.1
Other	14.8	11.8	10.1	7.1	8.4	8.1
Total	100.0	100.0	100.0	100.0	100.0	100.0
Total ($million)*	1,857.6	2,168.3	2,211.7	2,284.8	2,598.1	2,786.6

* Total sales and not merely sales from continuing operations.
† Motor products (formerly power tools and floor care).
SOURCE: Corporation accounts.

Table 3. Performance Data for Singer UK Subsidiaries: The Singer Manufacturing Company Ltd (to 1970); The Singer Company (UK) Ltd (from 1971 onwards)

		Sales (£000)	Net profit* before tax (£000)	Net profit before tax as % of sales	Exports (£000)	No. of employees
	1980	56,166	141	0.3	18,361	2,614
	1979	71,703	(1,901)	—	33,784	5,856
The Singer	1978	73,943	(1,830)	—	39,181	7,152
Company	1977	74,721	(2,246)	—	46,259	8,009
(UK) Ltd	1976	62,081	1,841	3.0	41,001	8,702
(Clydebank Factory	1975	66,278	1,545	2.3	31,834	8,915
plus other UK	1974	62,816	2,707	4.3	28,973	10,300
operations)	1973	52,625	4,480	8.5	24,470	10,500
	1972	42,251	2,658	6.3	22,163	9,900
	1971†	38,576	2,197	5.7	18,000	9,734
	1971†	18,445	1,312	7.1	15,092	6,197
The Singer	1970	17,219	1,111	6.5	13,734	7,129
Manufacturing	1969	19,463	2,516	12.9	15,934	7,520
Company Ltd.	1968	15,478	1,388	9.0	12,227	6,909
(Clydebank	1967	11,826	(183)	1.5	n.a.	n.a.
Factory)	1966	n.a.	(117)	—	n.a.	n.a.
	1965	n.a.	(889)	—	n.a.	n.a.

* Profit figures exclude exceptional or extraordinary items from 1971.
† On 30 September 1971 The Singer Manufacturing Company Ltd went into liquidation, being acquired by The Singer Company (UK) Ltd. 1971 figures are shown for The Singer Manufacturing Company as if it were a separate company.
SOURCE: Company accounts; Extel Statistical Services.

Table 4. Analysis of Turnover and Pre-tax Profits (Unadjusted) for The Singer Company (UK) Ltd

	1973	1974	1975	1976	1977	1978	1979	1980
				(% of total)				
Turnover								
Sewing machines	67.7	66.1	58.9	66.8	77.5	78.1	75.2	50.4
Tufting machinery	12.5	10.4	14.7	–	–	–	–	–
Business machines	12.6	15.2	17.0	–	–	–	–	–
Flight simulation	7.2	8.3	9.4	15.4	19.8	18.1	20.8	43.7
Discontinued operations	–	–	–	17.6	–	–	–	–
Gas metering products	–	–	–	–	2.7	3.8	4.0	5.9
	100.0	100.0	100.0	100.0	100.0	100.0	100.0	100.0
					(£000)			
Pre-tax Profits								
Sewing machines	2,497	1,751	(1,074)	621	(4,744)	(3,824)	(3,172)	(1,245)
Tufting machines	770	128	1,314	–	–	–	–	–
Business machines	509	398	1,077	–	–	–	–	–
Flight simulation	362	133	(389)	859	1,300	839	364	904
Discontinued operations	–	–	–	(2,858)	–	–	–	–
Gas metering products	–	–	–	–	358	418	460	381
Total	4,138	2,410	928	(1,378)	(3,086)	(2,567)	(2,348)	(40)

SOURCE: Extel Statistical Services.

NOTES AND REFERENCES

1. There were numerous American foreign direct investments during the first half of the nineteenth century, mainly in S. America and Canada but also elsewhere in the world. The forerunners of the present day multinational corporation were, however, the manufacturing firms which began to exploit their technological leadership through establishing production plants in Europe from the 1850s onwards. See Mira Wilkins, *The Emergence of Multinational Enterprise: American Business Abroad from the Colonial Era to 1914*, Harvard Univ. Press (Cambridge, Mass.) 1970, chapters 1–3.

2. ibid., p.30.

3. Years later, the Singer Company acquired Wheeler & Wilson.

4. Wilkins (n.1), p.41. This section also draws on R.B. Davies, 'Peacefully working to conquer the world: the Singer Manufacturing Company in foreign markets, 1854–1889', *Business History Review*, vol.43(3), 1969, pp.299–325.

5. ibid., p.316.

6. ibid., p.325.

7. The company name was changed from I.M. Singer & Company.

8. The information in these paragraphs is mainly derived from: 'Singer Company (B)' in J. Fayerweather & A. Kapoor, *Strategy and Negotiation for the International Corporation*, Ballinger (Cambridge, Mass.) 1976.

9. For details of the mid-1970s reorganisation of the company, see 'Singer's gamble turns into a loss', *Electronics*, 22 January 1976; 'How the directors kept Singer stitched together', *Fortune*, December 1975; 'Why the profits vanished at Singer', *Business Week*, 30 June 1975.
   In 1977 the world market was estimated at Yen 100 billion, with Japan accounting for half, according to the *Financial Times*: 'Electronics the key for Singer plant', *Financial Times*, 16 November 1977.

10. The figures in this paragraph were derived from: *Financial Times*, 16 November 1977; 'The Scottish thorn in Singer's side', *Financial Times*, 10 January 1979.

11. With respect to capital investment, between 1976 and 1978 Singer provided for over $90m. in depreciation for its sewing business assets, but spent only $75m. on investment. Internationally in the five years to 1978, Singer lost $81m. in foreign exchange adjustments, failing to make a gain in any of these years, indicating lack of central management control. See *Financial Times*, 19 November 1979.

12. 'Bringing an 80-year-old factory up to date', *Financial Times*, 24 November 1966.

13. 'Singer Company (B)' in Fayerweather & Kapoor (n.8).

14. Mira Wilkins, *The Maturing of Multinational Enterprise: American Business Abroad from 1914 to 1970*, Harvard Univ. Press (Cambridge, Mass.) 1974, p.25.

15. 'Bringing an 80-year-old factory up to date', *Financial Times*, 24 November 1966.

16. 'Regeneration in practice', *Financial Times*, 19 January 1979. The article went on: 'The question is – is this a terminal disease or is it possible, by decisive action on the part of all the people concerned, to effect a cure?'

17. 'The Scottish thorn in Singer's side', *Financial Times*, 10 January 1979.

18. 'Behind the Snafu at Singer', *Fortune*, 5 November 1979.

19. The following points are derived from: 1977 Annual Report of the Singer Company; 'Singer in Scotland – Who's to Blame?', *The Economist*, 23

December 1978; 'The Scottish thorn in Singer's side', *Financial Times*, 10 January 1979.

20. The Report also went on ominously: 'These production problems will continue to be the subject of intensive study and corrective measures during 1978'. As figure 1 indicates the Singer Company lost $3.7m. on industrial machines for the full year, although this was partly due to production difficulties in the Centurion sewing machine line.

21. It was estimated that 500 redundancies would be entailed, the rest of the reduction in manpower being achieved by natural wastage and early retirals.

22. The £8m. also included redundancy payments.

23. The S D A provided two-thirds of the finance and the workers subscribed £0.50 each.

24. Four options were actually presented in the report involving the saving of different numbers of jobs but this was the favoured option.

25. 'The Scottish thorn in Singer's side', *Financial Times*, 10 January 1979.

26. For details of the stormy meeting at which the workers overturned their original decision, see 'Singer factory saved', *The Guardian*, 18 January 1979.

27. *The Evening Times* (Glasgow), 12 October 1979.

28. *Singer (Clydebank) Ltd, A Cost Minimisation Study*, Department of Physical Planning, Strathclyde Regional Council, December 1978. See also T. Stone, 'Aspects of the impact of major employment loss, the case of the Singer Company, Clydebank', Fraser of Allander Institute, University of Strathclyde, *Quarterly Economic Commentary*, no.4, April 1979, pp.38–50.

CHRYSLER & PEUGEOT IN LINWOOD[1]

This case stands apart from the others reviewed in this section because of the sheer scale of public attention focused on the Linwood car plant during its brief 18-year history. Certainly Linwood was the biggest multinational employer of labour in Scotland during the 1970s, with 7,500 people still working at the facility in 1979 after years of problems. But the reasons for the constant glare of publicity surrounding the operation go much further than mere size. Linwood was the only car factory in Scotland, and when the Hillman Imp began to roll off the production line in May 1963, this was the first Scottish-produced car since 1928. The location of the manufacturing facilities also contributed. The economic and social problems of Clydeside have been and remain particularly severe. Linwood was in a position where it could partially alleviate (or exacerbate) these difficulties. In addition, despite its short life, Linwood had three owners, two of which were foreign multinationals. From 1964, when Chrysler Corporation first took a minority shareholding in Rootes Motors Ltd, the American corporation was involved with the British Government. This did not change when P.S.A. Peugeot-Citroen (now Peugeot s.a.) acquired Chrysler's European operations. The amount of parliamentary time consumed by the affairs of both these multinationals has ensured that Linwood has never been far from the public eye.

Background of the Multinational Owners

As in the other cases studied, the position of the multinational parents of the Scottish affiliate had an important influence on the course of events at Linwood. This was particularly true of Chrysler. As Appendix, table 1 reveals, Chrysler was, and despite its horrendous difficulties of recent years, is still one of the largest us industrial corporations. At a peak in 1973, the corporation rated number 4 in the Fortune 500. Yet the company has consistently been a poor third among the major automobile manufacturers in the us and at times has been well out of touch with market trends, particularly the trend towards compacts and subcompacts in America. Thus the data also show a very volatile profit performance, with poor profit figures in 1969 and 1971 and losses in 1970, 1974, 1975 and 1978–80. This explains, in part, a number of the policies pursued by the corporation in Europe:

market entry through the acquisition of ailing national producers in Europe;

Chrysler's policy of self-financing for its European subsidiaries (individually);

the inability to integrate the operations in Britain, France and Spain;

the need to seek government support at various points in time – British support in 1975/6, us and Canadian support in the late 1970s;

the requirement to sell-off affiliates, such as those in Europe, in the late 1970s.

The financial problems of the Chrysler Corporation were very much in evidence when the decision was taken to divest in Europe in 1978, but the appalling state of the company did not make the headlines until a little later. When Chrysler first took its problems to the us Government in August 1979 it owed \$4.8 billion to 350 banks in 15 countries. After months of negotiations a rescue package was approved involving £1.5 billion Federal loan guarantees and \$2.03 billion raised by Chrysler in the form of concessions by lenders, sales of assets, deferred pension payments etc. This was the biggest intervention by the Federal Government in the history of American business.[2]

Such problems are relevant to the position of the second multinational owner of the Linwood plant, Peugeot s.a. The latter group was created when Peugeot took control of Citroen in April 1976. In this form the European combine was profitable and the management earned the reputation for toughness and efficiency. But in the belief that the world motor industry of the 1980s would belong to only a few giants, Peugeot plunged into the big league with the acquisition of Chrysler's European operations for \$230 million cash and 15 per cent equity in the French concern in 1978. The latter was the beginning of what was to become increasingly closer involvement between the two groups: in 1980, Chrysler put up Peugeot stock as collateral for a \$100 million loan from the French car maker; agreement was reached for Peugeot to supply engines to Chrysler in deals worth \$400 million and the two companies made plans for a new small car for the us market. Peugeot's growing involvement with Chrysler was occurring at a time when it faced severe difficulties in the European market, in part at least caused by digestion of the acquired Chrysler Europe: in 1980 Peugeot lost \$350 million.[3] Not for the first time, speculation began to mount about the future of Linwood and on this occasion there was to be no saviour.

The Linwood Story

In considering the history of Linwood, it is possible to distinguish a number of periods in the years from 1963 to 1981, all of which, while distinct, share the common theme of hopes raised and hopes dashed.

Period I – Establishment. Amidst great enthusiasm, on 1 October 1960, Lord Rootes announced plans for the Linwood factory. For the Rootes company the plant represented a £23¼ million gamble, to take the manufacturer into the volume car business. The car to be built at Linwood was the Hillman Imp, a completely new mini car which was to be sold in competition with the B M C Mini; the latter, launched in 1959, had a strongly established market position. The plant was built on a greenfield site directly across the road from the Pressed Steel Fisher factory, which extended its pressings to supply the necessary car bodies. To meet the needs of the factory, nearly 2,000 new homes were built in the village of Linwood and road and rail links and shopping facilities were all improved. Aside from the economic advantages which were hoped to accrue from the plant, the local member of parliament, Norman Buchan, also saw social benefits, arguing that the project would 'contribute to curing the cancer of Glasgow housing'.[4]

The Rootes move to Scotland was part of the dispersal of the motor industry undertaken by the Government as part of the more active regional policy of the early 1960s. By refusing Industrial Development Certificates for proposed expansions in existing locations, mainly in the West Midlands, the motor manufacturers were steered towards the North and West. Ford and Vauxhall, however, located their new plants on Merseyside, fairly close to their existing operations; and only Rootes was persuaded to move to Scotland, 250 miles north of their other car production facilities at Ryton (assembly) and Stoke (engines) and the administrative offices and technical centre at Whitley (also in Coventry). Labour supplies, the availability of transport and dock facilities and particularly the fact that Pressed Steel already had a plant on an adjacent site in the village were all mentioned as reasons for choosing Scotland.

In retrospect the theory underlying the dispersal of the motor industry proved to be incorrect. The view was that the motor industry, as a location leader, would attract supporting investment in ancillary and components' industries. In Scotland, at least, this never occurred and the green fields surrounding the Linwood plant bore witness to the failure of the concept. In this lay one of the principal problems facing all owners – British, American and French – of the Linwood facilities. The cross-hauling of bodies, components and completed vehicles added significantly to production costs at Linwood. The operations which were undertaken at Linwood were those which were transport-cost sensitive, that is, the stamping of body shells (after Chrysler acquired the Pressed Steel Fisher plant in 1966) and the assembly of complete vehicles.

The early euphoria over the Linwood plant evaporated soon after the commencement of manufacture in 1963. In February 1965, the *Glasgow Herald* was calling the Linwood factory a 'running sore', as plant operations were disrupted by a plethora of labour disputes. It was in these very early years that Linwood's strife-ridden reputation was forged. But even now it is difficult to be certain of the true reasons for the labour problems. Among the various factors which have been cited are: inexperience on the part of middle management and the trades unions; the background of the labour force, many of whom came from the traditionally militant shipbuilding and coal-mining industries; the very different production techniques in the motor industry as compared with those more traditional sectors; and failure to make adequate provision for the necessary large-scale retraining and reorientation of workers' attitudes. On top of such issues, which primarily related to the newness of the facility, Rootes was experiencing other problems linked to the failure of the Imp to sell in planned volumes. While these may also be attributed in part to the inexperienced labour force and other start-up problems, the basic difficulties derived from fundamental design faults in the car. In the first full year of operation (1964), Linwood was operating at under one-half of capacity, and a four-day week was introduced at the factory in August of that year. Such uncertainties, after the initial high hopes, were hardly conducive to good industrial relations.

Period II – A New Beginning: The Chrysler Takeover. The events at Linwood had an important bearing on Chrysler's entry to the UK market, for it was the deteriorating financial position of Rootes, accentuated by the failure of the Imp, which virtually forced the British company to link up with Chrysler. Chrysler Corporation in the early 1960s had no overseas car manufacturing capacity. When Chrysler acquired Dodge in 1929 it took over the small-scale activities of Dodge trucks in the UK. But this was the sole foreign presence until the corporation purchased 15 per cent of the shares of Simca in 1958. Even then, major developments did not really commence until 1963, by which time corporate profitability in the US was improving and Chrysler had a new chairman whose declared aim was major expansion into Europe. The acquisition route was chosen, partly because the costs of establishing a new plant and facilities were prohibitive and partly because of the company's late entry to the European market. In the space of four years, Chrysler entered Europe and took majority or complete ownership of three separate firms: Simca in France, Barreiros in Spain and Rootes in the UK.

Chrysler's purchase of 30 per cent of the voting shares in Rootes in June 1964 came only after a number of other efforts to establish a manufacturing foothold in the UK had been rebuffed, including approaches to Standard and Leyland Motors. Rootes was neither the first approach nor the first choice. The Rootes–Chrysler arrangement aroused mixed emotions within the country and in Parliament. Since exchange control consent was required, the Government was a party to the deal and under pressure from the Opposition, the Conservative Government insisted that Chrysler should not increase its holdings in Rootes without first consulting the Government. The financial situation of Rootes continued to deteriorate after 1964, with losses rising from £2.1 million in 1965 to £2.6 million in 1966 and £10.7 million in 1967 (on a turnover of £171 million); the loss for Linwood alone in the latter year amounted to £2.4 million. The then Labour Government sought a 'national solution' for Rootes by bringing the company into partnership with an indigenous motor manufacturer. This idea was rejected by the Minister of Technology, Wedgwood-Benn, because the Government 'did not believe that Rootes, by itself, was a viable organisation with or without government money, owned or not by a British company'.[5] Chrysler, understandably anxious to introduce its own management and ideas, was, therefore, permitted to increase its voting interest in Rootes to 66 per cent.

As part of the 1967 takeover Chrysler agreed to a number of conditions, which were made public. Some of these 'undertakings' were fairly innocuous and were mere window-dressing, referring to the expansion of employment and exports and the maintenance of a 'British interest' in the company. The main political element in the package was the agreement to focus expansion on Linwood: 'Chrysler confirms the plans of expansion covering development work at various factories and especially at Linwood in Scotland where the major development will take place and where it is planned to increase employment by several thousands . . .'.[6] It is perhaps at this point that the multinational dimension of the Chrysler case first emerges. Chrysler were in a strong bargaining position. Linwood was already showing itself to be the albatross around the neck of the UK operations. And yet Chrysler undertook to centre expansion there. The only interpretation is that Chrysler saw in Linwood an even more important bargaining card for the future.

Following the takeover, Chrysler tried to stem the decline in the British company. A major capital investment programme was instituted, directed towards rationalisation, in-sourcing, facility updating and volume. How far this was well planned is, however, debatable. A former employee of the company, speaking of this period, said that 'Rootes/Chrysler UK seemed to be regarded more as a disposal bin for surplus funds than a commercial venture'.[7] To increase the capacity utilisation of Linwood, the Scottish plant took over body production which had been previously undertaken by Pressed Steel Fisher Ltd at Cowley. Linwood thus became the source of body shells for all of Chrysler UK. Assembly of the Arrow range (principally the Hillman Hunter and variants) was shifted to Linwood from late 1979; and with the launch of the Avenger, Linwood benefited to the extent that the transmission, rear axle and front suspension were scheduled for manufacture in Scotland. From being the Imp plant, Linwood was developed into an integrated facility with a complex product mix covering the entire Chrysler UK range.

Yet profitability for Chrysler UK, and particularly for Linwood, proved elusive for a variety of interrelated reasons. First, the investment programme upon which the company embarked laid too much emphasis in the early years on the improvement of plant facilities to the detriment of investment in new models. The only new car to be built by Chrysler in Britain between 1967 and 1976 was the Avenger, launched in 1970 from Ryton. A number of other models were introduced in other parts of Europe at this time. With both the Chrysler 180 and the Chrysler Alpine the declared intention was to launch these models from the UK. But early in 1970 the decision was taken to transfer manufacture of the 180 to France, and again in 1974 output of the Alpine was switched to France. Production switching, of course, requires multinationalism.

The reason given by the company for moving production out of Britain was industrial relations problems. Thus a second major reason for Chrysler's failure was that it failed manifestly to handle labour relations in the UK. Apart from the short unofficial disputes which plagued the British motor industry as a whole, Chrysler was beset by a variety of incidents which led to lengthy stoppages. At Linwood, the first of these occurred in 1968 as the company tried to improve production and eliminate differences in grade structures and payments' methods between the original Linwood plant and the pressings facility nearby. Having the agreement of the two major unions but frustrated by lengthy negotiations with the other unions, the company simply tried to implement its plan. This exacerbated the dispute and eventually a court of enquiry was set up, headed by D.J. Robertson. The three major points made by Robertson are worthy of note since they epitomise the labour relations of Chrysler at Linwood:

1. 'We conclude that in terms of payment and related benefits this is an Agreement which reasonable men should be able to accept without difficulty.'
2. But 'urgent attention should now be given to creating adequate machinery for negotiation and consultation'.
3. And the company was criticised for implementing an agreement when only the two larger unions had signed it. It was concluded that Chrysler 'acted with rapidity in a situation requiring patience'.[8]

These same three points emerge time and again in the history of Chrysler's labour relations. The company attempted to introduce far-reaching, well-meaning and innovative changes in labour relations practices, which were undoubtedly in the interests of the UK operation. But procedures were inadequate and the company seemed often to over-react in its handling of disputes. Attempts to end disputes were frequently accompanied by threats to redirect investment in the UK, to switch investment to other European locations or, indeed, to withdraw entirely. As an American-based corporation, Chrysler failed to understand labour-relations in the British motor industry. Some of their problems emerged from the employment of middle and senior managers more in line with practices in the United States than in Europe. The situation may also have been worsened by the intervention of Detroit but there is little evidence of this. On the other hand, union officials at Linwood have frequently complained about the inability of local management to make decisions without higher-level approval.

The worst year for stoppages at Linwood (in terms of manhours lost from internal disputes) was 1973 – see table 1 opposite. The prevalence of short stoppages is very evident, and throughout the years Linwood accounted for about 60 per cent of stoppages lasting less than four hours. In 1973, as in other years, the stoppages tended to occur at particularly unfortunate periods such as when the market was booming or when the company was running losses for other reasons.

A third major factor in the 1970s was shortage of finance both at subsidiary and corporate levels. Chrysler's financial policy for its European subsidiaries (individually) was that of self-sustenance. Investment in new

Table 1. Disputes Record at Linwood in 1973

	Under 4 hours	Under 1 shift	Under 1 week	Over 1 week	Total	% of Chrysler UK Total
No. of disputes by duration at Linwood	261	48	15	0	324	54.0
Manhours (000) lost because of:						
Internal factors	731					
External factors	110					
Total	841					
% of Chrysler UK total	25.6					

SOURCE: S. Young & N. Hood, *Chrysler UK: A Corporation in Transition*, Praeger (New York) 1977, p.243.

models and in plant and equipment was thus dependent upon profitability. Such a requirement produced a 'Catch 22' situation for the British affiliate, which was unable to make profits for lack of new models, and unable to finance new models because of lack of profits. Even if the corporation wished to help (which it undoubtedly did not), it was unable to assist financially because of its own weak position in the USA. Financial data both for the UK operation as a whole and for Linwood are given in Appendix, tables 2 and 3. 1973 was the year in which the company made record and almost acceptable profits and was one of the few years in its history that Linwood was profitable. Ironically, this was the same year that the fate of Chrysler UK was effectively sealed. The optimism built up by the reorganisation and re-equipment programme and the launch of the Avenger in 1970 had evaporated.[9] The decision was taken in June 1973 to halt investment because of labour disputes 'until we have demonstrated over a reasonable period of time, that we can work out our problems in a constitutional manner while continuous production is maintained'.[10] The onset of the oil crisis late in the same year, together with these other factors, sounded the death knell for the American subsidiary.

Period III – The 1975/6 Rescue, Another New Beginning. Speculation about the future of Linwood and the other operations of Chrysler UK began to mount in the press during 1974 and adversely affected company sales. UK banks started to refuse to renew short-term loans or require Chrysler Corporation guarantees. In spite of huge losses in the US, the American parent was forced to pump $38 million into the British operation between December 1973 and February 1976. An application to Finance for Industry for cash to reschedule loans proved unsuccessful. Finally, and dramatically, on 3 November 1975, 'the Government (were) presented with a pistol to their head . . .'[11] as the Chrysler Corporation Chairman outlined three possibilities to the UK Prime Minister: first, liquidation of Chrysler UK as of the end of November 1975; second, Chrysler would give the UK company to the Government; or third, Chrysler would transfer a majority interest to the

Government. The first inkling of forthcoming events had come only five days previously when, at a press conference in Detroit, the Chairman and President of Chrysler had made fairly explicit suggestions regarding the disposal of the British operations.[12] This was multinational imperialism.

Given the circumstances, the UK Government was almost bound to have to save Chrysler. Economically, serious effects on the level of employment (estimated at 55,000 directly or indirectly for the UK as a whole) and on the balance of payments, principally due to the loss of an important contract to supply car kits to Iran, were the major factors. Politically, Linwood was the key: the Scottish National Party (SNP) had won 11 seats at the previous general election and were second to Labour in 35 out of its 41 seats in Scotland. Chrysler was more or less asked to state its terms.

A number of options for saving the UK company were considered. Almost all hinged around the retention of Linwood in some way. Agreement was eventually reached on a deal which involved the closure of Ryton, but the retention of the Stoke engine plant, Linwood and the truck facilities. In a display of magnanimity, Chrysler Corporation proposed that, in addition, production of the Alpine should be transferred from France to Ryton, to prevent the closure of the latter. (But the reality of the situation was that Chrysler were short of capacity in France.) Under the terms of the deal, the UK Government committed itself to supporting Chrysler UK up to a maximum of £162.5 million between 1976 and 1979, in comparison with a potential corporation commitment of £64 million. These sums of money were to cover possible losses and to finance specific capital projects, principally five 'new' or improved models (for details, see Appendix, table 6).

Linwood was to become the heart of Chrysler UK under the new arrangements: production of an improved Avenger was to be undertaken at Linwood; a new small car, the Chrysler Sunbeam, was to be launched from Linwood in 1977; and a new light car was to be manufactured and launched from Scotland in 1979. While job losses were to occur at Linwood, they were to be far fewer than at other locations in Britain, as table 2 indicates.

Table 2. Chrysler UK Rescue Operation: Plant and Employment Forecast

Plant	Actual employment (Dec. 1975)	Planned employment (Aug. 1976)	% Change
Linwood	7,000	5,500	− 21.4
Stoke, Coventry	6,300	4,000	− 36.5
Ryton, Coventry	4,300	1,600	− 62.8
Whitley, Coventry	1,700	1,400	− 15.6
Other*	5,800	4,400	− 24.1
Total	25,100	16,900	− 32.7

* Includes truck manufacturing operations.

SOURCE: Eighth Report from the Expenditure Committee, Session 1975–6, *Public Expenditure on Chrysler UK Ltd.*, HC 596(I), HMSO (London) July 1976, p. 92.

The Corporation's agreement with the Government expressed laudable sentiments regarding integration: 'products and model ranges will be planned as an integral part of Chrysler's overall worldwide product plan so that CUK's (Chrysler UK) products will be complementary to, and have a specific and definable position within, the total Chrysler worldwide product offering'.[13] Transfer prices were to be determined on an 'arms-length basis'. The Government had the right to appoint two directors to the board of Chrysler UK and required the company to provide quarterly management accounts and other financial information for use by government departments in monitoring. Finally, the company agreed to negotiate a Planning Agreement with the Government and the unions (Chrysler, as it turned out was the sole private firm to sign a Planning Agreement before the fall of the Labour Government in 1979).[14] All of this, of course, smacked suspiciously of some of the commitments made by Chrysler in 1967 at the time of takeover.

Virtually all authoritative opinion was of the view that the government rescue of Chrysler UK would not enable the company to attain long-term viability. And in the context of later events, Chrysler's agreement to continue in Britain may be seen as a cynical attempt to improve the saleability of the UK affiliate. But ostensibly, at least, Chrysler took their commitments seriously and embarked upon a large-scale restructuring and reorganisation programme in 1976. The Avenger face-lift was duly implemented out of Linwood, and the Sunbeam (mainly using Avenger and Alpine components) was launched in July 1977.

Reaction to the Sunbeam was favourable: 'If it is marketed properly, proves reliable and is available on demand, the new Sunbeam should prove a success and the saviour of Chrysler Scotland and Chrysler UK.'[15] There were hopes that the Planning Agreement would usher in a new era of harmonious labour relations. On the other hand, an unofficial 12-day strike by 450 men in K block (so-called 'Crazy-K') in March 1977 over an apparently trivial issue suggested that little had been learned over ten years.

Period IV – The End of Chrysler, Enter Peugeot–Citroen. It was obvious that it would be no easy task to create a viable Chrysler operation in the United Kingdom. The company recorded losses of £42.6 million in 1976 and £21.5 million in 1977. These were largely covered by the terms of the rescue agreement with the Government, but into 1978 the need to earn profits began to be of crucial importance. Without profitability there could be no hope of financing new model development after the rescue agreement expired. A small profit in the first quarter of 1978, as the Sunbeam established itself, gave promise of brighter things. But in the second quarter Chrysler UK plunged back into the red, primarily because of a sharp increase in disputes at some of the English factories. A major dispute then erupted at Linwood late in June 1978, which, while directly involving only 550 paintshop workers, led to the lay off of a further 5,000 of the plant's employees. For the whole year losses amounted to another horrific £20 million.

Speculation over Linwood's future began to mount again. In France, Chrysler launched a new car, the Horizon, which in appearance was very similar to the Sunbeam. While selling at a similar price to the latter, it was a front-wheel-drive car (against the Sunbeam's conventional drive), and it had five doors (against the Sunbeam's three) and generally was more sophisticated. The Sunbeam was a car for the UK market, given the Continental European preference for front-wheel drive, but it was also faced with competition from the Horizon in the British market. The futility of a rescue programme for Chrysler UK in isolation was very apparent: Chrysler's long-term planning clearly did not foresee any integration between its various European subsidiaries. By leaving the UK operation as a separate entity, the option always existed of selling it or liquidating it without affecting the rest of the European facilities. The second factor leading to renewed fears for the future of Linwood was the decision taken to transfer production of a new light car from Scotland to Ryton. As the rescue agreement indicated, this car was to have been launched from Linwood in 1979. Finally, there were rumours that Chrysler were having talks with Mitsubishi Motor Corporation about the possibility of the Japanese firm moving into Linwood to make cars.[16] What actually occurred was, again, completely unexpected. Early in August 1978 it was announced that P.S.A. Peugeot–Citroen would take over Chrysler's entire European car and truck operations in return for $230 million cash and 15 per cent of the shares in the enlarged French company. Just as the withdrawal ultimatum revealed the unacceptable face of multinationalism, so also did Chrysler's sell-out. The UK Government was given no prior warning of the proposed deal. This was in spite of Government financial support and in spite of the corporation's commitment to a Planning Agreement. The latter was specifically designed to involve unions and Government in any discussions which took place about the future of the UK affiliate.

The British Government had little leverage in its subsequent discussions with Peugeot–Citroen. Doubtless the French giant (now the largest manufacturer in Europe) would have preferred to leave Chrysler UK out of the deal. In essence, therefore, the Declaration of Intent between Chrysler and the British Government passed to Peugeot–Citroen. The commitment to the maintenance of employment made in the existing Declaration was, however, weakened with the addition of the phrase 'to the extent consistent with prevailing economic conditions'. The Government agreed to continue its support programme for the British company and the loan guarantees passed intact to the new parent corporation. The Planning Agreement was also to continue. The one addition in the Declaration was the agreement to allow British component suppliers to compete for business within the Peugeot–Citroen group as a whole.[17]

Complete control did not pass to the French multinational until 31 October 1980, but in July 1979 the name of Chrysler in Europe was changed to Talbot as the French combine began the enormous task of restructuring. The motive for the acquisition of the UK arm of Chrysler Europe was seen by many as being access to the dealer network in Britain. Ostensibly, Peugeot s.a. set about trying to create a viable Talbot production operation in the uk. Environmental factors were hardly helpful to these efforts: political turmoil in Iran led to the suspension of the major contract to supply car kits; continuing recession conditions led to a further diminution of the size of the uk car market, and the growth of Japanese imports reduced the market share available to domestic suppliers. On top of this, the launch of the Solara, a saloon car version of the Alpine, from Ryton in 1980 proved singularly unsuccessful. Linwood had no new models and this time no political saviour. In the face of massive losses for the Peugeot s.a. group as a whole, the closure of the Scottish factory took place on 22 May 1981. The uk Government's attempts to save the plant were half-hearted. Cynically, the 4,700 Linwood workers added only imperceptibly to the 2½ million already unemployed in the uk. Even among the workers there seemed to be a feeling of inevitability – that time had ultimately run out. To the dismay of the Scottish tuc, the Linwood workforce, by a 2–1 majority, rejected their shop stewards' advice to fight the closure.

Postscript, November 1981. The national media and political spotlight returned to Linwood in November 1981 as what was called the 'Sale of the Century' got underway at the plant. Plant and machinery from the factory went under the auctioneer's hammer in Europe's most extensive ever industrial sale. Buyers from countries all over the world were unimpressed by demonstrators trying to hold up the sale. One German buyer commented 'the people should have concentrated on better industrial relations when the plant was going . . . Shouting is worth nothing.'[18] Even so, feeling against the sale ran high, as activists pointed out that Linwood's multinational owners, having received large sums in government money to equip the plant (see Appendix, table 5) were then able to benefit again from the machinery sale. As one remarked, 'I am appalled at the give-away prices. It is out and out madness selling this machinery to faceless foreigners. . . . Surely a means could have been devised to use it to regenerate the engineering industry here.'[19]

The Causes of Failure

In terms of its performance over the years, Linwood was an obvious target for closure. At the level of operation of Talbot in the uk there was no need for car assembly plants both at Linwood and at Ryton; the latter, being closer to sources of supply and to markets was the clear choice. It is ironic, nevertheless, that Ryton, which was so near to closure at the time of the government rescue in 1976, survived into the 1980s at the expense of Linwood. As the data in Appendix, tables 2 and 3 reveal, Talbot (Scotland) Ltd recorded losses in every year but two in the 1970s. During these years, the cumulative value of losses totalled £73.4 million or 8.6 per cent of turnover. For the years 1976–9 alone Linwood losses amounted to £61 million, almost half of the total losses incurred by Talbot (uk) Ltd; whereas the Scottish facility accounted for just one-fifth of turnover. It is necessary to be cautious in accepting these figures at their face value. The Linwood plant was operated as a cost centre not a profit centre and performance was measured against the manufacturing expense budget. And in evidence before a House of Commons Trade & Industry Sub-Committee, the plant manager at Linwood agreed that he 'does not know whether in fact that plant is making money or losing it . . . only . . . whether he is meeting targets or not'.[20]

In assessing the reasons for failure, a number of factors may be identified. The first of these concerns the inability of the many owners of Linwood to get to grips with the basic economics of the industry in Europe. In the same year that Chrysler took a majority stake in the British company, Ford introduced their 'Ford of Europe' concept. The rationale underlying this was that to obtain maximum benefit from the size of the European market, integration of country subsidiaries was necessary. Only in this way could the economies of scale in the production and marketing of motor vehicles be fully exploited. It took Ford ten years before the results of their European integration programme bore full fruit in the form of the Fiesta, with its engine blocks from Dagenham, transmissions and axles from Bordeaux, carburettors from Northern Ireland and engine machinery from Valencia in Spain. Chrysler Corporation policy should, from the beginning, have involved the development of an integrated car and commercial vehicle facility for the whole of Europe. This would have required the manufacture of a European product range, with component production and assembly centralised so as to maximise output at any one location. Together with this, a European marketing and distribution network should have been a major priority. Within such a system Linwood would have had a clearly defined European role. Given its peripheral location, this role would probably have been specified in terms of component manufacture.

Instead of this, Chrysler pursued a strategy for its European subsidiaries which stressed the independence of national units and the self-sustenance of these units. Even after the Government rescue this same policy was still being pursued, witness the Horizon and the Sunbeam. It is arguable that given the precarious financial position of Chrysler in the USA, this was the only possible strategy. Chrysler may have hoped that with the restoration of its European affiliates to profitability, the funds made available could be used to finance integration. But if this was the policy, then it was still based on misconceptions, that is, that US managerial expertise and experience was the main ingredient required to restore Chrysler UK to profitability; and that investment in new plant and equipment was more important than investment in new models. For their part, Chrysler argued that the problems in the British affiliate prevented integration. The then Managing Director of Chrysler UK commented that: 'The labour-climate, the consistency of supply, whether it be machined parts or built-up cars, did give us difficulty in convincing people that we were a good base to be integrated with.'[21] For Peugeot, still struggling to digest Citroen when it acquired Chrysler Europe in 1978, integration was an even greater necessity. The French group clearly had this as their objective but were blown badly off course by the recession of 1980. At this strategic level, with decisions taken by multinational owners hundreds even thousands of miles away, Linwood was but a pawn in a much bigger international game.

At the second level, Linwood failed because it didn't at any time have a winning model. Peak production of the Imp in 1964 was 72,000 cars, less than 50 per cent of theoretical capacity at the plant. After the Chrysler takeover, the product mix at the plant became more complex, but in 1969 assembly of the Arrow range was transferred to Linwood. The range, based on the Hillman Hunter, was by this time past its best. Following the Government rescue of Chrysler, a rejuvenated version of the ageing Avenger was moved to Linwood; and finally, Linwood obtained a new but only stop-gap model in the Sunbeam. Despite the euphoria of motoring correspondents, the Talbot Sunbeam was not a winner. In 1980, it came eighteenth in the best-seller lists in the U K and was out-sold by the Horizon from Talbot in France. Although the poor image that the plant had built up in the early years may have affected sales on a continuing basis, the fundamental reasons for model failure were outwith the control of Linwood itself.

Only at the final level, namely that of performance of the plant itself, does responsibility for failure rest with Linwood and its management, unions and workforce. Certainly in the early days, the position was almost anarchic. Labour relations up to the crisis of 1976 were appalling. Productivity levels constantly failed to meet targets. Poor performance was thus one ingredient in the failure mix. Having said all of this the Linwood plant never overcame the logic of distance from both its principal suppliers and its major outlets. It was this primarily which led to the situation where the plant required to be operated at about 90 per cent capacity to achieve viability.[22] The availability of grants, incentives and more direct government support did not affect the inherent problems of being in an environment with little means of supporting a car plant.

Lessons of the Linwood Case

As with the other cases in this section, it would be wrong to try to generalise the Linwood experience to all multinationals in Scotland. Even so, there are a number of lessons which may be drawn from the operation of first, the American and then the French multinational concern.

One lesson relates to the question of Government involvement in an M N E. Successive governments patently failed to secure a viable future for Linwood, in spite of the large sums of money ploughed into the facility (see Appendix, table 5). The explanation in part seems to lie in lack of understanding of the operations of multinational enterprises. Consistently, negotiations undertaken between the British Government and the two multinationals have focused on the viability of the U K company as a separate entity. The focus of negotiations should at least have been Europe-wide in their dimension. Given the failure of Chrysler (in particular) to implement an integration strategy, the British Government's responsibility was clearly to push the company in the direction of greater integration. On successive occasions, however, commitments extracted from the American corporation seemed to presume that Chrysler UK was a national company rather than merely one arm of a multinational. Yet the Government were fully aware, as far back as 1967, that Rootes was too small to survive as an independent unit. To quote Wedgwood-Benn again, 'if we had nationalised Rootes we should have been left, even then, with a company which, in technological terms, was not on a scale which could survive at a critical time'.[23] During 1975, moreover, the Government had the evidence of three reports on which to draw, all of which emphasised size and scale economies.[24]

Another issue which emerges from the Linwood case concerns the financial health of the parent MNE. The past track record and financial position of multinationals requires investigation both before investment decisions are made in Scotland and subsequently. Chrysler may have been seen by governments as a desirable parent for the UK operation because it was large and because it was American. Yet its volatile record in the US was evident to even a casual observer. And during the entire period in which Chrysler was operating in Europe, the financial weakness of the corporation in its domestic market had an important bearing on its inability to succeed in Britain. Finance was less of a problem for Peugeot–Citroen initially. Yet in acquiring Chrysler Europe before it had fully assimilated the takeover of Citroen, the French MNE was taking an enormous gamble. In the end, because of continuing recession conditions, the financial resources of Peugeot–Citroen were severely strained.

Along with many other multinationals in Scotland, Linwood was a branch plant. The Chief Executive at the factory was the plant manager who was responsible to the director of manufacturing at Coventry, with an expenditure authorisation limit of £15,000.[25] As already noted, the plant was operated as a cost centre, and Linwood was completely dependent on outside decision-making for its existence and expansion. Naturally, if the factory had been integrated on a European-wide basis, it would not be possible nor would it be desirable to have decentralised decision-making in most functional areas. Labour relations may be the one exception, where this is better handled in a decentralised manner by management on the spot. Centralised decision-making in this area may have exacerbated labour relations problems at Linwood.

The other lessons from the Linwood experience relate to regional and industrial policy. With the benefit of hindsight, Linwood, a new factory with a new labour force, should not have been asked to build a new car. There were too many imponderables and possibilities for error in this situation. A smaller-scale, less ambitious venture would clearly have been preferable. The other misjudgement in the case of Linwood concerned its potential for attracting ancillary industry. This was a major gamble which failed.

APPENDIX

Table 1. Performance Data for Chrysler Corporation

Year	Sales ($000)	Assets ($000)	Net income ($000)	Shareholders equity ($000)	Employees	Net income as % of shareholders		Rank (by sales) in Fortune Directory
						Sales	Equity	
1980	9,225,300	6,617,800	(1,709,700)*	(104,000)*	92,596	–	–	32
1979	12,001,900	6,653,100	(1,097,300)*	1,605,400	133,811	–	–	17
1978	16,340,700	6,981,200	(204,600)*	2,926,500	157,958	–	–	10
1977	16,708,300	7,668,200	163,200	2,924,600	250,833	1.0	5.6	10
1976	15,537,788	7,074,365	422,631	2,815,326	244,865	2.7	15.0	10
1975	11,699,305	6,266,728	(259,535)*	2,409,209	217,594	–	–	10
1974	10,971,416	6,732,756	(52,094)*	2,660,473	255,929	–	–	11
1973	11,774,372	6,104,898	255,445	2,727,702	273,254	2.2	9.4	4
1972	9,759,129	5,497,331	220,455	2,489,012	244,844	2.3	8.9	5
1971	7,999,339	4,999,720	83,660	2,268,913	227,397	1.0	3.7	7
1970	6,999,676	4,815,772	(7,603)*	2,155,621	228,332	–	–	7
1969	7,052,185	4,688,214	88,771	2,100,891	234,941	1.3	4.2	6
1968	7,445,251	4,398,092	290,729	2,066,324	231,089	3.9	14.1	5
1967	6,213,383	3,854,714	200,434	1,834,761	215,907	3.2	10.9	5
1966	5,649,505	3,148,543	189,223	1,701,267	183,121	3.3	11.1	5

* Bracketed figures indicate losses or negative values.
SOURCE: 'The Fortune Directory of the 500 Largest US Industrial Corporations', *Fortune*, various editions.

Table 2. Talbot (Scotland) Ltd and Talbot (UK) Ltd:* Profits, Turnover and Capital Employed (£000)

	Talbot (Scotland) Ltd			Talbot (UK)Ltd		
Financial Period†	Pre-tax profits (Losses)	Turnover	Capital employed	Pre-tax profits (losses)	Turnover	Capital employed
1980	n.a.	n.a.	n.a.	(75,071)	588,000	111,806
1979	(14,063)	137,339	22,423	(41,142)‡	575,000	101,640
1978	(16,261)‡	158,395	18,862	(20,204)‡	610,000	106,323
1977	(22,262)‡	79,745	20,773	(21,472)‡	458,000	93,378
1976	(8,463)‡	52,174	23,645	(42,599)‡	322,000	76,544
1975	(8,188)	58,173	16,784	(35,453	351,000	22,940
1974	(5,821)	75,429	19,363	(17,734)	313,000	51,766
1973	4,249	87,865	17,666	3,724	322,000	59,514
1972	(1,636)	70,763	2,212	1,641	281,000	66,445
1971	(3,640)	82,724	4,475	405	320,000	66,549
1970	2,724	48,294	10,219	(10,613)	179,000	69.572
1969	2,278	36,473	8,730	707	165,000	66,933
1968	(3,573)	21,448	8,393	3,804	176.000	59,751
1967	(2,359)	14,654	12,084	(10,716)	171,000	60,029

* The previous names of the Scottish company were: Chrysler (Scotland) Ltd., Rootes Motors (Scotland) Ltd. and Rootes Pressings (Scotland) Ltd; the U K company has gone through a similar series of name changes. Note: Since Talbot (UK) Ltd. is the holding company, the figures for Talbot (Scotland) Ltd. are incorporated into the former.
† Years ended July 31 until 1970. The 1971 period covers 16 months to November 1971; and 1973 covers 13 months to December 1973. Thereafter financial period is the calendar year.
‡ Net losses wholly or partly funded by government grants in these years. Value of government grants to Talbot (Scotland) Ltd. as follows (£000): 1976 – £8,463; 1977 – £10,000; 1978 – £7,500; and to Talbot (U K) Ltd: 1976 – £41,501; 1977 – £10,000; 1978 – £7,500; 1979 – £5,000.
SOURCE: Company accounts.

Table 3. Talbot (Scotland) Ltd: Year-End* Balance Sheets† (£000)

	1967	1968	1969	1970	1971	1972	1973	1974	1975	1976	1977	1978	1979
Fixed assets	11,122	16,953	19,014	18,214	16,433	15,592	14,320	13,323	12,210	13,941	13,851	13,444	13,125
Unamortised special tools	441	1,351	2,101	2,200	1,382	864	20	146	317	1,582	175	810	1,971
	11,563	18,304	21,115	20,414	17,815	16,456	14,340	13,469	12,528	15,523	14,025	14,254	15,095
Current Assets													
Balance at bank and cash	87	2	23	24	23	23	25	25	26	26	30	13	13
Debtors and prepayments	1,130	961	4,427	3,402	612	578	1,487	1,182	1,096	1,500	1,838	1,631	2,587
Amounts owing by holding co. and fellow subsidiaries	533	–	6	69	· · · ·	–	1,447	1,613	1,181	16	13	20	199
Inventories	2,143	3,391	3,936	6,915	6,741	8,436	11,401	10,251	7,002	19,200	22,659	27,781	25,435
	3,893	4,354	8,391	10,411	7,376	9,037	14,361	13,070	9,305	20,741	24,539	29,445	28,234
Less Current Liabilities													
Bank overdraft	–	365	484	634	3,068	3,585	1,727	–	–	–	–	–	–
Trade creditors and accrued charges	877	2,961	6,177	7,303	6,393	10,140	8,542	6,453	4,357	9,020	13,948	20,704	18,694
Amounts owing to holding co. and fellow subsidiaries	2,325	10,780	12,720	11,294	9,437	8,863	–	–	–	2,917	3,169	3,469	1,831
Current position of long-term debt and deferred liabilities	–	–	1,236	1,236	1,736	736	704	672	650	650	650	650	650
Accrued interest on loan capital and deferred liabilities (secured)	170	160	159	139	81	47	62	51	41	–	23	15	5
	3,373	14,266	20,776	20,606	20,715	23,372	11,035	7,176	5,048	12,619	17,791	24,838	20,906
Net current assets	520	(9,912)	(12,385)	(10,195)	(13,339)	(14,335)	3,326	5,895	4,256	8,122	6,748	4,608	7,328
Net capital employed	12,084	8,393	8,731	10,219	4,475	2,212	17,666	19,363	16,784	23,645	20,773	18,862	22,423
Financed by													
Issued ordinary share capital	5,000	5,000	5,000	5,000	5,000	5,000	5,000	5,000	5,000	5,000	5,000	5,000	5,000
Accumulated deficit	3,401	(6,974)	(4,696)	(1,972)	(5,612)	(7,230)	(2,981)	(8,802)	(16,990)	(16,990)	(29,251)	(30,513)	(44,577)
Shareholders' investment	1,599	(1,974)	304	3,028	(612)	(2,230)	2,019	(3,802)	(11,990)	(11,990)	(24,252)	(25,513)	(39,577)
Long term debt and deferred liabilities	10,485	10,367	8,427	7,191	5,087	4,351	3,647	2,975	2,325	1,675	1,025	375	–
Holding company loan	–	–	–	–	–	–	12,000	20,190	26,449	33,960	44,000	44,000	62,000
	12,084	8,393	8,731	10,219	4,475	2,121	17,666	19,363	16,784	23,645	20,773	18,862	22,423

* July in 1968 and 1970; November in 1971 and 1972; thereafter December. † Balance sheets are derived from accounts relating to year in question. Any amendments made after the end of the year in question have been ignored. SOURCE: Company accounts.

Table 4. Output Figures for Talbot (Scotland) Ltd. and Talbot (UK) Ltd (000 units)

	'67	'68	'69	'70	'71*	'72	'73†	'74	'75	'76	'77	'78	'79
Talbot (Scotland) Ltd													
Output	47	44	33	125	127	145	143	157	154	40	60	98	71
Built-up	45	43	31	68	76	88	81	72	35	n.a.	n.a.	n.a.	n.a.
Knock-down‡	2	1	1	57	51	57	62	85	119	n.a.	n.a.	n.a.	n.a.
Talbot (UK) Ltd Output§	210	214	245	249	308	288	292	287	246	159	185	214	121

* 16 month period.

† 13 month period.

‡ Knock-down units mainly consisted of supply of Hunters to Iran.

§ Cars and commercial vehicles.

SOURCE: S. Young & N. Hood 'Multinational and Host Governments: Lessons from the Case of Chrysler UK', *Columbia Journal of World Business*, 12(2), 1977, pp. 97–106; Company sources.

Table 5. Some Items of Government Assistance to Linwood (£000)

1.	1963 Board of Trade loan payable by instalments until 1980 5½% secured		7,850
2.	Government grants following 1975 rescue:	1976	8,463
		1977	10,000
		1978	7,500
3.	Value of Investment Grants and Regional Development Grants in Fixed Assets (as at Dec. 31st 1979)		4,821
4.	Value of Investment Grants and Regional Development Grants in Special Tools (1969–1976)		3,479
5.	Regional Employment Premium		4,400*

* Partly estimated.

SOURCES: Expenditure Committee, Session 1972–73, *Regional Development Incentives*, HC 327, HMSO (London) June 1973, p. 44; Company accounts.

Table 6. Financial Arrangements Agreed between the UK
Government and Chrysler Corporation

Potential Government Commitment	
£50 million maximum share of loss in 1976	⎫ Funding of
£10 million maximum share of loss in 1977	⎬ possible losses*
£12.5 million maximum share of loss in 1978 and 1979	⎭
£28 million loan for capital development in 1976–77 (guaranteed by Chrysler Corporation)†	⎫
£27 million loan for capital development in 1978–79 (secured on Chrysler UK)†	⎬ Loans to finance specific capital projects
£35 million medium-term bank loan facilities guaranteed by government (and counterguaranteed by Chrysler Corporation)	⎭
£162.5 million	
Potential Chrysler Corporation Commitment	
£10 million maximum share of loss in 1976	⎫ Funding of
£10 million maximum share of loss in 1977	⎬ possible losses*
£12.5 million maximum share of loss 1978 and 1979	⎭
£10–12 million for the C6 (Alpine) model introduction	
£19.72 million waiver of loans (and interest) made to Chrysler UK.	

* Government responsible for first £40 million of losses in 1976. Equal sharing of further losses in 1976 and possible losses in 1977–79 up to maximum figures shown.
† Government loans repayable in ten semi-annual instalments between 1985 and 1990.
SOURCE: Young and Hood, *Chrysler UK*, pp. 315–17.

NOTES AND REFERENCES
1. Apart from other references, this article relies heavily on S. Young & N. Hood, *Chrysler UK: A Corporation in Transition,* Praeger (New York) 1977; N. Hood & S. Young, 'The Linwood experience: Chrysler and Peugeot–Citroen in Scotland', in *Scotland, the Multinationals and the Third World*, Scottish Education and Action for Development (Edinburgh) 1982.
2. 'Chrysler on the brink', *Fortune*, 9 February 1981; 'How the banks were driven to bail out Chrysler', *Financial Times*, 25 June 1980.
3. 'Peugeot and Chrysler: ties that hinder?', *Business Week*, 15 June 1981.
4. N. Buchan, 'Linwood story', *New Statesman*, 4 December 1964.
5. Cited in Young & Hood, *Chrysler UK*, p.83.
6. ibid., p.102.
7. J.G. Norman, 'The crippling of Chrysler', *Management Today*, February 1981.
8. *Report of a Court of Inquiry under Professor D.J. Robertson into a Dispute at Rootes Motors Ltd. Linwood*, Cmnd 3692, HMSO (London), July 1968.
9. Sales of the Avenger were boosted by imports into the United States, where it was sold on the East Coast as the Plymouth Cricket. Chrysler Corporation were also at this time importing a similar car from Mitsubishi, the Colt, which was marketed on the West Coast. On the basis of quality comparisons, the Avenger showed up poorly and eventually all imports were halted in favour of the Colt.

10. *The Times* (London), 7 June 1973.
11. Young & Hood, *Chrysler UK*, p.282.
12. ibid., p.281.
13. ibid., p.315.
14. The Planning Agreement system was to involve the company, employees' representatives and the Government in regular discussions concerning the future of the enterprise. In particular the company and the Government would exchange information to ensure that their separate plans and projections were compatible.
15. 'Sunbeam is Linwood's ray of hope', *Glasgow Herald*, 18 July 1977.
16. 'Chrysler pressed to sell Linwood plant to Japanese', *Sunday Times*, 2 July 1979.
17. For further details see *The Economist*, 12 August 1978, p.69 and 30 September 1978, p.102.
18. 'Linwood under the hammer', *Glasgow Herald*, 17 November 1981.
19. ibid.
20. Expenditure Committee (Trade & Industry Sub-Committee), *Public Expenditure on Chrysler UK Ltd, Minutes of Evidence*, HC104–xx, 29 April 1976, paras.3911–2.
21. Eighth Report from the Expenditure Committee, *Public Expenditure on Chrysler UK Ltd*, H C596(I), Session 1975–6, H M S O (London) 1976, para.231.
22. Expenditure Committee (Trade & Industry Sub-Committee), paras.3998–4006 (n.20).
23. Young & Hood, *Chrysler UK*, p.83.
24. In time sequence, the three were: *British Leyland: The Next Decade*, H C342, H M S O (London) April 1975; Fourteenth Report from the Expenditure Committee, *The Motor Vehicle Industry*, H C617, Session 1974–5, H M S O (London) August 1975; Central Policy Review Staff, *The Future of the British Car Industry*, H M S O (London) 1975.
25. Expenditure Committee (Trade & Industry Sub-Committee), para.3920 (n.20).

HOOVER IN CAMBUSLANG

The Growth of The Hoover Company[1]

The Hoover Company started in North Canton (then Berlin), Ohio in the late nineteenth century as a manufacturer of harnesses, saddles and leather goods. With the beginning of the decline of the horse and carriage era, the Hoover family were looking to diversify, and in June 1907 a local inventor and relative of the Hoovers brought a model of his electric suction sweeper to them. On the basis of the prototype, the Hoovers formed The Electric Suction Sweeper Company in 1908, and the Hoover business was turned over entirely to the manufacture of domestic appliances after the end of World War I.

Internationally, The Hoover Company opened an assembly plant in Windsor, Ontario, Canada in 1911, and in 1919 Hoover Limited was registered in Britain and a sales office set up. Employing a handful of people, the first dealer in Britain was Selfridges of Oxford Street. From this date, the British company became the hub of Hoover's European and indeed international operations. The first British Hoover factory was built at Perivale, Middlesex in 1932, and in 1937 Hoover Limited became a public company, with shares listed on the London Stock Exchange. Aside from the establishment of further manufacturing plants in the UK, Hoover also set up a production facility at Dijon, but this and other sales and marketing companies in continental Europe and elsewhere are owned through Hoover Ltd. Thus the latter has wholly-owned subsidiaries in Austria, Portugal, Australia, South Africa and the Scandinavian countries. It also has a 50 per cent share in Hoover (Holland) BV which is a holding company for operating units in Holland, Belgium, France, Germany, Italy and Switzerland. As a consequence of these developments, at a peak in 1978, UK employees of Hoover Ltd accounted for 60 per cent of total employment in The Hoover Company; when employees of Hoover Ltd's overseas subsidiaries and associated companies are added in, this proportion rose to over 70 per cent. As at 1981, The Hoover Company had a 58 per cent shareholding in Hoover Ltd, a slightly higher equity interest than had been normal in earlier years.

Hoover is and has remained a family business. For years it was said that any male Hoover who wanted a job at North Canton could and did have one.

As at 1979 more than 100 Hoovers owned about 3.6 million shares or around 30 per cent of the company's outstanding stock. Moreover, it was not until 1967 that a non-family member became chief executive officer of the firm. The corporation built up a brand name which was synonymous with vacuum cleaners, and a 100,000 outlet marketing network. Yet the reputation which emerged was one of conservative, slow-moving management. The market for vacuum cleaners, the company's base business in the USA, is mature and therefore stagnant. In the mid-1960s, Hoover introduced numerous new small appliances, such as toasters and blenders, and in 1969 acquired a manufacturer in this product area. This venture was unsuccessful and Hoover divested itself of the business in 1977.

Returns fell sharply in the mid-1970s (Appendix, table 1) and the then head of Hoover, Felix Mansager took early retirement and was replaced by Merle Rawson. This is relevant to subsequent events at Hoover Ltd because as *The Times* commented: 'Hoover's UK involvement was very much junior's (F. Mansager) pigeon and played a part in his removal. Part of Rawson's job will be to meet head on the old jibe that Hoover Ltd is something that headquarters at North Canton, Ohio can neither own nor control.'[2] Despite the introduction of new management, Hoover's solid assets but lack-lustre performance made it an obvious takeover target. The not unexpected bid came in 1979 from Fuqua Industries Inc., an Atlanta-based conglomerate, with interests ranging from cinemas to lawnmowers. Owing, reportedly, to family squabbles, Herbert W. Hoover Jr, the grandson of the company's founder and a former chairman, announced that he planned to accept the Fuqua offer for his 8.2 per cent of the outstanding shares, a move which could have opened the way to a successful acquisition. In fact The Hoover Company had the right of first refusal on any sale, bought-out these shares and in the process managed to repel the takeover bid.[3] But the battle was a bruising one and almost inevitably would seem to push Hoover itself in the direction of greater expansiveness and aggressiveness, both in controlling costs and in developing products, with implications for Hoover Ltd in Britain. In the 1980 Annual Report, thus, The Hoover Company reported its immediate aims as:

> continued reallocation of resources and rationalisation among production facilities in Europe;
>
> broadening of our product base in Europe with further introduction of home security products;
>
> continuing strong research and development efforts to completely restyle appliance models to enhance our competitive position;
>
> diversification of our US product base by further expansion in the industrial cleaning field and also by seeking other opportunities to expand . . . including acquisitions.[4]

Ominously, the 1980 Annual Report also noted that Hoover was taking steps to lessen its dependency on its UK plants.

The Early Years of Hoover in Britain

Perivale was Hoover's sole manufacturing base in Britain until the end of World War II, although during the war the American company's engineering expertise was enlisted by the Ministry of Supply to produce equipment for the forces in 17 factories around London and in Scotland. It was in 1943 that the Hoover organisation started to manufacture aircraft wiring equipment at Rutherglen. With the ending of hostilities, Hoover accepted a government proposal to stay in the area as part of the latter's policy to encourage the establishment of light industry in the Clyde Valley. Thus the first government-built factory in the West of Scotland under the 'spacing of industry' scheme was leased to Hoover at Cambuslang and opened on 3 May 1946. Opening the factory, Sir Steven Bilsland, Vice-Chairman of the Scottish Council on Industry, said that: 'the mainstay of Scottish prosperity would always be in heavy industries, but in the altered conditions of world trade light industries must be developed on a wide scale'.[5] The Cambuslang plant was used to produce fractional horsepower motors for washing machines, refrigerators and similar electrical appliances, which had previously been imported from Hoover Canada; although in the early days a government contract for a small rotary transformer was also being fulfilled. Initial employment was 500, many of whom had previously worked at the Rutherglen factory which was vacated.

The story of Hoover at Cambuslang is again one of expansion in the post-war years, although growth was somewhat limited until the late 1960s, and there were fairly frequent hiccups. In 1947, for instance, output fell to less than half of capacity because of shortage of steel supplies. The problem arose because supplies of electrical steel at this time were being limited to firms which had used the product before the war. After this temporary setback, plans were announced in May 1948 for a 25 per cent increase in production area and in employment (the workforce at the time was 700, of whom 500 were women). But confirming the instability of economic conditions in this period there followed, in 1949, 150 redundancies, in what was then known as Hoover Electrical Motors Ltd, Cambuslang, because of restrictions on imports by countries abroad.

Aside from Cambuslang and Perivale, the third Hoover production base in Britain is at Merthyr Tydfil in Wales. This factory opened on St David's Day in 1948 to produce washing machines. Cambuslang supplied motors for the entire production of the Welsh plant, but at this time 60 per cent of output was also exported to Continental Europe and the Commonwealth. On the basis of this wide market area, employment in Scotland rose to over 1,000 in 1951 and up to 1,600 in the following year, before dropping back sharply (see figure 1). Cambuslang's role within the group was extended in 1963 so that apart from supplying motors to Merthyr Tydfil, the operation became responsible for a complete vacuum cleaner, a new fan heater, elements for electric irons and the programme timer and keyplate for an automatic washing machine. Aside from its role as a component supplier, therefore, a company spokesman commented that Cambuslang was 'destined to become an important production centre in the company's long-term plans'.[6]

Expansion continued to be somewhat halting, nevertheless. It was announced in April 1965 that Cambuslang was to be doubled in size over the following five years with the labour force increasing from the then 2,200 to 4,000 in a three-phase programme. Yet in 1966 employment was down to 1,600 and the second and third phases of the development plan were shelved owing to a slump in washing machine sales consequent on a tightening of credit controls by the Government. By the close of the 1960s, employment at Cambuslang was just under 2,500, but Hoover entered the new decade with

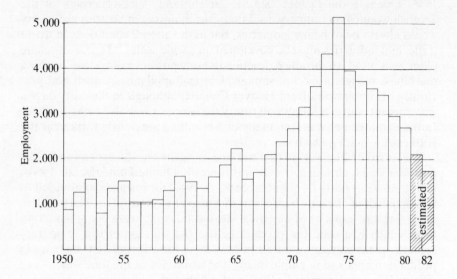

Figure 1. Employment at Hoover Cambuslang from 1950.

a potential for rapid growth, assuming as the company argued, that consistent credit controls could be operated and greater positive export incentives provided.

The Domestic Electrical Appliances Industry in Britain in the 1970s and the Position of Hoover Ltd

In considering the difficulties in which Hoover Ltd subsequently found itself, however, it is necessary to review the overall state of the British electrical appliances industry during the recent past. In its 1979 Progress Report, the National Economic Development Council noted five conditions or changes which were essential to the prosperity and development of the industry. These were:

a) A fiscal background in which domestic appliances are not discriminated against compared with most other durables;

b) An increased and concerted effort by all parties to tackle the problem of imports which have one-third of the UK market;

c) Urgent moves to ensure that the industry's products make the fullest use of micro-electronic technology, particularly in the home laundry sector, so as to remain relevant to changing consumer requirements both at home and abroad;

d) Greater effectiveness of the industry's export efforts, partly through enhanced Government support schemes;

e) Improvements in the sector's productivity in order to compete more effectively at home and abroad.[7]

These points summarise very clearly the major problems of the British industry, although not all are difficulties associated with the 1970s. As noted, changing government policies, as regards hire purchase terms and subsequently rates of VAT, have been a problem for industry planning since the early 1950s, as the consumer durable sector was used as a short-run economic regulator. This partly explains why employment at Hoover has been much more volatile than in some of the other multinationals even when, as in the years through to 1974, the overall trend in employment was upwards. In recent times it was not until the 1979 budget that higher rate VAT, with its discrimination against appliances, was removed.

The problem of import penetration, which rose to a figure of 78 per cent for fridge-freezers, 52 per cent for freezers, and 49 per cent for automatic machines in 1977,[8] cannot be disassociated from other issues such as productivity levels in the sector and the application of micro-electronic technology. The Italian industry was able to put on the UK market, automatic washing machines at a landed price of £99 in 1978 compared with an average factory rate price of £150 for a British machine. Despite charges of dumping, investigations into the efficiency of the Italian industry in fact revealed that cost competitiveness was a result of:

low product unit costs derived from high capacity utilisation;

low labour costs, although not low wage rates in comparison with the UK;

generally low level of overheads.

Investment in automation was a major factor underlying these low costs, although the difficult position of the UK industry was exacerbated into 1980 by the rise in the value of the £ sterling. As the Hoover 1980 Annual Report noted, Italian washing machines were 4 per cent cheaper in Britain in 1980 than in 1979 purely because of currency movements. Conversely, based on a Hoover export weighted value for the £, the landed costs of Hoover products in Europe rose by almost 10 per cent simply because of the appreciation of sterling.[9]

Problems of import competition do not apply solely to Italian washing machines. The British industry has also faced severe competition in vacuum cleaners. In this instance, the growth of low-priced imports from Eastern

European countries such as Poland led to a dumping complaint and an investigation towards the end of 1981 by the Commission of the EEC.

As the figures in Appendix, table 2 reveal, Hoover's financial position in Britain deteriorated sharply in 1974; after some improvement in the three subsequent years, profits slumped again from 1978 onwards and in 1980 the company reported its first-ever loss before taxation. In the first six months of 1981 the position deteriorated further with losses of £6.08 million compared with a profit of £1.56 million for the corresponding period in 1980, with redundancy costs contributing about half of this loss.

It has been argued that while Hoover shared the problems of the UK industry as a whole, in general the company has been even less competitive than some other manufacturers located in Britain. In comparison with Electrolux Ltd, the British subsidiary of Swedish Electrolux AB, the performance of Hoover Ltd in 1980 was poor as the following indicators reveal:

	Turnover (£000)	Pre-tax profits* (£000)	UK employees	Turnover per employee (£000)	Profits per employee
Hoover Ltd	206,744	(1,397)	10,706	19.3	(130)
Electrolux Ltd	130,529	2,389	3,718	35.1	642

* Excluding exceptional and extraordinary items.
Bracketed figure indicates loss.   SOURCE: Extel Statistical Services.

The difference is partly a reflection of Electrolux success in diversification notably into the lawnmower field with its Flymo machine. Until very recently, Hoover diversification was into smaller electrical appliances where intense competition exists. At time of writing, the company was moving into fire safety equipment, although their aim was still to 'improve our position as Britain's leading manufacturer of domestic appliances'.[10]

Hoover in Britain into the 1980s and the Role of Cambuslang

At the start of the 1970s, Cambuslang had entered a period of rapid and sustained growth (see figures 1 and 2). So on 16 June 1972, the 25th birthday of the plant, Lord Polwarth, Minister of State at the Scottish Office officially opened Hoover's eighth extension and broke the ground for a ninth extension of 109,000 sq. ft. At the ceremony, Mr Felix Mansager, the Hoover Chairman, remarked that: 'We have a long experience of manufacturing in five continents and I can categorically state that the Scot, given the right circumstances, is second to none in reliability and workmanship.'[11]

There were some signs of industrial unrest when the factory was shut down at the end of 1971 as the workforce pursued a wage claim; and early in 1973 production was halted as workers sought parity in wages with their colleagues in England. Demand continued strong, nevertheless, and in that

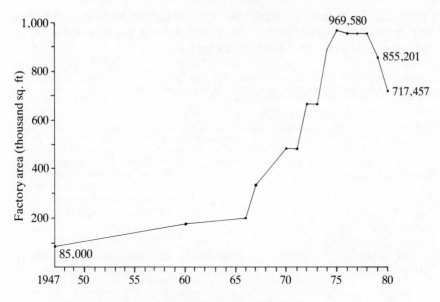

Figure 2. Factory space at Cambuslang (000 sq.ft).

same year the former Hamilton plant of Rolls-Royce was taken over by Hoover. Unable to wait for another factory expansion at Cambuslang to come on-stream, the company started to manufacture vacuum cleaners at this 137,744 sq. ft. Hamilton facility, taking on another 400 personnel in the process. Optimism was further boosted on the company announcement in October 1973 of a £30 million growth programme in Britain, the largest expansion undertaken by Hoover anywhere in the world. Once the new factories were in full production in 1977, it was envisaged that 6,000 new jobs would have been created, half in Merthyr Tydfil, half at Cambuslang. The importance of this for the West of Scotland was that the announcement occurred at almost the same time as the decision to run down the steel works in the area; there were hopes, therefore, that redundant steel workers would be retrained and employed by Hoover. Mansager, the Hoover Chairman commented again: 'This is a measure of our confidence in Britain and its people. I cannot think of a better place to invest than here in Britain. We believe that the British workers are some of the best in the world.'[12] Apart from the influence of Mansager, as an Anglophile, on the decision to locate yet more manufacturing capacity in Britain (and increase the company's vulnerability in the event of production stoppages), relatively low wages and the floating £ were believed to have further tipped the balance in favour of existing U K locations. The aim of the expansion programme was therefore to take advantage of British entry into the Common Market as well as to provide the capacity to meet anticipated demand within the U K itself. The latter was expected because of the relatively low penetration of domestic appliances in Britain at that time in comparison with the EEC and Scandinavian countries. Rightly or wrongly Hoover Ltd was perceived as the jewel in the crown of The Hoover Company.

Table 1. The Manufacturing Facilities of Hoover Ltd in 1973

Factory	Factory area (sq. ft.)	Employment	Manufacturing role
Cambuslang (& Hamilton), Scotland	700,000	5,400	Washing machine motors, fan heaters, irons, toasters, hair dryers, kettles, timers for washing machines, vacuum cleaners (mainly cylinder models)
Merthyr Tydfil, Wales	1.1 million	5,374	Washing machines, spin dryers, tumble dryers, dishwashers
Perivale, Middlesex, England (HQ)	700,000	2,565 (manufacturing only)	Vacuum cleaners (upright models) and electric motors for vacuum cleaners

The Role of the Hoover Plants in Britain as at 1973. As at the end of 1973, Hoover's British production capacity was located, and utilised as indicated in table 1. Hoover operated on the basis of product specialisation by plant, with Merthyr Tydfil the base for washing machines and other heavy appliances, Perivale the centre for most vacuum cleaners, and Cambuslang the base for small appliances, some vacuum cleaners, and components, particularly washing machine motors. Some parts were produced in each plant and then moved to the other operations so as to exploit economies of scale in component manufacture, with the main flow consisting of washing machine motors from Cambuslang to Merthyr Tydfil, and vacuum cleaner motors from Perivale to Cambuslang. These plants served the European market chiefly, and although there was another factory at Dijon, France, this was not linked to the British operations. It was also a small almost marginal operation which, so the story goes, effectively shut down for several months each year at wine harvest time! The headquarters of Hoover Ltd was at Perivale. It can be assumed that Hoover Ltd had a good deal of autonomy in its activities but this did not affect the Merthyr Tydfil and Cambuslang facilities which were essentially branch operations. On the other hand, there was a product development department at Cambuslang.

The Problems of 1974. 1974 was a watershed in the history of Hoover in Britain. Early in the year, *The Scotsman* was arguing that the huge expansion programme announced by the company would take employment at Cambuslang to over 8,000 and make it the biggest manufacturing facility in the West of Scotland.[13] Later in the year, however, there was a long unofficial strike at Cambuslang over a local wage claim. Agreement was reached between management and workers on a £3 per week wage rise, but the stumbling block proved to be the date on which this increase was to be paid. As a consequence of the Cambuslang strike, which lasted 11 weeks, 4,500 workers were laid off at Merthyr Tydfil because the supply of electric motors was halted. At Perivale, meantime, 1,900 workers were laid off by another unofficial strike by 150 craftsmen. The disputes ended in November 1974, but for the whole year the company lost over half a million working days (table 2).

Table 2. New Employees Engaged and Days Lost through Disputes and Associated Lay-offs at Hoover Ltd

	New employees	Days lost
1977	2,186	6,068
1976	888	1,908
1975	912	27,303
1974	3,122	541,215
1973	4,767	53,388

SOURCE: Hoover Limited, *Report and Accounts 1977.*

The ending of the dispute coincided with the retirement of Mansager as Chairman of The Hoover Co. and almost immediately there was an announcement from Mr P. Budd, General Works Manager at Cambuslang that: 'As a result of the long strike in Scotland, we lost credibility with our customers and it is because of this that we will be phasing out the manufacture of certain motors, hair dryers and fan heaters and trimming back some other work. In the longer term to safeguard future supplies of motors to Merthyr Tydfil, we plan to establish a motor manufacturing facility at the Welsh plant as with those at Cambuslang and Perivale. At this point I cannot predict any long-term growth in the number of people required at Cambuslang or the necessity for a further extension of the manufacturing facility there. It depends on the demand for our products which has been reduced in recent months.'[14] Six hundred jobs were to be lost at Cambuslang as a result of these changes.

Under pressure from the STUC, the company issued a further statement in February 1975 noting that Cambuslang had had a record in the immediate past of not producing the required quantities and of operating inefficiently with excessive costs and overmanning. On the decision to transfer motor manufacturing to Merthyr Tydfil it was argued that this was partly a desire to improve the self-sufficiency of each of the manufacturing complexes and thereby reduce their vulnerability to disputes and partly a change in relative manufacturing costs. Cambuslang had for some years held a production cost advantage over Merthyr because of the female content in the manufacture of motors (and the lower rate of pay for females) which more than compensated for the transport costs. With legislation on equal pay and rising transport costs following the Arab-Israeli war, it was argued that the cost advantage lay with Merthyr Tydfil. This loss of motor manufacturing capability (for washing machines) at Cambuslang was partly compensated for by the transfer of some vacuum cleaner motor capacity from Perivale to Cambuslang, to reduce the Scottish plant's reliance on the English facility. In response to Union efforts to prevent the transfer of motor manufacturing from Cambuslang, the management retorted that: 'The alternative . . . will be to force us into seeking another manufacturing location and progressively closing Cambuslang.'[15]

In interpreting the events of 1974, it is necessary to stand back and look at the general economic conditions of the time. The 1971 and 1972 budgets were reflationary and these, added to an expansive monetary policy and a rapid rise in money wages, led to a huge boom in demand for all types of consumer durables. Into 1973 price reductions following the introduction of a Value Added Tax and the absence of hire purchase controls until December of that year created highly favourable trading conditions. It seems likely that the company's decision in 1973 to embark upon its largest-ever expansion programme was heavily influenced by these short-term events. Equally, the subsequent decision to halt or postpone this programme was at least as much to do with the ending of the boom conditions in the UK and elsewhere and increasing competition from domestic and foreign appliance manufacturers, as it was to do with the stoppages of 1974. In the UK, the April 1975 budget raised the rate of VAT on domestic electrical appliances from 8 to 25 per cent and the economic recession had a marked adverse influence on sales of consumer durables throughout Europe. As to Hoover's competitive position, it does seem that the company had relied for too long on its name and had neglected product development. In fairness, even so, the long strikes of 1974 did allow other manufacturers and importers to gain market share, as the following figures show:

	Share of European vacuum cleaner market (%)	Share of UK vacuum cleaner market (%)
1972	12.4	52.3
1973	11.9	46.4
1974	9.9	40.7

SOURCE: STUC, *Annual Report 1975.*

The company's market share in the UK in 1974 was its lowest for 15 years and in the process Hoover lost its market leadership for the first time to Electrolux.

As noted earlier, the company bitterly attacked the overmanning and

Table 3. Employment Breakdown for Hoover Limited

	No. of Employees as at 31 December								
	1981 (estimated)	1980	1979	1978	1977	1976	1975	1974	1973
UK Manufacturing – Perivale	1,300	1,518	1,716	1,851	1,978	2,061	2,151	2,376	2,565
– Cambuslang*	2,100	2,675	2,890	3,342	3,714	3,605	3,900	4,958	5,400
– Merthyr Tydfil	3,000	3,786	4,047	5,098	5,411	4,618	4,826	5,017	5,374
Other UK – Marketing, distribution, engineering, admin.	2,000	2,245	2,498	2,629	2,783	2,797	2,829	2,860	2,953
	8,400	10,224	11,151	12,920	13,886	13,081	13,713	15,225	15,892
Overseas subsidiaries and associated companies	n.a.	2,803	2,676	2,785	2,778	2,858	3,287	3,675	3,408
Total	n.a.	13,027	13,827	15,705	16,664	15,939	17,000†	18,900†	19,300†
UK employment as % of total	n.a.	78.5	80.6	82.3	83.3	82.1	80.7	80.6	82.3
Cambuslang employment as % of total	n.a.	20.5	20.9	21.3	22.3	22.6	22.9	26.2	28.0

* Employment figures for Cambuslang are presented on a different basis to those in Figure 1 and the two sets cannot be directly compared.
† Available data is in 000s in source. Employment for overseas subsidiaries and associated companies is derived as the difference between the total and UK employment figures.
SOURCE: Company accounts.

inefficient working practices at Cambuslang. It is difficult to sympathise with Hoover, given the circumstances which prevailed. In the boom conditions of the early 1970s the company were desperate for output, brought in large numbers of new employees (see table 2) and perhaps paid less than adequate attention to cost control. Meeting schedules may have become more important than the costs involved in doing so.

Post-1975 Events and a New Crisis for Hoover Ltd. The major change in company policy following the 1974 strike was to phase out unprofitable lines and increase the self-sufficiency of the three U K production centres, with the transfer of washing machine motor-production from Cambuslang to Merthyr being the principal element of the latter. In the event the transfer of motors did not take place, for whatever reason. On the other hand, fan-heater and hair-dryer production ceased at Cambuslang in 1975 and production of some motors was sub-contracted. On the positive side, some vacuum cleaner motor capacity was switched from Perivale to Cambuslang.

Demand for Hoover products revived following the halving of the luxury rate of V A T to 12½ per cent in the 1976 budget, and following the offer of substantial Government assistance the company, apparently, revived their expansion plans in respect of Merthyr Tydfil. It was also reported in the press that Hoover was seeking Government aid for a similar expansion at Cambuslang.

Reflecting the improved conditions, manufacturing employment at Hoover in Britain actually rose in 1977 for the first time for a number of years, to a figure of just under 14,000 (table 3). But this revival was short-lived, as the effects of economic recession and competition started to bite. Between 1977 and 1980, sales of floorcare products (vacuum cleaners etc.) dropped by over one-third in volume terms and laundry equipment sales declined by one-quarter, with exports being particularly severely curtailed (table 4).

Table 4. Hoover Ltd Sales Volume (1977–80)

	Floorcare (000 units)			Laundry equipment (000 units)		
	Home	Export	Total	Home	Export	Total
1977	940	839	1,779	544	142	686
1978	964	740	1,704	552	135	687
1979	899	602	1,501	502	107	609
1980	725	403	1,128	473	48	521
% change 1977–80	− 22.9	− 52.0	− 36.6	− 13.1	− 66.2	− 24.1

Aside from the impact of falling sales, a variety of internal problems were observed at Cambuslang:

absenteeism: among women, absenteeism apparently reached a level of 23 per cent at one time and was the highest at any Hoover factory in Britain. Male absenteeism, on the other hand, was less of a problem than at Merthyr;

low productivity;

wage niggles, over complicated wage and bonus payments;

pilfering;

management wastage: it was reported that thousands of electric irons were destroyed in Spring 1978 because they didn't comply with certain European safety regulations;[16]

problems of implementing new technology, particularly an automated armature connecting line which lay unused for about a year.[17]

The net result of internal and external difficulties was that Hoover's Hamilton plant was shut in 1978, while production of toasters was ended at Cambuslang in 1979 with the loss of 120 jobs. The latter represented the continuation of a trend which was to see the cessation of all small appliance manufacturing in Britain by 1982. With a further rundown of employment through natural wastage, rumours concerning the closure of Cambuslang began to mount in the Autumn of 1979. Following a meeting with the Unions, the company issued a statement that: 'It was their intention that Cambuslang should remain a strong and viable manufacturing unit ... A significant increase in productivity and a reduction in absenteeism is essential if products manufactured at Cambuslang are to be competitive and profitable.'[18] As Hoover's market and financial position deteriorated, however, redundancies continued: in August 1980, the twilight shift was ended at Cambuslang with the loss of 162 women's jobs and short-time working was introduced, with the plant operating for only three out of every four weeks. The shop stewards' convener, Eddie McAvoy said after the announcement: 'It is the most dangerous crisis we have ever faced. We have no doubt we are facing the same pressure applied on the Unions at BSR, Smith Clocks and Singer where they gave management all it wanted and were still massacred.'[19] In March 1981, this period of short-time working was replaced by 530 redundancies as part of a package of 1,000 redundancies for the UK as a whole. The cuts, coinciding with the announcement of Hoover Ltd's first loss since its stock market debut, brought employment at Cambuslang down to 2,100, the lowest level since 1968. The succession of events followed a depressingly *déjà-vu* pattern and the closure of Cambuslang seemed a likely next step.

The Reorganisation of Hoover Ltd in 1981. It was reported in the Summer of 1981 that Hoover had engaged a team of consultants to investigate the rationalisation of their manufacturing facilities in the UK, particularly as regards the production of floorcare products. The announcement in August 1981 that this exercise was essentially complete, was followed by a programme of meetings between management and unions at plant level. In the first of this series of meetings, management presented details of the options open to Hoover in respect of production rationalisation for the floorcare range.

The options were:

slim down Perivale and Cambuslang to manning and cost levels which bear international comparison;

concentrate floorcare manufacture at Cambuslang and close Perivale;

concentrate floorcare manufacture at Perivale and close Cambuslang;

consider alternative sites where floorcare will be manufactured at the minimum cost to the company.

Workers were also asked for:

a reduction in manning levels;

longer wage agreements, running for thirty months instead of the existing twelve;

no wage increases or industrial action until the company was making a profit.

These latter conditions were rejected by workers at all three of Hoover's U K plants. At Cambuslang, the shop stewards declared that no plans for saving money on the wage bill would be discussed until the directors clearly stated that the factory would remain open. The statement went on: 'If they do not do this and decide to close, the employees will take whatever measures are necessary to prevent them closing down or removing any plant from Cambuslang.'[20]

In spite of the aggressive response from Cambuslang, when the restructuring plans were announced, it was option 2 that was chosen, namely, closure of Perivale and concentration of floorcare manufacture at Cambuslang. In fact Cambuslang was a much more suitable location for several reasons. In the first place, the plant and equipment at Cambuslang were comparatively new and contained much of the company's latest investment in high technology equipment. Second, parts of the Perivale complex consisted of multi-storey buildings which were unsuitable for installing the most modern equipment. Thirdly, Perivale was located close to a residential area and there were problems with noise levels. Fourth, floorcare manufacture could not be combined at the Perivale complex without taking more space. Fifthly, Perivale was the only factory which the company owned; Hoover's financial position could thus be assisted by its sale. Finally, it was argued that the balance of other factors including productivity, industrial relations, absence levels, distribution to markets and quality levels also favoured Cambuslang.

Perivale's closure having been accepted at a mass-meeting at the plant on 1 December 1981, Hoover's plans for its British manufacturing plants were as shown in table 5 (compare table 1 on p.88). Basically the company planned to reduce its U K labour force to 5,800 compared with 10,224 in 1980 and a peak employment level of 15,892 in 1973. With the closure of Perivale, vacuum cleaner manufacture was to be transferred to Cambuslang and a new range of cleaners was to be launched from that location in mid-1982; an associated product, paper bags for cleaners, was to be switched from

Table 5. Plans for the Manufacturing Facilities of Hoover Ltd in 1982

Factory	Employment*	Manufacturing role
Cambuslang, Scotland	1,750	Washing machine motors; vacuum cleaners (upright and cylinder models); paper bags for vacuum cleaners
Merthyr Tydfil, Wales	2,000	Laundry products, especially washing machines; switch/timer manufacture for washing machines

* Total employment in Hoover Ltd (manufacturing and non-manufacturing) is planned to be around 5,800.

Merthyr to Scotland. Conversely, the plan called for the transfer of switch/timer manufacture from Cambuslang to Wales, but washing machine motor output was to remain in Scotland. All remaining small appliances (kettles and irons) were to be phased out from Cambuslang in 1982. With this decision, Hoover Ltd is to follow the path of The Hoover Company which divested itself of its small appliance interests in 1977.

How far this represents a stable, long-term as opposed to a stop-gap strategy is not known. What is pertinent is that the 1980 Report and Accounts of Hoover Ltd spoke of a major investment ($10 million) to produce cylinder cleaners in a highly mechanised facility at Dijon. The aim of this is to balance the company's over-dependence on the UK. It is possible (though obviously uncertain) that Hoover may retain both Cambuslang and Dijon as cleaner manufacturing facilities and base production allocations on relative exchange rates, inflation rates, etc. Another factor of relevance is that since 1978, Hoover has had an assembly facility in Portugal producing cleaners from parts imported from the UK. Developments here and elsewhere in Southern Europe, for example Spain, must be watched carefully. Even the short term poses difficulties, of course, for the company has first to reverse its sales decline of recent years and begin to solve its cash problems – at the beginning of 1977 the group balance sheet showed over £22 million in liquid funds; by the end of 1980 the position had changed to net borrowings of £15 million. On past evidence, the future of Cambuslang is far from secure. This is true, even assuming that the complex production reorganisation envisaged in the 1981 plan can be accomplished successfully, that worker-management cooperation is maintained and that the problems of earlier years, such as high levels of absenteeism can be overcome.

Postscript, April 1982.   As with the other cases in this section, the Hoover case covered the period up to the end of 1981. When Hoover Ltd published its financial results for the year 1981 a loss of £31 million was recorded. This was a good deal worse than anticipated and followed the UK company's first ever loss of £2.7 million in 1980. Speculation about the future of Cambuslang began to increase again during the Spring of 1982, after the announcement of these figures and a fresh outbreak of industrial relations problems. The latter concerned union rejection of the company's call for a wage freeze during 1982 and an electricians' dispute over the payment of allowances. The company in response warned that a £7 million investment at the plant in a new range of cleaners – the Euro Junior – was at risk. Among the options apparently being considered was the reopening of the Perivale factory and the use of an empty factory rented by the company in Wales. The story had a disturbingly familiar ring to it. Whether in this case events had so damaged company confidence in Cambuslang as to place the future of the entire operation in jeopardy was not apparent at time of writing.

Lessons of the Hoover Case

The underlying problems of Hoover in Scotland are fairly complex, relating as they do to environmental factors (Government fiscal and trade policies), company strategy and planning, and operational variables. Much has been written about the impact of changing Government tax policies and credit terms on demand fluctuations in the consumer durable sector, and certainly Hoover found difficulties in coping with the volatility of demand. Employment prospects, as a result, were very uncertain for the Hoover workforce in Britain. On the trade side, there is no doubt that Britain has maintained a very open market for importers. It is true that highly efficient Italian production is largely responsible for import expansion, but the Italians have not been without their difficulties. Indesit was recently rescued from financial problems and it is revealing to contrast the Italian Government's recognition of the need to keep the industry healthy with the inactivity of the Government in Britain.

At the level of corporate strategy, planning at Hoover seemed to be unsatisfactory, failing as it did to distinguish between short-term and long-term demand trends. On several occasions, large expansion programmes were announced in the wake of buoyant demand in the UK, only to be shelved when the next credit squeeze came around. Since 'stop-go' was such a common feature of British economic policy, presumably it should have been possible to predict. Failure to keep abreast of changing consumer requirements and production technology was also to prove highly costly; while continued investment in the UK, as Hoover's European production base, brought the corporation to the position where the entire Hoover Company was excessively dependent on its British operations. Hoover Limited was seemingly highly autonomous in its activities, and while many would view this as desirable, in Hoover's case greater objective American control could have led to a more geographically balanced investment policy in Europe. Since the departure of Mansager as Chairman at the end of 1974 and particularly since the later 1970s, Hoover Ltd has in fact been more closely controlled from the US. As part of a continuing process, in 1980 Hoover's export headquarters was moved from the UK to North Canton.

Operationally, Hoover found difficulty in managing the changeover from boom to recession and technological advance. It is easy to criticise the workforce for inflexibility, when management were faced with the need for much tighter cost control than in the late 1960s and early 1970s. But there is also a question whether different management styles and expertise are required for rationalisation and reorganisation. This is very relevant to the implementation of the latest Hoover plan.

The Hoover case does tend to confirm some of the allegations made concerning production switching by multinationals, although for most of the period studied Hoover was little different in this respect from a multi-plant national firm, given the distribution of its assets in Europe. But with the decision to build-up Dijon and perhaps other Continental European locations the issue may become a very real one in future. Given communications difficulties across national frontiers, the multinational company is able to at least partly evade public accountability and scrutiny of its actions.

Table 1. Performance Data for The Hoover Company

Year	Sales ($000)	Assets ($000)	Net income ($000)	Shareholders equity ($000)	Employees	Net income as % of shareholders		Rank (by sales) in Fortune Directory
						Sales	Equity	
1980	830,465	532,367	30,048	247,458	20,081	3.6	12.1	346
1979	754,324	491,091	39,263	227,714	21,523	5.2	17.2	339
1978	691,817	474,350	24,648	223,567	22,587	3.6	11.0	334
1977	590,740	425,981	23,462	209,220	23,370	4.0	11.2	348
1976	571,913	391,248	6,838	195,780	22,886	1.2	3.5	335
1975	593,747	391,489	11,903	199,071	23,713	2.0	6.0	294
1974	502,731	384,617	8,711	196,630	27,452	1.7	4.4	334
1973	534,655	399,076	33,035	199,901	27,947	6.2	16.5	283
1972	458,415	346,123	29,514	180,862	25,499	6.4	16.3	278
1971	402,282	309,094	21,673	159,810	22,578	5.4	13.6	281
1970	346,686	275,522	17,860	147,058	22,602	5.2	12.1	302
1969	309,319	259,828	17,025	138,500	21,231	5.5	12.3	303
1968	287,120	234,176	16,093	130,456	18,441	5.6	12.3	296
1967	267,682	206,314	10,166	119,906	17,243	3.8	8.5	295
1966	259,577	210,330	14,917	116,475	17,328	5.7	12.8	290

SOURCE: 'The Fortune Directory of the 500 largest US Industrial Corporations', *Fortune*, various editions.

Table 2. Performance Data for Hoover's U K Subsidiary – Hoover Ltd*

Year ended Dec. 31	Sales (£m)	Net profit before tax (£m)	Net profit before tax as % of		Govt. grants received	Exports	Average no. of UK employees (000)
			Sales	Shareholders' funds			
1980	206.7	(2.7)	–	–	567	28.7	10.7†
1979	203.7	1.9	0.9	2.0	532	38.9	11.8
1978	212.1	5.3	2.5	5.5	613	40.8	13.5
1977	191.0	12.2	6.4	15.1	560	38.1	13.5
1976	180.0	17.0	9.4	21.7	546	35.0	13.3
1975	162.9	20.7	12.7	28.8	556	29.6	14.2
1974	113.8	4.2	3.7	6.5	378	23.0	15.8
1973	121.0	24.0	19.8	36.3	344	22.3	14.9
1972	98.4	19.5	19.8	35.4	319	19.3	13.1
1971	82.3	11.0	13.4	25.2	351	17.1	11.5
1970	67.3	8.5	12.6	21.3	n.a.	n.a.	11.1
1969	59.0	7.7	13.1	20.6	n.a.	n.a.	9.8
1968	58.7	8.6	14.7	24.6	n.a.	n.a.	9.1

* Including wholly-owned subsidiary manufacturing companies in Australia and South Africa and marketing subsidiaries in seven other countries. Also includes 50 per cent stake in Hoover (Holland) BV.
† At year end 1980, U K employment was 10,224 and employment in subsidiary and associated companies overseas 2,803.
SOURCE: Company accounts.

NOTES AND REFERENCES

1. This early information is mostly derived from 'The Hoover Company Seventieth Anniversary, 1908–1978' and 'Hoover – A Worldwide Organisation', both issued by the company.
2. *Times Business News*, 8 November 1974.
3. See 'Fighting off Fuqua was an unsettling victory for Hoover', *Fortune*, 22 October 1979 and 'Hoover: How stodgy management made it a takeover target', *Business Week*, 18 June 1979.
4. The Hoover Company, *1980 Annual Report*.
5. *Glasgow Herald*, 2 May 1946.
6. *Scotsman*, 9 July 1963.
7. National Economic Development Council, *Domestic Electrical Appliances S W P, Progress Report 1979* (London) 1979.
8. ibid.
9. Hoover Limited, *Report and Accounts 1980*.
10. ibid.
11. *Glasgow Herald*, 17 June 1972.
12. *Glasgow Herald*, 19 October 1973.
13. *Scotsman*, 5 April 1974.
14. *Glasgow Herald*, 14 December 1974.
15. S T U C, *Annual Report 1975* (Glasgow) 1975, p.123.
16. *Glasgow Herald*, 8 August 1978.
17. The management blamed inability to reach agreement with unions over manning levels; the unions blamed technical difficulties.
18. *Scotsman*, 27 October 1979.
19. *Glasgow Herald*, 18 August 1980.
20. *Financial Times*, 18 September 1981.

NCR IN DUNDEE

Background of the Corporation

This American company was formed in 1884 by John H. Patterson who along with his brother Frank bought the National Manufacturing Company and changed the name to the National Cash Register Company. Less than one year after the establishment of the firm, overseas sales agents were appointed in various countries to market the company's cash registers, and by 1914 NCR had set up marketing companies in ten countries outside the USA. Domestically NCR had cornered 95 per cent of the market for cash registers, from its centre of operations in Dayton, Ohio, by the beginning of World War I. The internationalisation of the company continued in the inter-war years with NCR establishing three manufacturing factories in overseas countries. The product range was also diversified to include adding machines and accounting machines as well as the original cash registers. Manufacture in Europe commenced in 1946, and from its initial location in the UK, NCR set up manufacturing operations in three other European countries. Production began in Japan in 1957 and as at 1970 the corporation had twelve equipment manufacturing plants in ten countries.[1]

The progress of NCR from the mid-1960s is highlighted in App. table 1. Until 1969–70, expansion was the keynote: employment rose to 103,000 worldwide and NCR became the seventy-sixth largest industrial corporation in the USA; sales during the 1960s grew at an annual average rate of 12 per cent to reach $1.4 billion in 1970. Profits failed to keep pace but the company attributed this to the high costs of R&D, and as late as 1970 NCR was regarded as a glamour stock on Wall Street.

Yet this apparent success disguised fundamental weaknesses, particularly as regards the company's product range. Some of NCR's electro-mechanical products had been in existence for 20 years or more, and the company failed fundamentally to keep pace with technological change and identify the move towards electronic computers and computer terminals. NCR acquired a computer company in California during the 1950s but the first computers developed to compete with IBM were unsuccessful and were a major drain on corporate resources. More important than this was the fact that NCR failed to see the applications of computers to their traditional markets: electronic retail terminals could replace the mechanical cash registers and link up with central processors to provide a dramatic improvement in productivity and information availability among retail stores, banks, etc. Burroughs was proving to be NCR's major competitor in banking markets. Although Burroughs faced the same problems of converting to electronics, it had essentially completed the transition by the late 1960s. Longer term, the Japanese were to prove the major threat. NCR had ample warning of the challenge through their own subsidiary in Japan, which was the largest and most profitable of NCR's foreign affiliates and was itself developing the company's first electronic cash register. Once again, the tradition-bound attitudes within the corporation seemed to prevail, and NCR entered the 1970s in an extremely perilous position.[2]

The European and Dundee Operations[3]

NCR had sold its products in Europe from 1885 and a marketing operation based in London was set up after World War I. The company commenced its European manufacturing operations with the establishment of a factory in Dundee in 1946. Anticipating the end of World War II and the economic crisis and dollar shortage in Europe, NCR seemingly took the decision to consider a manufacturing base in Britain in 1944. After a nationwide survey Dundee was chosen primarily because of the low costs of doing business and labour availability – 'a spot in the East of Scotland viewed against the West thickly dotted with industrial sites'.[4] At the formal opening of the factory, Sir Stafford Cripps, President of the Board of Trade said of the decision to select Dundee that 'if he were to speak in the language of his very learned friend Justice Evershed, he would no doubt say it must be some form of "Oomph"'![5] Work on the factory started in November 1945 and production of a range of cash registers and accounting machines started in the Spring of 1946. In respect of accounting machines, this was the first time the product had been manufactured in the UK. Output was mainly intended for the British market, and the initial employment was 300 people, most of whom were women engaged in assembly work.

One year after the establishment of the Dundee operation, a production plant was set up in Augsburg (West Germany) and as will be shown, in spite of all the subsequent upheavals, these two operations have remained the major European manufacturing facilities of NCR. Later, further production units were built in Bulach (Switzerland), Massy (France) and at two other locations in Germany – Berlin and Giessen. In line with the expansion of the corporation as a whole, NCR's European operations developed rapidly. In Dundee, the first NCR factory occupied 146,000 sq.ft, and was basically an assembly facility using parts imported from the USA. But over the following years the product line was expanded to include a full range of business equipment, with many of the electro-mechanical component parts being produced in-house. Indeed by the late 1960s NCR Dundee had achieved virtual self-sufficiency, meeting all of its needs from raw materials and components through to assembly and testing. As table 1 shows, expansion in Dundee entailed an enormous demand for factory space. At the peak in 1969–70 the manufacturing division occupied 1.2 million sq.ft of space in nine factories and employed 6,500 people. The dramatic growth was accentuated in the late 1960s by the UK's switch to decimal currency (in February 1971) and the consequent boom in demand for new decimal adding

Table 1. Factories Occupied in Dundee as at 1969*

Name	Year	Size (sq. ft)
Camperdown†	1946	146,000
Beechwood	1949	48,000
Dryburgh	1952	264,000
Dunsinane	1962	185,000
Broomhill	1963	11,000
Kilspindie	1964	130,000
Lansdowne	1966	26,000
Birkhill	1967	53,000
Gourdie†	1968	350,000
		1,213,000

* All factories except one were leased from the Industrial Estates Management Corporation for Scotland.
† Factories occupied as at 1981.

machines and cash registers, and for the conversion of existing machines from £sd to £p.[6] This meant that the problems facing the corporation were slightly later in striking the UK subsidiary: it also meant that the downturn, when it came, was that much more severe. Commentators at the time praised the efficiency of NCR's personnel programme in Dundee in the face of rapid expansion and the limited labour pool in the surrounding area. Turnover of employees was low and figures quoted in 1967 indicated that 98 per cent of all apprentices remained with the company for a minimum of five years after completing their apprenticeship. Union membership at this time totalled about three-quarters of all NCR Dundee employees, but the company had suffered no major disputes. With the introduction of electronic accounting machines, a major retraining programme was instituted so that by the late 1960s between 400 and 500 people were undergoing training or retraining; again this seemed to be implemented fairly painlessly. If any voices of dissent were to be heard, they concerned lack of decision-making responsibility and the absence of R&D in the UK: 'Very little research work is done in Dundee ... and it does seem that a considerable amount of interest is compulsorily taken by the main US board of NCR in the Dundee operations, even although these have now reached full industrial maturity. The decision ... to make computers had to be referred to the us. The British board of NCR does, in fact, seem something of a cipher where decisions of this kind – which one would have thought it was perfectly capable of making – are involved.'[7]

Expansion of the other European subsidiaries was less impressive, but by 1970 6,100 people were employed in manufacturing in Continental Europe. Total employment was 15,300 including 2,500 systems specialists and salesmen, and 3,000 technicians, field maintenance personnel and computer engineers. In the uk, total employment in the same year was 12,800, made up of Dundee plus other activities in Britain, so that Europe as a whole accounted for nearly 30 per cent of NCR employment worldwide.[8] In addition, Appendix, table 2 indicates that, entering the 1970s, Europe accounted for just about half of the assets of NCR's international operations. By any standards, Europe was of prime importance to NCR.

With the production of mechanical machines, Dundee, as the largest international manufacturing plant outside the us, occupied a key role in NCR's European operations. Its role was that of a supply point for Europe and other non-us markets. The range of accounting machines was manufactured for European markets while the cash registers were sold to all non-us markets (except Germany for some machines). In total about 50 per cent of output was exported in the mid-1960s. The other major operation in Augsburg manufactured some of the same accounting machines for German markets, plus part of the range of cash registers not produced at the uk facility. The remaining European plants supplied components or had restricted market roles. A limited amount of design and development work for the electro-mechanical products was undertaken in Europe, but NCR's main R&D operation was in Dayton, Ohio. When NCR took its first steps into computer manufacture in the 1960s with its Century series, assembly of the central processor, using components from Augsburg and Bulach, was undertaken in Dundee.

NCR Corporation in the 1970s

The crash which came at NCR Corporation was apparently unexpected. The 1969 report for the corporation commented that NCR's product development programme had 'created for the company an extensive capability in electronic data processing . . . NCR is entering the 1970s well equipped to meet the challenges which the new decade will present . . .' and therefore 'the 1970s should be a period of steady progress'.[9] The reality was that NCR was completely unprepared for the take-off in electronics in the business machine sector. Earnings fell sharply in 1971: in part because of a 16-week strike in the us by the United Autoworkers Union, but also because the write-off of inventories for obsolete products and heavy costs relating to product modification and new product introduction caused major financial difficulties. The company's problems reached a peak in 1972 with a loss of $60 million, including a write-down of $135 million in obsolete plant, stock and tools and associated goods (Appendix, table 1).

In response to the crisis, a new President, William Anderson, the son of a

Scottish engineer, was brought in from NCR's Japanese subsidiary. Belatedly the principle was established that NCR's future was to lie in total business systems. This meant that the company was to become a supplier of electronic data processing systems and terminals, focusing on banking and retailing sectors, the markets in which NCR's strengths traditionally lay. Having established this broad strategy, three priorities were established, firstly, to decentralise manufacturing and move towards smaller plants (a plant with 1,000 employees being suggested as an efficient size) chartered for a limited line or group of products. Secondly, to reorganise the company's marketing operation in the US, and thirdly, to reorganise the international divisions.[10]

The reorganisation implied by the new strategy was considerable. Perhaps the key problem emerged from the fundamental differences between electro-mechanical and electronic products. With the mechanical products, large centralised plants were feasible; vertical integration and in-sourcing were stressed, even to the extent of manufacturing screws in-house. In the electronics field, corporate resources were inadequate to permit development work to be undertaken across such a wide-ranging and fast-moving area. Effective integration between the Engineering and Manufacturing Divisions, which had been notably absent previously, was crucially important in electronics. Thus NCR moved towards minimum rather than maximum vertical integration. This meant that whereas in the mechanical fabrication plants labour costs made up 75 per cent or more of product cost, in the electronics product plants 60–80 per cent of costs were represented by bought-in parts and materials.

A second important consequence of the move from mechanical to electronic products was that the latter required far fewer parts. Electronic machines had only 2,000–4,000 parts compared with as many as 25,000 for the mechanical products. As the 1975 report of the Corporation stated: '. . . we can now place in our Microelectronics Division microcircuits, not much bigger than the head of a pin, which contain up to 16,000 components. These replace mechanisms that required hundreds of individually machined parts and scores of space-consuming machine tools and manufacturing processes to produce them.'[11]

With the mechanical cash registers and accounting machines, the product lifespan had been considerable. Although it is arguable that this was one of the reasons why the corporation almost collapsed ultimately, one of NCR's cash registers maintained its same design from 1921 to 1959. In the move to electronics, flexibility had to replace stability because of the short product life cycle, estimated at perhaps 3–4 years between product introduction and product obsolescence. Equally, research and development became much more important, to enable NCR to keep pace with the rapid market changes. This was so in spite of the fact that the buy-in strategy excluded the necessity for basic materials' research.

The final requirement produced by NCR's changeover to business systems was for a reorganisation of marketing. The salesman's role had to be altered to that of a consultant to the customer. Inevitably a huge re-education process was also involved to train salesmen and particularly field-engineers in electronics. A further requirement was to ensure effective communications between the field engineers and the marketing organisation and also between the marketing and R & D divisions. Finally an expansion in marketing manpower was required.

The implementation of these changes necessitated enormous upheavals. The reorganisation began at the top: of the 35 corporate executives listed in the 1971 report, only seven survived. In NCR's main manufacturing facilities at Dayton, employment, which at a maximum had reached 14,500, was reduced to 850 by 1977. The effects on the local community in Dayton, a one-company town, were devastating. Worldwide employment was cut from 103,000 to 64,000 as NCR moved into a completely new, knowledge-intensive industry. Old product lines were phased out and data terminals and computer systems introduced. The progress NCR made with its new products was striking as figure 1 indicates: mechanical products, which

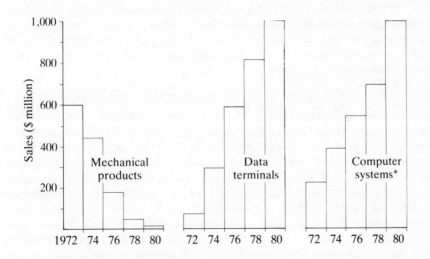

Figure 1. Equipment sales by product line. Source: *Annual Reports*, NCR Corporation.
* Change in classification in 1976.

accounted for two-thirds of equipment sales in 1972, made up less than 14 per cent of revenues by 1976. Research and development expenditures meantime rose from $50 million in the early 1970s to about $120 million in 1977 and were forecast to rise substantially in following years. The turnaround in profitability was also impressive, as the $60 million loss of 1972 was converted into a profit of $72 million in the following twelve months. And in the period up to 1977, returns on sales and equity were generally better than those attained during the best years of the 1960s.

It would be wrong to give the impression that all of the corporation's problems had been solved by the late 1970s. For example, during the boom period for its mechanical products in 1970, NCR had acquired the Appleton Coated Paper Company, a producer of speciality papers, in an attempt to further exploit its dominant position within the office machinery market. This acquisition was clearly less relevant when the conversion to electronics took place, and the company experienced a large fall in sales and profits; but it was not until 1978 that NCR was able to divest itself of this legacy of the past.[12] Because of its lateness into electronics and the subsequent period of transition, NCR has not been able to regain the market share it held with mechanical machines during the 1960s. On the other hand, given that the company had no point-of-sale terminal to offer at all in the late 1960s, NCR had recovered by 1977 to the position where it held about half of the market in retail stores and banks.[13] Into the 1980s, corporate strategy was beginning to stress the need to reduce the company's dependence on outside suppliers. The aim was to reduce purchases of components from non-group companies from 64 per cent of the total in 1980 to 40 per cent in 1984. To this end NCR, in common with its competitors such as Burroughs and Sperry Univac, is investing heavily in semiconductor manufacturing capacity; and the vertical integration programme continued with the acquisition of Applied Digital Data Systems, one of the leading suppliers of computer video-display terminals at the end of 1980.

NCR Europe in the 1970s and the Role of Dundee

Divestment and Rundown of Manufacturing Operations. The problems faced by the NCR Corporation were paralleled at the European level. Indeed the position was even more difficult in the UK given the stimulus which had been produced by the decimalisation programme. It is questionable whether NCR should have allowed its Dundee operation to build up so quickly and thereby produce a false sense of euphoria. The company had plenty of time to plan for UK decimalisation and could presumably have supplied the British market from Continental European facilities or the USA; although failure to meet demand could have had adverse repercussions in the longer term. In any event, the reorganisation and rationalisation programme of the 1970s to take NCR out of mechanical products and into electronics and total business systems was more far-reaching in Europe than in the US. With manufacturing facilities spanning several countries with different laws, languages and traditions and numerous subsidiary companies, the rundown of production capacity and personnel was bound to create fundamental difficulties.

The decision was taken to concentrate production in Europe in two locations, and the operations which were reprieved were NCR's main manufacturing bases in Augsburg and Dundee. This was a fairly logical decision. The greatest technical and managerial know-how existed at these operations, and both had already been involved in computers. Therefore the expertise existed to carry responsibility for electronic products. Wage levels and labour relations were deemed to be satisfactory. Moreover, with British entry into the EEC pending, a closer integration between the company's European operations would not be hampered by tariff and other trade barriers. The remaining factories in Berlin, Giessen, Massy and Bulach were closed. All four facilities were relatively small, employing under 400 people in each. By implication this meant that the depth of technical and managerial expertise was restricted, but there were other reasons for closure in particular cases. From a logistics viewpoint a factory in Berlin posed major problems, while Switzerland had become a high cost country on account of the strength of the Swiss franc, and its position outside the EEC was a disadvantage. The closures were not achieved without resistance at the national level: in France, for example, it was reported that the Government fought hard to retain the factory in operation and extracted additional redundancy payments from NCR for the workforce before agreeing to closure. In Berlin, in addition, long drawn-out negotiations took place with the Workers Council prior to the liquidation of the operation.

Although closure was avoided, the major job losses occurred in Dundee and Augsburg, and particularly at the former location (see figure 2). For the workers and their families at the Dundee plants, the 1970s was a traumatic decade, with the almost constant threat of redundancy existing. Decimalisation temporarily breathed some life into certain low price high volume products which otherwise would have been phased out before the end of the 1960s and delayed the transition to electronic machines. In addition it effectively wiped out the post-decimalisation market for Dundee's established mechanical products. In the Autumn of 1971 1,200 redundancies were announced as the start of what was to prove a long period of job attrition. The company were at pains to point out that these job losses compared with 7,500 redundancies in Dayton, and between 2,000 and 3,000 in Germany. A local union leader commented, however: '. . . we were a boom town. Now suddenly we are a doom town. It is the speed with which it has all happened which has shocked us'.[14] What was particularly disturbing from the viewpoint of the workforce was that the initial redundancy announcement coincided with a press report (denied by NCR) that the company were proposing to build a new factory in Portugal to take advantage of low labour costs.[15] A demonstration was held in the city centre to demand UK Government action and brief protest stoppages took place in the factories toward the end of 1971. The year ended with a union allegation that they had been told by the company that NCR might have had to 'close its doors' if a recent order for 18,000 machines had not been received.[16] Further redundancy announcements occurred at intervals through to 1978, with a total of 3,200 employees losing their jobs. But this was only a proportion of all jobs lost, for employment was reduced by a further 2,500 during the period by natural wastage, early retirals and voluntary redundancies. During these years, seven of the nine Dundee factories closed. From the company perspective the rundown was effected remarkably smoothly. Apart from token stoppages and demonstrations there was little worker

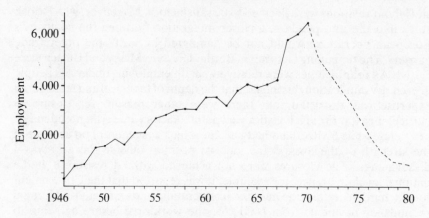

Figure 2. Employment at N C R Dundee. Annual figures available until 1970. After 1970, data available for occasional years from newspaper reports, journal articles, and other sources.

resistance to the redundancy programme. After one announcement of dismissals in 1976, a union official remarked: 'It is a disastrous decision by the management, but I cannot see it being reversed, no matter how hard we oppose it.'[17]

In part, the absence of disputes or stoppages may have been a reflection of the policies implemented by NCR, which emphasised retraining.[18] NCR permitted workers to shift jobs within the factory and retrain for the assembly and testing of electronic products. A 3- to 4-week training package was developed to enable instruction in the assembly and testing of specific electronic models to be overlaid on a general understanding of electronics. There were inevitable difficulties in trying to impart diagnostic skills to men accustomed to operating power presses or automatic lathes or to assembling purely mechanical units, but even disputes concerning the implementation of the retraining programmes were few. Draughtsmen and other technicians held a one-hour stoppage at one point to protest about the company's redeployment terms. They claimed they were being offered jobs as machine operators for which they would work five hours more per week but receive £10 per week less; even then, they alleged, there was no guarantee the company would accept them for retraining nor of continuity of employment for those subsequently retrained. But those on piecework or other incentive payments were assured that their previous level of earnings would be maintained. This programme reduced the extent to which new labour had to be hired while existing employees were becoming redundant. The motives were partly altruistic, given the scarcity of suitable skills existing within the company's normal recruitment area, but retraining brought its own problems to NCR which may only have become clear in the longer term, such as lower productivity among employees who had been more suitable for work on the fabrication of electro-mechanical products.

Apart from large-scale retraining, the company claimed that their strategy for the Dundee operation was agreed in advance with union representatives, and that their open style of management ensured that workers were kept fully informed. Yet, for example, the company statement accompanying the second round of job losses in 1971 was positively misleading, emphasising as it did the general economic environment rather than technological change: 'The expected improvement in the economy was taking longer than had been anticipated and this continued to have an adverse effect on the requirements for business equipment.'[19] And it was not until 1977, after several years of upheaval and uncertainty, that it became clear that NCR was targeting for a maximum employment at the plants of 1,000. Company strategy for the operation was never specifically defined, for as late as mid-1978 NCR announced further cutbacks in its 1,000-strong workforce. The reason given was that an earlier plan to build microprocessor boards in Dundee would not go ahead.[20]

Given the lower peak level of employment in Augsburg, the rundown of jobs was less severe. The restructuring of the German facility in terms of products was achieved earlier than in Dundee, and the target employment level of approximately 1,000 had been achieved by 1976 (at this time there were still 2,000 employed in Dundee). Employment among field engineers, computer engineers and salesmen was also affected by the overhaul of NCR's European operations. Apart from the loss of about 5,500 jobs in manufacturing in the UK between 1970 and 1977, approximately 2,500 jobs disappeared in other areas of business. In Continental Europe over 5,000 production jobs were lost (including the closures of the smaller facilities), but the number of non-production workers was relatively unchanged. In total in 1977 NCR employed 15,000 people in the European region, compared with 28,000 in 1970.[21]

Organisational Changes.[22] The employment rundown was only part of the restructuring programme for NCR Europe. Important organisational changes also took place. Previously, managers of the manufacturing plants reported to the chief executives in the country in which the plant was located. Under the new structure, plant managers of both domestic and international facilities reported directly to the USA. As from 1977 the General Managers in the Augsburg and Dundee plants were thus responsible to the Vice-President of the Computer and Communications Systems Division in America, given their product orientation towards computers. The aim of this was to integrate the European and other non-US plants into the company's overall production programme and strategy for supplying various markets. When mechanical machines were being produced, a high proportion of the output of NCR Europe was destined for European markets. Under the new scheme the product to market allocation was rejected as NCR planned to move towards a global system of production and supply.

Product and Market Strategy. NCR's overall strategy was to emphasise smaller plants chartered for a limited line or group of products.[23] Each of these plants would then serve world markets or at least significant parts of the world market with the products for which they were responsible. Similarly manufacturing plants would have their own resident engineering development groups so that product changes could be implemented quickly, a necessity in electronics given the short product life cycle. In essence, therefore, the second source role which the European plants had previously fulfilled, was being at least partially rejected.

The implementation of this strategy at the European level could not be done overnight, given the need to phase-out existing products and the heavy capital expenditures in introducing new products. At Dundee, for example, during 1977 and 1978 major reorganisation involved the scrapping of fifteen outdated product lines such as mechanical comptometers and older electronic cash registers.[24] It was only by the end of 1978 that the changeover to a fully electronics-oriented facility had been achieved. As the 1977 Annual Report of NCR commented, the Dundee facility 'will become the prime supplier of the Criterion Series of computers (I-8200 and 8500) for Common Market countries, the Middle East and Africa'.[25] In addition to this dual source role, Dundee was granted a unique product charter in the area of banking terminals, with an allocation of R & D funds for product development. The end result was the introduction early in 1979 of the 1780 Banking Terminal, an automatic teller machine, developed to replace a four-year-old model which had emanated from the USA.

Because of the earlier changeover in Germany, there were fears in the UK that Augsburg would replace Dundee as the chief non-US operation. As a newspaper article at the time commented: 'Augsburg has replaced Dundee as the prime source factory and the danger for the Scottish complex is that it will now be left to pick up the crumbs from the tables of the United States and West Germany.'[26] This perhaps represented a misunderstanding of the role which NCR envisaged for the various plants. The unique charter for Augsburg was to develop and manufacture a ledger card printing facility for small business systems and the plant had engineering responsibility for the I-8130 computer and supplied it and the I-8150 to the European and Middle East/Africa regions. As with Dundee's banking terminal, funds were allocated for research and development for the unique products which could be marketed worldwide.

The decentralisation of R & D to plant level was an important feature of NCR's strategy and a necessary adjunct to the allocation of unique product charters. From a European viewpoint it is highly desirable in that it reduces the reliance of European plants on the innovativeness of the parent corporation and on product allocations from the US. It also means, conversely, that the European operations will sink or swim by their own efforts, although the fact that financial control and investment allocations are decided in the USA means that Europe will be competing for funds with all other NCR subsidiaries worldwide. With respect to Dundee, while the level of employment has reduced dramatically since the electro-mechanical days, plant status has probably improved. From date of establishment, an

Engineering Service function existed at the complex and this subsequently evolved into an Advanced Engineering department. But it was only with the overhaul of the corporation's international strategy in the 1970s that Dundee developed a strong research and development unit, staffed by a substantial number of R & D professionals.

Concluding Comments. NCR Dundee thus survived the traumas of the 1970s, with a remarkably smooth transition into a completely new technology. Whereas Dundee's manufacturing operations used to start with blank metal, much of the current work is concerned with the assembly of bought-in components, and electronic modules have replaced hundreds of mechanical parts. Unlike the situation for the corporation as a whole, moreover, NCR in the UK never made a loss. In 1972, admittedly, profits fell by 55 per cent compared with the previous year, but at the same time the Dundee arm of the company was awarded its second Queen's Award to Industry for its export achievements. As the data in Appendix, table 3 show, profits slumped again in the mid-1970s, primarily as a result of the phase-out of mechanical products from Dundee, before recovering strongly towards the end of the decade.

Such success has to be set against the problems and hardship for the city of Dundee created by the very large job losses at NCR during these years. Industry in Dundee was traditionally dominated by jute processing, but the position changed dramatically after World War II as table 2 indicates. Redundancies in this industry continued into the 1970s, with, for example, heavy job losses in Sidlaw Industries Ltd, the largest British jute manufacturer. Much store was placed on US inward direct investment in Dundee to

Table 2. Textile Employment in Dundee (1911–76)
(as % of total employment)

1911	1931	1951	1961	1976
48	41	23	18	8

SOURCE: Scottish Economic Planning Department,
Redundancies in Dundee, ESU Research Papers No.1,
July 1979.

improve the industrial structure and to expand employment opportunities during the post-war years. Apart from NCR, companies such as Dayco Rubber, Holo-Krome and Veeder-Root were significant employers of labour; but by far the largest was Timex, which at peak employed over 6,000 people in its five-plant complex in Dundee. Timex began operating in 1946 in Dundee, only a few months after NCR, and like the latter grew rapidly in the immediate post-war years. From the late 1960s the watch manufacturer was faced with major and continuing labour relations problems in Dundee and the switch from electro-mechanical to solid state technology for electronic watches adversely affected the operation. Despite efforts to diversify and seek sub-contract work, employment had been reduced to 3,900 by 1981, and whether this can be sustained in the future is open to considerable doubt. The decline of employment at NCR was thus accompanied by job losses at other American factories. The result was an alarming upward trend in unemployment as shown in table 3.

Table 3. Number and Percentage of Working Population Unemployed

July figures	Dundee Number	%	Scotland Number	%
1969	2,569	2.8	78,966	3.6
1970	4,406	4.9	90,598	4.2
1971	6,454	7.4	128,730	6.0
1972	6,932	7.4	136,509	6.5
1973	5,013	5.3	95,207	4.4
1974	3,783	4.0	89,840	4.2
1975	6,137	6.5	129,836	6.0
1976	7,687	7.9	165,649	7.5
1977	9,219	9.4	194,271	8.6
1978	8,890	9.1	191,906	8.5
1979	9,079	9.3	187,431	8.3
1980	11,677	11.9	236,326	10.5
1981	15,168	15.5	318,215	14.1

SOURCE: Manpower Services Commission, Edinburgh.

For NCR Dundee, itself, by the start of the 1980s the basis seemed to have been laid for a sound if fairly limited-activity future. Rather disturbingly, after the industrial calm of the 1970s, in the Autumn of 1980 the company had a five-week strike which was estimated to cost £2 million in lost output. Then in March 1981, 250 redundancies were announced taking employment to only 750; the problem was reported to be the high value of sterling which had led to the almost total collapse of one of NCR's second-source products, the class 8200 computer. Even if these immediate problems can be overcome, short product life cycles for electronic products mean that future success depends crucially on the ability to anticipate market trends. Given NCR's commitment to growth, production expansion will be necessary but this is more likely to take the form of new plants rather than the build-up of existing European operations, such as that in Dundee. There must indeed be a doubt whether any such new facilities will be built in Europe at all, given wage trends, etc. The effects of the reorganisation of the company have been to increase the relative importance of Japan and the Far East in NCR's international operations: as Appendix, table 2 indicated, the relative decline in net assets in the European region was matched by a build-up in Australia and the Far East, and any new plants are perhaps more likely in the latter region.

While the future of NCR Dundee rests more firmly in its own hands than in the past, given its product responsibility in the area of automatic teller machines, trends within the corporation overall will inevitably influence the progress of the Scottish operation. A number of issues are particularly relevant to this. First, the R&D requirements necessary to keep pace with the fast-moving technology will continue to make heavy demands on corporate resources. Secondly, NCR's actual as compared with desirable position within the market is still being debated. Thirdly, the corporation is trying to increase the amount of in-sourcing through backward integration. In such a dynamic situation, the future offers many problems and challenges as well as potential for NCR Dundee.

Implications of the NCR Case

Some of the issues raised by the NCR case also emerge with Goodyear and Honeywell. The first question of importance relates to the huge build-up of employment by NCR in Dundee and elsewhere in Europe during the 1960s. Some might argue that this represented a ruthless attempt by NCR to exploit short-term circumstances, while being aware that cutbacks and job losses would inevitably follow. While there is some evidence of this in respect of the UK decimalisation programme, it does appear that the failure to anticipate the growth of electronics was a genuine, albeit a highly costly, miscalculation. In any event, responsibility must partially lie with national governments for failing to consider the security of the employment being created.

A second issue of importance relates to the policies to be pursued when divestment and job loss became inevitable. In this NCR can hardly be faulted, and a reasonable balance between commercial objectives and concern for long-serving employees seems to have been attained. Retraining programmes, natural wastage, assistance to redundant personnel in job-hunting and full discussions with the unions were undertaken in order to try to minimise the dislocation costs to the workers.

The question of intra-European competition for jobs when NCR was restructuring did not appear to be particularly important. It is possible that strong pressures were created by national governments in the attempt to preserve jobs, although these were not made public. The attempt by the French Government to retain the operation at Massy has already been noted, and, under pressure from the unions, there were certainly meetings between the British Government and NCR. More generally, this case throws some further light on the factors which influence multinationals when decisions are taken on rationalisation and divestment. The factories closed by NCR in Europe were the smallest, least-well established operations and those lacking any depth of technical and managerial experience. The comparison with Goodyear in Drumchapel is worth noting.

Table 1. Performance Data for NCR Corporation

Year	Sales ($000)	Assets ($000)	Net income ($000)	Shareholders equity ($000)	Employees	Net income as % of		Rank (by sales) in Fortune Directory
						Sales	Shareholders equity	
1980	3,322,370	3,366,455	254,686	1,704,483	68,000	7.7	14.9	108
1979	3,002,640	2,918,435	234,602	1,476,313	67,000	7.8	15.9	111
1978	2,730,166	2,596,161	318,004	1,299,585	62,000	11.6	24.5	104
1977	2,521,626	2,340,626	143,620	1,023,285	64,000	5.7	14.0	98
1976	2,312,713	2,311,795	95,644	888,848	67,000	4.1	10.8	96
1975	2,165,607	2,194,722	72,491	798,287	72,000	3.3	9.1	96
1974	1,979,003	2,110,417	87,165	732,572	81,000	4.4	11.9	97
1973	1,816,281	1,833,916	71,961	645,167	81,000	4.0	11.2	86
1972	1,557,699	1,689,304	(59,612)*	580,712	90,000	–	–	86
1971	1,465,701	1,689,298	1,284	610,068	95,000	0.1	0.2	79
1970	1,420,576	1,644,600	30,246	612,700	98,000	2.1	4.9	76
1969	1,254,641	1,444,528	44,115	576,110	103,000	3.5	7.7	87
1968	1,102,178	1,117,582	35,860	519,684	91,000	3.3	6.9	86
1967	955,455	1,010,145	35,320	391,569	84,000	3.7	9.0	89
1966	871,305	566,440	27,219	241,004	79,000	3.1	9.4	91

* Bracketed figures indicate losses.
SOURCE: 'The Fortune Directory of the 500 Largest US Industrial Corporations', *Fortune*, various editions.

Table 2. International and European Operations of NCR Corporation

International operations	1969	1970	1971	1972	1973	1974	1975	1976	1977	1978	1979	1980
Revenues ($000)	n.a.	642,567	686,848	727,607	895,430	1,014,373	1,124,013	1,133,391	1,362,379	1,574,603	1,774,322	1,975,396
% of corporate revenues	n.a.	45.2	46.9	46.7	49.3	51.3	51.9	49.0	51.0	53.1	52.2	51.2
Operating income ($000)	n.a.	76,837	69,232	80,857	133,092	148,746	153,890	170,389	147,067	168,068	188,660	249,046
% of corporate operating income	n.a.	52.2	68.7	53.3	52.0	46.7	53.8	49.9	47.1	41.0	40.6	46.3

European operations*	1969	1970	1971	1972	1973	1974	1975	1976
Net assets	106,704	123,135	127,280	125,951	156,185	166,596	169,225	158,222
% of total net assets in international operations†	49.1	47.1	46.3	43.8	45.6	46.7	43.0	38.0

European operations*	1977	1978	1979	1980
Revenues	627,060	746,108	891,936	1,064,119
% of total revenues from international operations	46.0	47.4	50.3	53.9
Operating income	50,642	83,548	97,152	108,325
% of total operating income from international operations	34.4	49.7	51.5	43.5

* Consistent series not available for whole period.
† The decline in net assets in Europe in relation to net assets in international operations as a whole contrasts with the position of Japan, Australia and the Far East. In 1969 the equivalent figure for the latter region was 22.8% and in 1976 30.9%.
SOURCE: Corporation accounts.

Table 3. Performance Data for NCR's UK Subsidiary – NCR Ltd*

Year ended 30 November	Sales (£000)	Net profit before tax (£000)	Net profit before tax as % of sales	Exports (£000)	No. of employees
1980	103,618	11,474	11.1	32,000	4,246
1979	82,422	10,073	12.2	23,300	4,257
1978	76,649	12,199†	15.9	22,600	4,200
1977	75,690	3,849	5.1	22,500	4,800
1976	66,000	2,608†	4.0	19,000	5,500
1975	71,091	3,638†	5.1	29,000	6,600
1974	65,589	6,824	10.4	27,000	7,400
1973	52,797	6,631	12.6	13,500	7,800
1972	46,169	3,847	8.3	13,800	8,700
1971	63,299	8,774	13.9	16,200	11,183
1970	70,971	9,916	14.0	15,600	12,825
1969	50,787	6,497	12.8	9,609	12,609
1968	40,793	5,499	13.5	7,669	11,067

* Including subsidiary companies in Kenya, Tanzania and Cyprus, but excluding subsidiary in Ghana.

† After exceptional costs of £1.6 mill. in 1975 and £1.5 mill. in 1976 incurred as a result of phase-out of certain mechanical products in Dundee factories. In 1978 exceptional profit of £1.9 mill. earned on sale of company's right to future royalty income.

SOURCE: Company accounts.

NOTES AND REFERENCES

1. The information in this section was derived from company PR material and the 1970 Annual Report of NCR Corporation.
2. This discussion draws on: 'NCR's new strategy puts it in computers to stay', *Business Week*, 26 September 1977; 'What happened at NCR after the boss declared martial law?', *Fortune*, September 1975.
3. *Glasgow Herald*, 2 September 1976; 'NCR tackles growth problems', *Financial Times*, 10 April 1969.
4. *Glasgow Herald*, 2 September 1976.
5. *Scotsman*, 12 June 1947.
6. 'The US invaders strike it rough', *Management Today*, October 1971.
7. 'Pacemakers of the East Coast', *Scotland*, April 1967.
8. 1970 Annual Report of NCR Corporation.
9. 1969 Annual Report of NCR Corporation.
10. *Business Week*, 26 September 1977, p.102.
11. 1975 Annual Report of NCR Corporation.
12. Reported in *Electronics Weekly*, 19 July 1978.
13. *Business Week*, 26 September 1977, p.101.
14. *Scotsman*, 27 September 1971.
15. *Scotsman*, 14 September 1971, quoting a report by Dundee International Socialists.
16. *Scotsman*, 10 December 1971.
17. *Scotsman*, 2 September 1976.

18. 'Re-training helps NCR avoid the big drop', *Business Administration*, November 1974.
19. *Glasgow Herald*, 4 December 1971.
20. *Scotsman*, 3 June 1978.
21. Quoted in 1976 Annual Report of NCR Corporation.
22. Company PR material.
23. *Business Week*, 26 September 1977, p.102.
24. *Financial Times*, 31 January 1979.
25. 1977 Annual Report of NCR Corporation.
26. *Glasgow Herald*, 2 September 1976.

HONEYWELL IN LANARKSHIRE

Honeywell Inc. is a corporation with interests in the fields of information processing, automation and controls. The company started as a manufacturer of control systems incorporated in Delaware in 1927, and control systems is still the main part of Honeywell's business, accounting for two-thirds of corporate revenues in 1980 (see Appendix, table 2). Within this business segment, the company currently supplies domestic and industrial markets with temperature control equipment such as clock thermostats; process control equipment for petrochemical and other industries; micro-switch products for the automotive, machine-tool and material handling industries; test instruments; and equipment for the aerospace and defence industries. The other area of Honeywell's business is information systems, in which the company manufactures and markets computer products and services. The development of this business segment is very recent; indeed it was not until 1970 that the Information and Control Systems Divisions emerged as separate, autonomous entities within Honeywell.[1]

The Scottish and European Operations of Honeywell Pre-1970

Honeywell commenced overseas activity in the inter-war period with a base in Britain. Here the company was established through the acquisition of Brown Instrument Ltd in 1934; in its first full year of operation (1937), sales by Honeywell-Brown Ltd were valued at £18,600. Seeking to expand in Europe after World War II, Honeywell opened its first manufacturing factory outside North America at Blantyre in 1948. In the 30,000 sq.ft. factory at the Blantyre Industrial Estate, about 60 people were employed initially making industrial products such as temperature and pressure recorders and controllers. Thirty years on, the Chairman of Honeywell in the UK said of the decision to locate in Blantyre: 'When we were first looking for a place to start . . . the Board of Trade recommended Lanarkshire as a location with a stable, skilled workforce; a tradition of education and training on which to build future management; good communications; and, of course, the status of a "development area" . . .'.[2]

The company expanded rapidly on the basis of domestic sales and sales to

118

Sterling Area and Continental European countries and employment rose to 350 by 1953, two-thirds of whom were male. With the Blantyre factory bursting at the seams, Honeywell-Brown moved a few miles along the road to a 66,000 sq.ft. facility at Newhouse, Lanarkshire. Speaking at the formal opening of the factory on 18 September 1953, Mr Gordon Jackson, Scottish Controller of the Ministry of Supply said: 'Scotland desperately needs the new skills which have been brought to this country by companies such as Honeywell-Brown, and we must do everything possible to encourage them. They came to Scotland to train us in the new techniques required by industry . . . There is growing up in Scotland a new generation of skilled craftsmen, skilled in a way their parents never imagined . . .'.[3] A second Newhouse factory was occupied in 1956 to accommodate micro-switch production; and a third was opened in 1958 for modurol manufacture, in the same year as the British company was renamed Honeywell Controls Ltd. Expansion was continuing elsewhere in the U K during this same period. Thus a factory was established at Hemel Hempstead for industrial and temperature control systems manufacture in 1961 and in the following year a computer marketing operation was established in Britain. Within the Honeywell organisation, the pattern was to replace imports by local manufacture when the market size was deemed to be large enough and when there was pressure from the local Honeywell marketing organisation On the basis of these factors, computer manufacture commenced at Newhouse in 1963. Growth continued unabated on the controls side of the business, with further factories at Bellshill (1967) to produce temperature controls, and at Uddingston (1969) for industrial products. Employment in Scotland peaked at just under 6,000 in the late 1960s, of which 1,950 were employed in computer operations at Newhouse, and the remainder in the Control Systems Division with factories at Newhouse, Bellshill and Uddingston.

Part of the reason for employment expansion in computers was the fact that Newhouse represented Honeywell's sole European manufacturing capability for a number of years. With the rapid growth of the computer market in Continental Europe, however, a manufacturing base was required and a new operation was established at Heppenheim in Germany, with the technical help of management personnel from Newhouse. In addition a systems engineering centre was established in the South of England, at Hemel Hempstead. In the controls area, growth in Scotland was partly matched by expansion on the Continent, and manufacturing operations were set up in Holland, Germany, France and Spain.

By the end of the 1960s, Honeywell was at its peak in terms of scale of activity in Scotland. The 1970s, by contrast, was to prove one of consolidation, rationalisation and massive technical change as the Honeywell Corporation sought to establish itself as a world force in information and control systems and assimilate the electronics revolution.

The Reorganisation of Honeywell in the Early 1970s

Information Systems:[4] *Links with General Electric.* The operations of

Honeywell in the 1970s cannot be understood without also considering the activities of another American corporation, General Electric (GE). The latter had decided in the 1960s to enter the computer industry, but its problem, like that of Honeywell, was to achieve a viable position in a market dominated by IBM. The decision was taken to expand in Europe where IBM was less firmly entrenched. So between 1964 and 1968 GE acquired Olivetti's computer division, renaming the company General Electric Information Systems Italia. The decision of Olivetti to sell its computer interests to GE stemmed from the losses being made by the division, management difficulties and internal disputes within the company.

Around the same time, GE made an offer to acquire a stake in the ailing French firm, Compagnie des Machines Bull. The French Government rejected the American solution in favour of an alternative French solution, but the French interests to which Bull was to be linked were not able, or willing, to implement the proposed agreement. Meantime Bull's finances were deteriorating, and, bowing to the inevitable, the French Government completely reversed its previous position and permitted GE to acquire 50 per cent of Bull in July 1964. GE's experience with Bull was not a happy one. Losses continued until 1969, by which time GE had sunk something like $200 million into General Electric-Machines Bull, including investment, operating losses and loans. What is important in relation to Honeywell's subsequent strategy was that GE maintained Bull's R&D facility, which employed 1,200 people in 1969/70.

As independent computer manufacturers, both Honeywell and GE were too small to survive in the long term: each had about 5 per cent of the market compared with IBM's 70 per cent. In 1970, therefore, Honeywell acquired General Electric's computer business, and with this the GE operations in France and Italy. Within Honeywell, the view was that GE provided a 'better fit' than outsiders recognised, for a variety of reasons. First, although the product ranges of the companies were competitive and far from totally compatible, Honeywell's main strengths were in medium-sized computers, whereas GE was particularly strong on large and small machines. Honeywell was marketing the 200 Series, a range of medium-sized general purpose computers, which had been developed in the US but were being built for European markets at Newhouse and Heppenheim. General Electric contributed four separate computer ranges, including a simple computer for first-time buyers and a range of large computers. Secondly, Honeywell's main success was in domestic US markets; by comparison, two-thirds of GE's sales were outside the US. Thirdly, Honeywell was strong in the marketing area, while GE was probably superior in technology.

It was the purchase of GE that decided Honeywell to split its operations into two fairly separate entities, viz. Honeywell Information Systems and Honeywell Control Systems. At the European level, a new company was established in the UK – Honeywell Information Systems Ltd.; in Italy, Honeywell Information Systems Italia was formed; and in France, Compagnie Honeywell-Bull was set up on 1 October 1970, in which Honeywell owned 66 per cent of the capital and Compagnie des Machines Bull 34 per cent. The French company had manufacturing plants at Angers and Belfort, a development centre in Paris, and in addition it controlled the Heppenheim facility. In Italy, the R & D centre was located at Pregnana, Milan, and the manufacturing facilities at Caluso, near Turin. Finally, the UK operation consisted of the production plant at Newhouse, and the software development division at Hemel Hempstead.

Reorganisation of Information Systems. Once the Honeywell–GE agreement was formally completed, Honeywell Information Systems (HIS) was faced with the daunting prospect of planning to build a coordinated product line. The aim of this strategy was to enable the company to compete across the board from small to very large systems. While Honeywell had computer manufacturing operations in the UK and Germany only, its strategy had been to use its European facilities as second source points. The product line manufactured in the USA was also produced in Scotland (the role of the West German operation was more restricted) for European and Commonwealth markets. The plan for HIS was to move towards single-sourcing for world markets.

After considerable internal debate, 'mission assignments' were designated for 23 major development projects ranging from printers to large control processors. Within Europe, the Pregnana Centre of HIS Italia was given the task of developing a small to medium series of computers; this included responsibility for hardware development and for all systems software. Compagnie Honeywell-Bull had full responsibility for the development of the smallest of the series of computers, and shared responsibility with the USA for the critical middle-range model. The two largest models in the line were to be the responsibility of Honeywell's operations in Phoenix (Arizona), which had been GE's major computer manufacturing facility. Finally, programming languages and software systems were shared between the US and the UK; the software division in Hemel Hempstead had the responsibility for the development of software for Europe, given the differing needs and requirements of the latter market.

The carve-up between the various operations seemed perfectly rational, capitalising upon existing R & D strengths; and observers at the time praised the fact that Honeywell had moved further than any other American-owned computer company to give its European subsidiaries real autonomy.[5] But it is difficult to know how far political pressures influenced the choice of locations: this is particularly relevant in the case of Honeywell-Bull. What is interesting is that neither Newhouse nor Heppenheim – the original Honeywell manufacturing locations in Europe – were given product development responsibilities. Although this would have entailed the formation of R & D centres from scratch, the fact that these operations were left on the sidelines had obvious implications for the subsequent roles (if any) of the plants as manufacturing bases.

The fruits of the Honeywell–GE merger appeared in the Spring of 1974 when HIS launched the Series 60 family of computers. The manufacturing allocation basically reflected the fundamental development work which had been undertaken. Thus Italy was to manufacture the Level 62 (small systems) and France the Level 61 (machines for first-time users) and Level 64 machines (medium range offering), with the Levels 66 and 68 (large systems) being produced in the USA. The United States was also involved in minicomputers and, along with the UK (Hemel Hempstead), in software. These Honeywell facilities became single-source points for the supply to world markets of the particular computer concerned.[6]

Control Systems. The Control Systems Division of Honeywell in Europe was faced with different reorganisation pressures in the 1970s. The need for change emerged from three sources. The first was because European plants were basically established as supply points for local national markets. With the prospect of British entry into the EEC, this entailed unnecessary duplication and so a programme of rationalisation and relocation of product charters was instituted. The aim of this was to bring about product specialisation on a plant basis. Secondly, in some areas of business, electronics were replacing electro-mechanical controls, thereby reducing required labour inputs. Thirdly, and finally, complicating the picture were government pressures in Europe. These were particularly important on the computer side of Honeywell's business, but inevitably decisions taken within the Controls Division had to take account of possible repercussions in computers. There was some speculation, for example, that Honeywell might have preferred to close its controls plant in France, but it kept the facility open to prevent problems with the French Government, which would have affected the position of Honeywell-Bull (and the successor to this company CII – Honeywell Bull).

Honeywell in Scotland during the 1970s

Information Systems. The first hint that the days of unrestrained expansion in Scotland were over came in 1971 when the redundancies of 350 hourly-paid employees was announced, spread evenly between the Information Systems and Control Systems Divisions. Honeywell stressed that the job losses were not related to the merger with GE which, if anything, had 'strengthened the position',[7] but rather to the recession. While this may have been true, longer term, the reorganisation of the US corporation's computer business had obvious adverse consequences for operations such as Newhouse, which were not allocated product development and manufacturing responsibilities. Production facilities were closed in Bowmanville, Canada and at Lowell and Framingham, Mass. The small Heppenheim facility, moreover, had been closed soon after the Honeywell–GE merger. In spite of much speculation, the Scottish plant did not suffer the same fate, although the product role which was granted to the operation with the launch of the Series 60 computers made it fairly likely that substantial cutbacks in employment would occur. Newhouse was to become a second-source plant for the large Level 66 computer which had been developed and was produced at Phoenix in the USA. The markets to be supplied from Scotland were the UK, Italy and France. The role of this operation was thus at odds with Honeywell's overall product strategy, the key to which was single-sourcing for world markets.

The reason for retaining a computer manufacturing presence in Britain at all is difficult to establish. The single tender policy operated by the UK Government, which prevented companies other than indigenous firms like International Computers Ltd (ICL) from competing for government business, has been a long-standing source of complaint by Honeywell. In 1972 the Department of Trade and Industry in the UK announced that most official contracts would henceforth be put up for tender, and there was speculation that this decision was taken to persuade Honeywell to retain a manufacturing presence in the UK. The issue did not end at this point, because government contracts continued to elude Honeywell, leading to a warning as late as 1976 by the Managing Director of HIS Ltd that manufacture of the Level 66 computer at Newhouse would have to switch to Europe unless the Government amended its policy of preference for ICL. The point was made that the export ratio from Newhouse, estimated at 85 per cent, was not sustainable unless Honeywell had a strong base in the UK home market.[8]

Two hundred and fifty staff redundancies were announced in 1972 and a further 250 early in 1974; but the crunch decision came on 1 November 1974 when it was announced that 1,150 people were to be paid off within a week, 800 of these in the computer division. There were angry protests from a variety of sources: government ministers criticised the behaviour of Honeywell as 'completely irresponsible'; it was argued that the situation had emerged without warning or notice and had been aggravated by the failure of the company to enter into meaningful discussions with the unions about the reasons for their decision and the alternatives which might be considered. The unions for their part occupied the factory for 10 days in protest against the redundancies, which they argued had been achieved by 'blackmail and coercion', and their take-over ended only when management conceded the principle of allowing the redundancies to be voluntary.[9]

In considering the subsequent progress of HIS in Scotland, it is necessary once again to take a European view of Honeywell's operations, specifically focusing on the American company's activities in France. In the Spring of 1975, the French firm Compagnie Internationale Pour L'Informatique (CII) merged with Honeywell-Bull to form a new company CII-Honeywell Bull (CII-HB) in which Honeywell Information Systems held a 47 per cent interest (the background to the merger and the terms of the deal are discussed in the Appendix p.127). As part of this deal CII-HB was given the right to manufacture any product in the common line with decisions based on 'the economic feasibility of local production'.[10] Among the other Honeywell Information Systems companies in Europe, serious concern was expressed at the merger. In Italy it was feared that this would lead to the down-grading of HIS Italia, and similar concerns were voiced in Scotland, particularly when HIS cut employment at its Newhouse plant from 400 to 300 early in

1976. The company stated that Newhouse would continue to export to France for the 'foreseeable future'. However, there was a suspicion that CII-HB might try to justify the manufacture of the Level 66 computer in France (as permitted under the terms of the agreement, provided that this was viable) and thereby end UK exports to France. In the event the French firm did implement its right in respect of this model, which until then had been main-sourced in Phoenix and second-sourced at Newhouse.

The effect of the decision was that the market area to be supplied out of Newhouse was reduced: instead of markets in the UK, France and Italy, Level 66 computers would be marketed in the UK and Italy alone. Fears about the future of Newhouse were, nevertheless, allayed by an announcement from HIS in 1978 that the Level 6 range of minicomputers would be third-sourced at that plant for the UK market. The decision to manufacture the Level 6 product line in Scotland was related partly to the fact that this minicomputer was selling well in the UK; local manufacture could provide a further marketing advantage. Additionally, without another product the viability of the Newhouse operation must have been questionable, and there may have been UK Government pressures on Honeywell to retain the plant. But it does seem also that the excellent performance record of the Newhouse facility from the mid-1970s had a significant bearing on the decision, and company reports in the UK have stressed the consistency of the operation in meeting scheduled delivery dates. To bring the story completely up-to-date, 1980 saw Newhouse establishing production lines for the new DPS 8 large computers, to replace Level 66 production which came to an end in December of that year. Employment by 1980 was down to 283, a much reduced, but for the time being, stable job level. Even so, the European operations of Honeywell seem likely to continue to be affected by external events and political factors, witness the possibility of nationalisation of CII-HB by the Mitterand Government of France. In fact as at end 1981, Honeywell was negotiating to sell 27 per cent of CII-HB to the French Government.

Control Systems. At the start of the 1970s, the Control Systems Division in Scotland had the widest product range and the largest employment of any Honeywell operation in Europe. On the other hand, performance was unsatisfactory in comparison with some other European manufacturing units. It seems that the Division was carrying a good deal of fat from the boom days of the 1960s, on both the management and labour sides. In other ways too, Honeywell showed characteristics of the 'British disease', with restrictive practices and low productivity, and problems associated with product quality. Within this environment, technological innovation and the change-over from electro-mechanical to electronic products, together with product relocation programmes within Europe, created the climate for painful readjustment.

The initial redundancies occurred in 1971 when the manufacture of gas valves was transferred from Scotland to Holland. It is not known how far this was a function of poor performance in Scotland or the production relocation programme. In general, however, it does seem that in the early years of the 1970s, some newer electronics' products were being allocated to Honeywell operations in Germany as opposed to Scotland, leaving the latter with technology which was not state-of-the-art and with declining demand. Honeywell was thus set for a substantial reduction in jobs in Lanarkshire.

In late 1974, when 1,150 redundancies were announced, principally in the computer division, considerable under-utilisation of capacity was reported at Bellshill (temperature controls and thermostats) with some under-employment also at Newhouse (micro-switches). It was, therefore, not unexpected that some time later closure of the Bellshill factories was announced, with the temperature controls' products being transferred to Newhouse. The Managing Director of Honeywell Control Systems Ltd commented at this time that: 'We have long gone past the days of big labour increases. Technological change is sweeping through our industry and the need for assembly and manufacturing labour has unfortunately decreased more and more.'[11]

Honeywell seemed committed to making the Lanarkshire operation viable and competitive. Investment was high in 1977 and 1978, and in early 1979 a £1 million investment was announced for the production of electronic process control instruments, the first Honeywell factory outside the USA to make the equipment. This so-called High Technology Unit was officially opened in February 1980 with an initial staff of 35 but the potential for a further 90 jobs. This was followed by the establishment of a Solid State Application Centre, basically an R&D unit concerned with research into the application of advanced solid state electronics, in order to meet the needs of the European market. To quote Jim McGregor, the Managing Director of the Division again, 'the development of the Centre is a continuation of our investment in Scotland and follows our recent announcement to begin micro-computer production and micro-processor based product manufacture at Newhouse . . . Honeywell, in common with a number of other international companies based in Scotland, have been criticised in the past for setting up satellite plants with no real roots in the community. I hope that this will be seen as a move in the right direction.'[12]

The phase-out of older technology products, however, continued. In September 1980, the rundown and closure of the industrial products factory at Uddingston was announced. This affected 330 people at a location which had once employed 1,200. The reason given for shut-down was that the plant's products were electro-mechanical instruments overtaken by new technology goods produced elsewhere in the Honeywell group. The remaining newer technology products were to be consolidated at Newhouse, which, after the closure, became the sole manufacturing location for Honeywell in the United Kingdom. It was stressed that the economic climate (recession conditions curbing new house-building) and the high value of sterling had, in addition, produced a renewed emphasis on the need to reduce costs. These same factors were mentioned only a few weeks later when 1,300 workers at Newhouse in the micro-switch and residential divisions were put on a three-day week.

As at 1980, employment in the Control Systems Division in Scotland was 1,585, a reduction of about 2,400 people compared with the peak. It is not at all certain that this represents a stable, longer-term level of employment. Problems at time of writing, nevertheless, seemed less related to performance difficulties at the plants than with general economic problems in the UK. How far the replacement of electro-mechanical by electronic products has still to go is not known.

Concluding Comments. By 1980, Honeywell employed 5,181 people in Britain in comparison with 9,200 at the start of the previous decade (Appendix, table 4). In comparison with some other cases studied in this section, the job losses were not too traumatic overall in Britain; although almost all of this decline occurred in the manufacturing plants in Lanarkshire, with little change in marketing and administrative employment. In terms of performance, the company had a series of very bad years from 1972 to 1975, with cumulative losses totalling £20 million. A thirteen-week strike caused major problems in 1972 and the Control Systems Division was hit by the oil crisis and rise in energy costs from the end of 1973. Otherwise the major costs were concerned with transition in technology and plant roles. Unlike some other companies studied, Honeywell had not completely come through its difficulties by the end of the 1970s, although the new investment in controls systems was an encouraging sign.

One of the most likely developments in Honeywell Inc. in future is perhaps a closer relationship between the Controls and Information Systems Divisions. It has been argued by the Chief Executive of one of Honeywell's European subsidiaries that the company only went into computers to benefit the Controls side. Therefore 'as computers feature more and more in the control situation . . . there is a turnkey element in the business and it starts to generate a closer identification with our (the computer) business . . . The synergy between the two operations becomes more important.'[13] At the same time, Honeywell's computer strategies will continue to stress flexibility in Europe. The impact of both of these issues on Honeywell in Lanarkshire has yet to be seen.

Some Lessons of the Honeywell Case

Perhaps the main lesson from the Honeywell case concerns the ability of host governments to influence the behaviour of multinationals, at least in this particular industry sector. The key is to identify where a particular country's bargaining strengths lie and then to exploit these. The overall size of the market (in the UK), access to the R&D facilities and widespread distribution network of Machines Bull (for GE in France), and access to French Government business (for Honeywell-Bull in its link-up with CII) were all factors enabling European Governments to modify the strategy of Honeywell Information Systems in Europe. These bargaining strengths have then to be balanced against bargaining weaknesses, for example, the absence of an R & D department at the UK and German production facilities; the deterioration in the financial position of Machines Bull (following the French Government's refusal to allow GE to acquire a 20 per cent share in the company); and the continuing losses in CII, together with the failure of Unidata.

The effect of the above factors was that Honeywell's integration strategy, involving plant specialisation for world markets and single sourcing, was then followed by progressive dis-integration with the introduction of second and third sourcing. In responding to European pressures in this way, Honeywell may yet prove to have been in the forefront in devising a strategy for the 1980s. It remains to be seen whether the need to compromise on what it might have considered as an optimal strategy will adversely affect performance in Europe.

What emerges clearly is the role of research and development departments in determining the status of subsidiary companies in Honeywell. At the time of the rationalisation programme following Honeywell's takeover of GE's computer interests, the operations which were saved or retained as significant manufacturing bases were all those with R & D departments. Honeywell is rather unusual in that there are relatively few other American multinationals which operate world-based R & D programmes of this type. Nevertheless, there is a strong case for attempting to encourage US affiliate R & D in Scotland or even for persuading firms to set up technical support or service facilities: other evidence on US multinational R & D indicates that there is a good likelihood of such support or service facilities evolving into formal R & D units over time.

The significance of operational performance as a factor in determining corporate policy is again suggested in this case. In the 1970s Honeywell's computer operations at Newhouse performed successfully and thus survived when there were indications that the company could have been wound up. Conversely, poor performance in the Control Systems Division during much of the 1970s seems to have been a factor (along with technological change) in permitting the rundown of the Scottish facilities and plant closures. Indeed the Lanarkshire subsidiary may have been spared further employment shrinkage because Honeywell was experiencing difficulties with some of its other European factories in this product area.

Appendix. CII and the Honeywell Link-up

In 1966, in the wake of the loss of French control of Machines Bull, the French Government launched its Plan Calcul in an attempt to recreate a national computer industry. Le Plan Calcul hinged on Compagnie Internationale Pour L'Informatique (CII), the two major shareholders in which were (ultimately) Thomson-Brandt and Compagnie Générale d'Electricité (CGE). CII was thus a privately owned company, although heavily supported by the French Government through R & D contracts, preferential treatment in state purchasing and various loans and grants. In spite of this substantial support, by 1975 CII still only accounted for 8 per cent of the French market and less than 2 per cent of the European market. The firm was thus in desperate need of allies, given that a market share of about 10 per cent *Europe-wide* was probably the minimum necessary for profitability. It was partly this that persuaded CII to link up with Siemens of Germany and Philips of Holland in a joint company, Unidata, in June 1973.

From the beginning the prospects for Unidata were not encouraging. Thomas-Brandt and CGE, the main shareholders in CII, disagreed over participation in Unidata. CGE was believed to favour a link with Honeywell-Bull, and in 1974 was refusing to put up funds for Unidata, contrary to the wishes of CII, Thomson-Brandt and the French Government. There were French complaints that Siemens was refusing to sell CII products; and Siemens then took over AEG – Telefunken's computer division, whose models were in competition with those of CII. Apart from such factors, all the partners in Unidata were losing money heavily on computers.

Without a national solution (Machines Bull) for the computer industry nor a European solution (Unidata), France turned reluctantly to the only realistic alternative, namely a Franco-American solution. CII merged with Honeywell-Bull in the Spring of 1975 to form a new company CII-Honeywell Bull, in which Honeywell Information Systems held a 47 per cent interest and the remaining 53 per cent was shared between CII (17 per cent of the balance), the French Government (17 per cent) and the existing French shareholders in Machines Bull (66 per cent). The position with respect to the two companies prior to the merger was as shown in the table below.

The Partners in Compagnie Internationale pour L'Informatique CII-Honeywell Bull S.A. (CII-HB)

Date of Establishment	October 1, 1970	December 6, 1966
Shareholders	Honeywell Information Systems (66%), Compagnie des Machines Bull (34%)	Finifor* (59.6%), Institut de Developpement Industriel (23.8%), Schneider (14.6%), Kali Sainte-Therese (2.0%)
Employees	15,700 (10,500 in France)†	8,800
Plants	Angers, Belfort (France), Heppenheim (W. Germany)	Toulouse

* Finifor owned by Thomson-CSF (52%) and GCE (48%).
† The difference between 10,500 and 15,700 arises from the fact that Honeywell-Bull controlled all Honeywell interests in Europe, except Italy and the UK.
SOURCE: 'Computer Dating with a View to a Partner Swap', *Financial Times*, 14 May 1975.

The terms of the merger agreement were as follows:

Honeywell sold 19 per cent of its 66 per cent stake in Honeywell-Bull to Compagnie Générale d'Electricité and the French Government for approximately $58 million.

About 5,000 of CII's employees were transferred to the new company, giving it a total labour force of about 20,000 and an annual turnover of nearly £300 million. CII's Toulouse plant and its existing minicomputer, military and communications business was not included in the agreement, and was hived off to a new French company.

Subsidies of about $270 million were to be paid by the French Government to CII-HB over the four-year period commencing with the merger.

The French Government announced its intention to support product segments of the merged company in which it was a minority shareholder.

Regarding products to be manufactured, both Honeywell Information Systems and CII-HB were given the right to manufacture any product in the common line, with decisions based on 'the economic feasibility of local production'.

The ultimate ratification of the agreement was hailed as a victory by the French Government, with Honeywell-Bull reverting to majority national ownership eleven years after Machines Bull was first taken over by a US firm (General Electric). The new venture was Europe's largest computer group.

Table 1. Performance Data for Honeywell Inc.

Year	Sales ($000)	Assets ($000)	Net income ($000)	Shareholders Equity ($000)	Employees	Net income as % of shareholders		Rank in Fortune Directory
						Sales	Equity	
1980	4,924,700	3,892,600	293,500	1,904,200	97,200	6.0	15.4	71
1979	4,209,500	3,339,600	260,500	1,642,500	94,620	6.2	15.9	79
1978	3,547,800	2,826,100	201,400	1,386,900	86,328	5.7	14.5	77
1977	2,911,093	2,429,360	145,124	1,208,743	75,840	5.0	12.0	82
1976	2,495,295	2,203,728	113,053	1,128,024	70,775	4.5	10.0	88
1975	2,760,068	2,573,914	77,826	990,153	83,053	2.8	7.9	67
1974	2,625,683	2,679,385	75,768	938,227	92,173	2.9	8.1	68
1973	2,390,592	2,583,114	103,885	951,652	98,122	4.3	10.9	54
1972	2,125,445	2,240,787	82,327	852,658	96,652	3.9	9.7	50
1971	1,946,127	2,183,098	69,262	763,288	94,418	3.6	9.1	53
1970	1,921,194	2,018,678	61,650	588,319	100,230	3.2	10.5	49
1969	1,425,993	1,222,011	62,481	494,115	81,520	4.4	12.6	75
1968	1,281,300	987,398	50,545	421,613	74,483	3.9	12.0	72
1967	1,044,927	847,303	42,270	384,811	69,248	4.0	11.0	77
1966	914,384	772,055	45,280	356,024	64,148	5.0	12.7	87

SOURCE: 'The Fortune Directory of the 500 Largest US Industrial Corporations', *Fortune*. various editions.

Table 2. Revenues and Earnings for Honeywell Inc. by Line of Business ($ million)

	1972	1973	1974	1975	1976	1977	1978	1979	1980
Information systems									
Revenues	774	843	856	856	914	1,037	1,294	1,453	1,634
Earnings	42	53	34	40	41	79	106	152	186
Control systems									
Revenues	1,064	1,214	1,393	1,436	1,581	1,874	2,254	2,757	3,291
Earnings	130	153	143	127	181	229	283	326	339
Information systems as % of total									
Revenues	42.1	41.0	38.1	37.3	36.6	35.6	36.5	34.5	33.2
Earnings	24.4	25.7	19.2	24.0	18.5	25.6	27.2	31.7	35.4

SOURCE: Corporation accounts.

Table 3. Revenues, Profits and Assets for European Operations of Honeywell Inc.

	1976	1977	1978	1979	1980
Europe ($m)					
Revenues	521	634	784.4	864.2	1,113.8
Operating profits	33	63	84.5	99.6	146.0
Identifiable assets	488	571	680.2	721.2	900.9
Europe as % of					
International Operations					
Revenues	69.0	71.2	73.0	72.5	73.8
Operating profits	56.9	71.6	69.8	72.7	77.5
Identifiable assets	74.8	77.1	78.3	76.7	78.0
Europe as % of					
Worldwide Operations					
(excl. eliminations)					
Revenues	19.9	20.6	21.1	19.6	21.3
Operating profits	15.2	20.4	21.4	20.2	27.2
Identifiable assets	21.4	22.9	23.5	21.1	22.4

SOURCE: Corporation accounts.

Table 4. Performance Data for Honeywell's UK Subsidiary: Honeywell Ltd*

Year ended 31 Dec.	Sales (£000)	Net profit before tax† (£000)	Net profit before tax as % of sales	Govt. grants received (£000)	Exports (£000)	No. of employees
1980	146,830	15,946	10.9	971	23,014	5,273
1979	125,861	16,390	13.0	373	23,089	5,339
1978	118,678	11,307	9.5	306	21,174	5,300
1977	101,216	14,856	14.7	n.a.	25,100	5,134
1976	84,183	9,065	10.8	65	25,449	4,993
1975	71,151	(3,882)	—	46	20,550	5,283
1974	60,874	(8,840)	—	118	19,066	6,890
1973	58,781	(2,458)	—	128	17,972	7,397
1972	41,924	(4,876)	—	44	9,683	7,658
1971	51,539	698	1.4	310	17,035	8,415
1970	47,341	2,406	5.1	2,356	17,964	9,232
Performance Data for Honeywell Information Systems Ltd						
1980	69,109	7,689	11.1	235	6,481	n.a.
1979	51,968	2,945	5.7	—	6,081	n.a.
1978	50,575	4,120	8.1	18	5,537	n.a.
1977	42,948	6,265	14.6	17	12,297	n.a.
1976	33,491	3,563	10.6	108	13,582	n.a.
1975	31,574	(2,507)	—	—	13,117	n.a.
1974	23,642	(8,539)	—	40	11,987	n.a.
1973	29,291	(4,794)	—	98	11,403	n.a.

* Incorporates a number of subsidiary companies, including Honeywell Information Systems Ltd. Some accounting information for the latter is included in the second part of the table.
† Excludes exceptional and extraordinary items.
SOURCE: Company accounts; Extel Statistical Services.

NOTES AND REFERENCES

1. Although attempts are now being made to link the two operations in order to exploit synergy.
2. *Glasgow Herald*, 23 June 1978.
3. *Glasgow Herald*, 19 September 1953.
4. This section draws on Y.S. Hu, *The Impact of US Investment in Europe: A Case Study of the Automotive and Computer Industries*, Praeger (New York) 1973, chapter 6. See Also OECD, *Impact of Multinational Enterprises on National Scientific and Technical Capacities: Computer and Data Processing Industry*, DSTI/SPR/77.39 – MNE (Paris), 27 December 1977.
5. See, for example, 'Why Honeywell came to Europe for its challenge to IBM', *Financial Times*, 24 April 1974.
6. There were some amendments to this principle. For example, Level 62 computers were manufactured in Japan under licence from HIS Italia.
7. Quoted in the *Guardian*, December 1971.
8. With respect to the comments by the Managing Director of HIS Ltd, see *Guardian*, 1 December 1976. Frustrated by its exclusion from public sector business, the company ultimately sought to establish its position through the courts. The particular contract in question was that of the Anglian Water Authority. Honeywell had submitted the lowest tender and an advisory team recommended buying the HIS computer, but the contract seemed likely to be placed with another company. In a long court battle the American company sought to establish that 'Buy British' was not a factor to be taken into consideration in awarding contracts. Although Honeywell lost the case, it subsequently gained the contract and this may have influenced other bodies.
9. *Glasgow Herald*, 16 November 1974 and 18 December 1974.
10. *Financial Times*, 5 February 1976.
11. *Glasgow Herald*, 23 April 1977.
12. *Glasgow Herald*, 11 September 1979.
13. Reported in 'European makers told to unite', *Electronics*, 20 December 1973.

GOODYEAR IN DRUMCHAPEL, GLASGOW

Company and Industry Background

The Goodyear Tire and Rubber Co. was established in 1898 in Akron, Ohio, operating, so company history goes, in an abandoned strawboard factory. The company was named after the man who had discovered the vulcanisation process but had died penniless thirty years earlier. The original product line of the firm consisted of bicycle tyres, carriage tyres and horseshoe pads, to which were added automobile tyres in 1899 and pneumatic rubber aircraft tyres ten years later. Expansion was rapid: the company's first subsidiary and foreign plant was acquired in Bowmanville, Canada in 1910, sales branches were opened in Australia, Argentina and South Africa in 1915, and in 1916 Goodyear acquired a rubber plantation in Sumatra. By this time Goodyear had become the world's largest tyre company. Further plants were established in Europe, Australia, Brazil, Argentina and Indonesia in the inter-war period and in numerous other countries after 1945. Similarly, until synthetic rubber was developed, Goodyear expanded its rubber plantations, and diversified into a variety of fields such as airships, shoe products, packaging films, industrial rubber and flooring and counter products.[1]

Not only has Goodyear retained its position as the biggest tyre producer worldwide, it has also emerged as one of the largest companies in the world, being ranked in the Top 25 US corporations in most recent years. The overall performance of the corporation over the years from 1966 is indicated by the data in Appendix, table 1. In this period Goodyear expanded its turnover by over 12 per cent per annum. On the other hand, as the table suggests, Goodyear (in common with other tyre producers) had mixed fortunes in the 1970s, with particularly poor years since 1973. With others, Goodyear performance was affected in 1976 by a 130-day strike by the United Rubber Workers, which covered 15 of its US plants as part of the bargaining for the three year wage contract; for the whole year profits fell by 25 per cent in comparison with 1975. The year 1979 was another poor one for the corporation, particularly in the United States, as a consequence of escalating labour and raw material costs and consumer concern over the future of the economy and fuel availability.

At the end of the 1970s and into the 1980s, Goodyear performance in its foreign operations was a major lifeline for the company: in 1979, for instance, sales and profits abroad both set all-time records, contributing over half of corporate profits and two-fifths of sales. As the Chairman's report for the year noted, 'The foreign performance underscores the value of geographical diversification which tends to even out the ups and downs of individual national economies'.[2] In 1980, Goodyear operated 54 production facilities in the United States and 47 plants in 27 foreign countries. And, out of total employment of 144,500, about 73,500 people were employed outside the United States.

Although Goodyear's foreign operations as a whole were very profitable in the late 1970s, for much of the decade the reverse position had been true. As table 1 reveals, net foreign earnings as a percentage of net foreign assets showed a consistent decline from 1971 to 1976. The company's European operations were a particular problem, and indeed the difficulties in Europe continued until the very end of the decade (table 2). A large part of the company's overseas investment was in Europe because of the sophistication of the market, which required extensive retooling for radial tyre production. European sales, however, continued to be depressed owing to low economic growth and problems in the automotive industry.

These developments have taken place against a background of transition in the strategies of the major US tyre manufacturers.[3] In marked contrast to its major competitors, Goodyear is still highly dependent on the tyre business, as table 3 shows. Faced with a declining domestic market (the US market fell from more than 200 million tyres in 1973 to 187 million in 1976 and 180 million in 1980) and increased competitiveness, most of its leading US competitors have taken considerable steps towards diversification. At least two of them, Goodrich and Uniroyal, view chemicals as their prime targets for internal growth and acquisition, while General Tire & Rubber Company owns radio and T.V. stations, a rocket systems subsidiary, an airline and seven drink-bottling plants as well as chemical activities. Goodyear's investment strategy has taken them in the opposite direction, namely towards product development and increased market share for tyres. Through heavy investment in automated plant for the production of radial tyres, the aim of the company has been to strengthen its market leadership and profitability in a highly competitive industry. In the face of poor profit performance compared with some of its more diversified competitors, Goodyear announced plans in 1979 to diversify into new businesses – probably energy or services.[4] Whether it will be able to do this in the short term is in some doubt since the company's debt burden, arising from its capital expenditure programme on tyres, may restrict its ability to borrow to finance a meaningful diversification programme.

The other crucial variable dominating strategic planning in the tyre industry has been technical change, and particularly the replacement of crossply tyres with longer lasting radials. Reflecting market demand at the time and the high investment cost, US tyre producers were slow to convert to

Table 1. Goodyear: Foreign Assets and Earnings (1971–80)

	1971	1972	1973	1974	1975	1976	1977	1978	1979	1980
Net foreign assets ($m)	555.3	647.3	722.4	825.5	825.5	814.1	934.0	1,098.3	1,168.4	1,326.6
Net foreign earnings ($m)	57.4	59.0	64.5	49.3	49.0	11.1	34.6	62.2	75.5	165.8
Net foreign earnings as % of net foreign assets	10.3	9.1	8.9	6.0	5.9	1.4	3.7	5.7	6.5	12.5

SOURCE: Corporation accounts.

Table 2. Goodyear: European Operations

	1976	1977	1978	1979	1980
Financial data for Goodyear's European Operations ($m)					
Revenue	810.6	889.0	1,027.6	1,250.3	1.440.2
Operating income	(6.0)	41.8	35.9	31.8	99.0
Identifiable assets	713.9	790.5	887.2	911.0	897.5
European operations as % of total non-US operations					
Revenue	36.5	37.3	37.0	38.1	37.8
Operating income	–	22.2	15.7	13.1	27.7
Identifiable assets	38.9	40.4	45.6	39.7	36.9
European operations as % of Goodyear's worldwide operations					
Revenue	13.6	13.1	13.5	14.8	16.6
Operating Income	–	7.0	5.5	6.5	16.2
Identifiable assets	16.5	17.3	17.3	17.4	17.2

SOURCE: Corporation accounts.

Table 3. Major US Tyre Producers

	% of 1977 operating income from		
	Tyres and related activity	Chemicals/Plastics	Other
Goodyear	84	9	7
Firestone	64	8	28
Uniroyal	52	39	9
General Tire	26	17	57
Goodrich	53	23	24

SOURCE: *Business Week*, 28 August 1978.

radial ply construction in the American market. Thus at the start of the 1970s European tyre manufacturers, notably Michelin and Pirelli, were responsible for stimulating radial demand for standard-sized US cars. Only then were they followed by the US car makers specifying radials. Ford had first put radials on its US models in 1970, and had about 25 per cent so equipped in 1973 and 75 per cent by 1974. By 1978 and after very heavy investment betweeen 1972 and 1975, half of the US industry's annual output was radial. As evidence of the capital required for this transformation, General Tire, the fifth largest US tyre producer, spent nearly 20 per cent of the gross value of its plant in 1973 alone, largely to bring in new radial capacity. Goodyear's announcement of major investment plans for the US in 1978 constituted the beginning of the second round of development and the reinforcement of its distinctive strategy. With the new plants operational in 1981 Goodyear increased its capacity for car radials by around 50 per cent compared with 1977, when it had the capability to produce 25 million radials a year. This is estimated to enable the company to supply another 5 per cent of US demand for car tyres. Even without this type of expansion by Goodyear and some of the other manufacturers, the prospect of considerable overcapacity in the US remains, with resultant changes in the structure of the industry.

Goodyear and the Tyre Industry in Europe

Although Goodyear had been exporting in volume to Europe since 1914, the first European manufacturing plant was not set up until 1927 in the UK (Wolverhampton). This was the beginning of a European manufacturing strategy which was heavily based on the UK. Work began on a plant in Norkopping, Sweden, in 1938, but the first major Continental European facility was not established until 1949 in Luxembourg. In part this later entry into mainland Europe was a function of the concentration of the motor industry at time of entry, but it also reflected an apparent consideration of the UK and the Continent as two distinct markets. Following this, it was not until the 1960s that Goodyear engaged in further major expansion outside the UK by, for example, building a plant and acquiring that of Fulda in Germany and developing manufacturing facilities in France, Sweden, Italy and Luxembourg. Even with these additional activities, around a half of Goodyear's European employment and a third of its European assets were still in UK plants in 1965.

The development of the EEC did, of course, entice the more marketing oriented US companies to expand within the six member states. Firestone for instance, like Goodyear, had a UK base dependent on Ford and Vauxhall business but subsequently built new plants in Italy and France. Similarly, Uniroyal concluded an agreement with Esso to sell its tyres under the Esso label and also expanded its manufacturing plants into Benelux, France and Germany. This process was aided by the fact that the domestic European tyre industry was still largely operating on a national basis. The most significant attempts at international operations by European companies were by Dunlop with plants in the UK, France and Germany, and Michelin with plants in France, UK and Germany. For these reasons, together with marketing expertise, the US tyre producers were in a good position to benefit from the EEC and expand their market share. Some of these pressures from the Americans led to the Dunlop-Pirelli merger in 1971, as both producers were facing considerable competition in their respective domestic markets. Dunlop, once sole supplier to the then BMC, was having to share its position with Goodyear and Pirelli following the adoption of revised purchasing policies; while Pirelli's share of the Fiat business had declined following Michelin's purchase of equity in Fiat in 1971.

Many of the other contextual elements discussed previously with reference to the US were relevant in the formulation of the European strategies of Goodyear and the other tyre producers in the 1970s. But the more rapid penetration of radials, and the low car market growth as a result of higher oil prices and overcapacity were additional elements. The pace of technological change had not slowed down, for by 1978 the steel-belted radial (estimated to last 25 per cent longer than the earlier textile-belted radial) had become almost standard, thereby further reducing the unit size of the replacement market. The final ingredient lay in the growing imports into Western Europe from the Eastern Bloc countries, often developed through the export of Western technology: Taunus tyres from Hungary (using technology from Semperit in Austria) and the agreement between Dunlop-Pirelli and the USSR were only two examples of this.

The end-result of these various factors were moves, at first tentative but then positively sweeping, to rationalise manufacturing activity and slash capacity in Europe. The initial steps were taken by Firestone and Goodrich which closed plants in Switzerland and West Germany respectively and Goodyear which shut its operation in Belgium, but these were relatively small facilities and only the beginnings of more fundamental reorganisation. It was not until 1979 and later that the dramatic steps were initiated: in the Spring of 1979, the number three American tyre manufacturer, Uniroyal, sold its entire European operation to West Germany's leading producer, Continental Gummi-Werke (included in which was Uniroyal's plant at Newbridge, Midlothian). Around the same time, Germany's second largest manufacturer, Phoenix, took the decision to pull out of the tyre market; and in August 1980 Firestone announced that it would end all production in Britain by the end of that year. Plant closures by Dunlop, including factories at Speke and Inchinnan and the dissolution of the Dunlop-Pirelli merger was yet further evidence of the scale of the transition taking place.

It is within this environment of severe retrenchment that the restructuring of Goodyear's activities in Europe and ultimately the closure of its Glasgow plant on 18 May 1980 has to be seen. Goodyear's corporate performance in Europe fell well below acceptable levels from the early 1970s. Europe was largely responsible for the situation in 1976 when, for the corporation as a whole, overseas business accounted for 38 per cent of tyre and tube turnover but only 9 per cent of after tax income. The region moved from a position as one of the best overseas operations to bottom of the corporate league on almost all measures. Performance was particularly poor in terms of return on capital employed, reflecting the very high capital investment required to keep pace with technological advance. While the product dimension has been highlighted, this was only one element of the problem. Poor returns continued after 1973 by which year over 80 per cent of Goodyear passenger tyre production in Europe was radial and 50 per cent of that was of steel-belted construction. The crux of the performance problem lay in the fact that the effects of the large investment in Europe of the late 1960s did not show in production capacity until 1972–3, when the market went into slump.

Against this background Goodyear adopted a progressively more central-ised system of organisation and control for their European operations. Europe, as with the other areas, was represented by strong regional management at corporate headquarters in Akron, Ohio. Until 1974 the corporation operated through a European headquarters in Brussels, but the inter-plant rationalisation process which took place in Europe led to this being dismantled. The only function which remained at European level was production planning. Overall planning and marketing strategy was deter-mined in Akron, but advertising, sales management and other operational matters were dealt with on a country basis. Technically, the European operations hinged on the Technical Centre-Europe at Colmar-Berg, Luxembourg, which employed in excess of 2,000 staff. Set up in the late 1960s, this major facility was established in Europe because of the technical advance within the market and the pace of technological change, and in recognition of the differences existing between us and European require-ments.

The product/plant strategy adopted towards Europe was to develop the plants to supply European markets, and only in the u к did a significant non-European export business continue. This reflected exports built up in earlier years based on Commonwealth preference. While the bulk of investment funds in Europe were directed to the tyre business, some diversification into two other fields took place. Goodyear established various chemical plants, on their own behalf – in France, and in conjunction with other firms – in the u к (with i s r) and in France (with Michelin). In the latter case this involved a joint company (51 per cent Goodyear) with Michelin Cie to manufacture polyisoprene at Le Havre. Production capability was also expanded in both the u к and Germany for the 'vita film' packaging film. The other significant non-tyre area for development has been industrial rubber products – based at Craigavon, Northern Ireland. This plant, established in 1968, is responsible, in addition, for coordinating the marketing of all industrial rubber products in Europe, and houses the technical centre for this product area, which includes conveyor and power transmission belting, hose and packaging film. While all of these activities constitute continued movement to a more diversified European strategy, they form a relatively small proportion of European turnover. In Europe, as in the US, Goodyear based its future on gaining a higher market share for tyres through product development and aggressive marketing.

Some changes did take place in the company's production strategy for tyres in Europe. In common with a good number of other US multinationals, Goodyear had developed in Europe by treating the UK and the Continent as separate market areas. With British entry into the EEC, this distinction was no longer real and thus at Goodyear the major European plants were partially reorganised so that about one-third of output was exported to other Goodyear subsidiaries for distribution, as part of a programme of product specialisation. Even with this reorganisation, redundancies were relatively small (except in the Swedish plant) and the European labour force of Goodyear in fact increased by about 10 per cent between 1970 and 1977. In 1977 the corporation employed 24,000 in Europe, 45 per cent of whom were in the UK plants. By the mid-1970s, nevertheless, it had become clear that Goodyear had too many European factories, and that in terms of overall scale of operations the firm was likely to suffer from being too small to achieve the economies of scale available to major competitors such as Dunlop-Pirelli and Michelin. Moreover, some of Goodyear's earlier expansion within Continental Europe in the 1960s had been based on the German plant on grounds of labour quality. The rise in value of the DM during the 1970s seriously weakened any strategy relying on Germany as an export base and so added a further dimension to the transition required. Given the distribution of Goodyear's European assets, nevertheless, it was inevitable that if the corporation were to fulfil their rationalisation aims, this would have particularly serious implications for the Goodyear Tyre & Rubber Company (Great Britain) Limited.

Goodyear in Britain

The first Goodyear factory in the UK began operating in Wolverhampton in 1927 and this location has remained as the head office and centre of manufacturing operations for Goodyear in Britain. For a long time after establishment, the company's story was one of continuous expansion and growing demand for their products. In the years before World War II, the company's range of products was gradually extended to include aircraft wheels, tyre equipment, rubber soles and heels, industrial rubber products and chemicals, and frequent factory extensions were necessary to keep pace. The post-war boom in the motor industry increased the demand for tyres both as original equipment and as replacements, but while Goodyear growth continued unabated, most of the initial developments took place at the Wolverhampton location. The one exception was in 1949 when part of the aircraft division moved to a new factory at Wallasey.

The reasons for moving away from their Midlands base to establish a manufacturing unit in Scotland are not known in detail. Work on the factory at Drumchapel commenced on Boxing Day, 1955, which was really some years before the Government began to use Industrial Development

Certificate (IDC) policy vigorously. It seems likely, moreover, that the reason was more related to site constraints such as shortage of land in Wolverhampton than a desire to diversify geographically within the UK. Numerous sites were apparently inspected in Scotland and Northern Ireland before the Drumchapel location (about seven miles West of Glasgow city centre) was chosen, on the basis of 'a good water supply and the proximity of a vast housing estate from which it was expected to draw an adequate labour force'.[5] Water supplies were undoubtedly a factor since the factory was estimated to draw and return 1 million gallons of water a day for cooling purposes from the Forth and Clyde Canal. Although it would be interesting to link the establishment of the Goodyear tyre plant to the Linwood car factory of Rootes, the plans for the latter were not announced until October 1960 and the BMC truck and tractor manufacturing operation at Bathgate only commenced production in 1961–2. It is possible that government intentions to steer the vehicle manufacturers towards the Development Areas, such as Scotland, were apparent at the time of the Goodyear locational decision, and this may have had some minor influence on site selection. Certainly the West of Scotland was an obvious location for a car plant within Scotland given the existence of the Pressed Steel factory at Linwood (operating from 1947) and the announcement in 1958 to build a wide strip mill at Ravenscraig.

Opening the plant on 26 September 1957, as the sixty-first Goodyear production unit worldwide, the President of the Goodyear international organisation referred to the factory as: 'The best I have seen in Goodyear, or indeed in the rubber industry of the entire world' – it was also, of course, a factory for producing *crossply* tyres! Lord Strathclyde, Minister of State at the Scottish Office commented that: 'The opening marked the culmination of an important phase in Glasgow's development, and the beginning of another phase which would lead us into the future. As Glasgow grew between the wars and large numbers of people were rehoused on its outskirts, it became clear that room must also be found for industry outside the congested city centre so there would be jobs as well as homes in the new districts. Thus the new large housing areas, built in the outlying parts of the city in the last twelve years, had been matched by new industrial estates.'[6]

The cost of the Scottish plant was put at £2.75 million, with a planned daily output of 1,200 car and truck tyres; 300 people were employed initially, with a total of 600 to be employed when the factory was in full production on a 24-hour basis.[7] The role of the facility was to produce tyres for all kinds of vehicles, mainly for the Scottish and Northern England markets but also for markets overseas.

From the start, thus, the Scottish plant was a small factory with a very limited market role, that of an additional supply point for the UK market for crossply tyres. The capacity of the Wolverhampton factory was five or six times as great as that of Drumchapel and, in fact, the latter was the smallest facility in Europe except for that in Greece. In many ways the Scottish operation was a classic branch plant: the Plant Manager in Scotland was responsible to the UK Production Director and through him to the UK Managing Director, both of whom were located in Wolverhampton; Marketing and Finance was handled out of Wolverhampton; and while every Goodyear factory has a development department, the only responsibilities for that in Scotland were concerned with the achievement of specifications and the servicing of the production group.

In considering the background to the problems of the Scottish plant and its ultimate closure, a distinction needs to be made between factors which were common to all Goodyear operations and indeed to all tyre manufacturers in the UK and those with a particularly Scottish dimension. The declining overall UK market size in the 1970s concomitant on the oil crisis and economic recession falls into the former category. Goodyear's policy of UK plants supplying the UK market tended to exacerbate these difficulties. On the other hand, the switch to radial tyres (see table 4) was a factor which damaged the position of Goodyear in Scotland more markedly than Goodyear in Britain as a whole, in spite of the fact that in the 1970s production at Drumchapel had been reorganised to facilitate the manufacture of both crossply and radial tyres. As the table indicates, UK output of crossply tyres fell by nearly 60 per cent between 1973 and 1977.

Table 4. Car and Van Tyre Output in the UK (000 units)

	Crossply	Radial	Total
1973	9,828	16,095	25,923
1977	4,071	20,510	24,581
% change	− 58.6	+ 27.4	− 5.2

The second issue of general significance in the UK concerned the threat from cheap imports. Between 1975 and the first half of 1978, import penetration of the UK replacement market rose by 55 per cent for car tyres, 70 per cent for lorry and bus tyres and 39 per cent for tractor tyres.[8] In part this simply matched rising import penetration in the vehicle market, but the factor which caused most concern was the startling rise in imports from Eastern Bloc countries and in particular imports by the same companies with manufacturing operations in Britain. It was alleged that Dunlop was importing Romanian tyres through its wholesaling and retailing arm, National Tyre Services, until the end of 1977 without informing the unions. Futhermore, Uniroyal was providing technical assistance and managerial advice to a high capacity plant in Poland, which was exporting much of its output to France in direct competition to British products. More than this, because of inflated inventories, tyres were being sold from mainland

European factories to brokers for disposal wherever they could; this led to tyres being sold in Britain at a lower price than a buyer would have to pay for an identical tyre made in the same manufacturer's British plant.[9]

The effect of these various factors on the performance of the Goodyear Tyre & Rubber Company (Great Britain) Ltd is shown clearly in Appendix, table 2. Profits slumped from £5.5 million on a turnover of £79 million in 1971 to an average of £2.4 million for the three years 1972–4; two years of even lower profits followed before the company plunged into the red. During the years 1977–9, losses were nearly double the cumulative value of profits earned during the previous seven years of the decade. Throughout the period the UK subsidiary continued to be highly dependent on the British economy and suffered severely from the low growth in that market. Thus, exports as a proportion of sales rose only modestly from 13.5 per cent in 1968 to just under 20 per cent in 1979. Meanwhile employment remained relatively static throughout the period.

Aside from external factors, dissatisfaction was expressed by the company at poor plant performance in the UK, the Scottish operation being a particular target for criticism. Labour disputes were an especial cause for concern, leading to the comment from the President of Goodyear International in 1976 that 'we've had a lot more labour problems in the last couple of years than we ever had in the previous 40 years we've been doing business in Britain'.[10] In Scotland, three major disputes, each involving one of the three unions in the plant, were claimed to have crippled the operation. The most important of these was a damaging 11-week strike which took place in 1974, concerning the demands of 570 rubber process workers for the ending of the Friday night shift. Management argued that the 3-hour reduction in the working week (from $38\frac{1}{3}$ to $35\frac{1}{3}$ hours) resulting from such a move would be harmful in a continuous process activity such as tyre making and would result in an 8.9 per cent drop in plant utilisation. The costly dispute was only finally settled by ending the late shift working and by the compromise that Friday evening working would be on a voluntary basis. Another major dispute occurred in the Autumn of 1977 over the move of five wage clerkesses from key-punch to computer operations and demands for regrading. The strike lasted six weeks, for more than half of which time production was completely halted and 700 workers laid off.

Goodyear, in common with other multinationals, issued warnings of plant closure on several occasions during industrial disputes. Midway through the 1974 strike at Glasgow, for instance, warnings were being circulated that a closure date would soon be set for the plant. And in October 1977, the company warned that: 'In the long term the strike obviously threatens the plant, in cash terms alone, if one is hit badly enough.'[11] Industrial action was not unique to Scotland at this time and in November 1977, the 1,000 workers at Goodyear's Craigavon facility in Northern Ireland were warned that the corporation would pull-out if industrial action over a pay claim did not cease. Again, threats were made regarding the Norkopping plant in Sweden in 1975, where the company was meeting considerable resistance in its efforts to increase productivity. In this case, the management scheme was accepted and Norkopping has been one of Goodyear's most successful European plants, albeit with a reduction of some 50 per cent in employment since the early 1970s.[12]

In the case of Goodyear's Scottish operation, however, labour disputes were not followed by changes in attitudes, and low efficiency together with inflexibility was to prove crucial when the company took decisions to try to stem losses in the UK. Claims were made that the Drumchapel factory had failed to meet its production targets throughout the 1970s, and that because of restrictive practices, manning levels were 15–20 per cent higher than in other Goodyear plants. The union response to this was that the low productivity argument was a smokescreen. The shop stewards' convener argued that Scottish workers produced 14 per cent more rubber per hour than their opposite numbers in Wolverhampton (21.1 kg as against 18.5 kg); the effect of this, it was claimed, was that it cost Goodyear £3,000 more to produce 1 ton of rubber in Wolverhampton than in Scotland. It was argued, therefore, that losses in Scotland were due to the company's own decision to freeze investment and to run the factory well below capacity.[13]

In March 1978, the company announced that over 500 redundancies would be necessary in the Glasgow and Wolverhampton plants in a bid to cut losses. For Scotland this was to involve 130–150 employees out of a total workforce of 830. This reduction in the labour force was announced as the beginning of a three-part programme designed to restore the company to profitability, involving reduction in wastage, production improvements and manpower savings. This action was followed by redundancies in Northern Ireland and, in the Autumn of 1978, by the closure of a small Goodyear plant in Barnsley which made earth-mover remould tyres. The plant had apparently lost money since it was opened in 1974 and involved 80 redundancies.

Further redundancies were announced in December 1978 involving 200 workers at Drumchapel and up to 1,000 at Wolverhampton; in the latter case, the plant had only recently returned to normal working following a five-week strike in protest at the company's previous redundancies. The announcement of these plans coincided with corporate action from the US to inject funds into the UK subsidiary, thus reducing its debt burden and providing working capital. There is little doubt that the corporation knew that labour was almost a fixed cost in the UK and anticipated considerable problems in trying to implement redundancies. It was also, in fairness, very much against corporate philosophy to close or run down plants until really necessary.

The rundown in the workforce at Drumchapel was linked to a series of management proposals designed to ensure the survival of the plant. These were:

a reduction in manning levels;
rationalisation of the types and sizes of tyres to be produced;
a minimum of 5-day, 3-shift working;

adherence to agreements reached between the company and the trade unions;

no wildcat strikes.

Goodyear said that if the programme was not implemented 'the Drumchapel factory would not be financially viable and could not, therefore, hope to exist in today's competitive markets ... The magnitude of the financial losses currently being sustained at Drumchapel cannot continue.'[14] Criticisms were once again levelled at plant performance: that it had the poorest quality record, the highest scrap rate (nearly twice as much as in other plants) and the greatest absenteeism (around 15 per cent per annum) and was the most unproductive in Europe.

The local union members at the Glasgow plant were bitterly opposed to this proposal and the conditions attached to it, although the corporation stressed that a similar plan had been accepted and implemented at the Swedish plant in 1975. There then began a process of bargaining and counter-bargaining between the corporation and the local workforce which continued over two or three months. The management offered a concession in February 1979 when faced with union criticism that the rationalisation would mean a major rundown of the products at Glasgow and especially the phasing out of radials. The concession involved an offer to retain radial tyre production in the plant (thereby reducing the number of redundancies required by 90), provided the labour force would accept 15-shift working and adopt greater flexibility in work systems. The former was the sticking point. The workers had only a few years previously been on strike for nearly three months to get rid of the Friday night shift; they were, therefore, in no mood to return to working this extra shift on Friday evenings. Company arguments, that their other major competitor in Britain, Michelin, worked 17 shifts a week and that in Japan plants operated 7 days a week for 350 days a year, were of no avail. The proposals were almost immediately rejected at the plant and a week later Westi Hansen, Chairman and Managing Director of Goodyear UK announced that the plant would be closed, 'During the 81 years Goodyear has been in business, this is the first time we have closed one of our tyre manufacturing plants.'[15]

Having seen the toughness with which management were approaching the situation, the unions subsequently reversed their decision and accepted the proposals made by Goodyear. But it was by then too late. Approaches were made to the corporation by Members of Parliament and Government Ministers, and discussions were held at European level with union representatives from other Goodyear plants.[16] All these pleas failed and the issue was closed with a final announcement from Ib Thomsen, the President of Goodyear International: 'The decision is final ... this Scottish plant is rated at the bottom of the totem pole in just about every respect. I am not apportioning blame, but we have failed either as a company, managers, shop floor or union.'[17] The local newspaper, for its part, was in no doubt where blame lay: 'The Drumchapel plant's industrial record is appalling in absenteeism and productivity alike ... The STUC might take its nominal socialism a bit more seriously and start telling Scottish workers to change the way in which they see the world and their work. Until they do so our problems cannot begin to be solved.'[18]

Concluding Remarks

In many ways Goodyear is a classic example of a US multinational commencing manufacturing in one country, and maintaining the largest part of its activity at that port of entry, until there was considerable corporate disadvantage in so doing. The disadvantages lay in the delayed expansion of manufacturing into Continental Europe, in the loss of technological superiority to European producers in the late 1960s and early 1970s, and in a relative change in national economic performance which made a low growth UK base a less favourable one than at time of entry. Simply because the corporation has not yet achieved an optimal balance of European locations and production activities, the full implications of this strategic lag are not yet obvious. The balance of both investment and employment is likely to move from the UK. This pattern is not exclusively found in Goodyear, as there are a number of other US corporations which, for historical reasons, have remained over-dependent on UK bases. Some of these companies were influenced by the delayed entry of the UK into the EEC which caused a postponement of decisions on the location of new plants.

The multinational dimension which looms large in this case (although Goodyear itself may not have been involved particularly) concerns the continued erosion of the UK market base through imports. As noted earlier, the unions have argued that between 1972 and 1978 around half of the tyre imports into the UK have come through the major producers themselves. Moreover, some of these imports reflect the transfer of technology from Western multinationals to Comecon producers. Such factors raise important questions regarding the extent to which multinationals can influence work flows especially in a situation of market transition, short-time working and redundancy in some of their own facilities.

As to the closure of the Drumchapel factory, it is difficult to escape the conclusion that this was justified in the light of continuing performance problems. Where multinationals have manufacturing facilities in different countries making similar product lines, performance comparisons are inevitable. The poorest performers, especially if these are small and strategically unimportant, are certain to be earmarked for closure when, as in the 1970s, times got rough.

Table 1. Performance Data for Goodyear Tire & Rubber Co.

| Year | Sales ($000) | Assets ($000) | Net income ($000) | Shareholders equity ($000) | Employees* | Net income as % of | | Rank (by sales) in Fortune Directory |
						Sales	Shareholders' equity	
1980	8,444,015	5,368,301	230,689	2,302,500	144,452	2.7	10.0	36
1979	8,238,676	5,371,239	146,184	2,163,350	154,061	1.8	6.8	28
1978	7,489,102	5,231,103	236,127	2,108,159	154,013	3.0	10.7	22
1977	6,627,818	4,677,908	205,781	1,973,854	152,890	3.1	10.4	22
1976	5,791,494	4,336,125	121,967	1,861,911	151,263	2.1	6.6	23
1975	5,452,473	4,173,675	161,613	1,816,051	148,225	3.0	8.9	23
1974	5,256,247	4,241,626	157,461	1,746,668	154,166	3.0	9.9	23
1973	4,675,265	3,871,043	184,756	1,673,506	152,929	4.0	11.0	19
1972	4,071,523	3,476,668	193,159	1,591,848	145,201	4.7	12.1	18
1971	3,601,565	3,183,547	170,223	1,455,993	139,152	4.7	11.7	19
1970	3,194,554	2,955,301	129,210	1,341,472	136,825	4.0	9.6	22
1969	3,215,334	2,763,456	158,202	1,266,673	133,524	4.9	12.5	20
1968	2,925,745	2,377,054	148,262	1,162,638	119,744	5.1	12.8	22
1967	2,637,710	2,082,667	127,066	1,060,562	113,207	4.8	12.0	21
1966	2,475,665	1,912,062	118,489	1,435,315	140,000	8.6	14.1	21

* Employment is average for each year.
SOURCE: 'The Fortune Directory of the 500 Largest US Industrial Corporations', *Fortune*, various editions.

Table 2. Performance Data for Goodyear's UK Subsidiary: Goodyear Tyre & Rubber Company (Great Britain) Ltd

Year ended 31 Dec.	Sales (£000)	Net profit before tax* (£000)	Net profit before tax as % of sales	Exports (£000)	No. of employees
1980	217,176	(717)	—	49,520	8,662
1979	206,318	(13,392)	—	40,960	8,998
1978	179,752	(21,401)	—	29,466	10,785
1977	187,571	(507)	—	31,932	11,432
1976	159,267	611	0.4	30,934	10,979
1975	131,715	92	0.1	22,255	11,212
1974	111,955	3,605	3.2	20,716	10,942
1973	91,330	1,343	1.5	14,413	11,135
1972	81,110	2,399	3.0	10,093	11,013
1971	79,148	5,535	7.0	12,915	11,150
1970	76,650	5,036	6.6	12,180	10,935
1969	64,075	3,619	5.7	9,459	10,208
1968	58,509	4,869	8.3	7,940	9,312

* Bracketed figures indicate losses. Prior to 1972 profit figures exclude extraordinary or exceptional items.
SOURCE: Company accounts; Extel Statistical Services.

NOTES AND REFERENCES

1. Information derived from *A History of the Goodyear Tire & Rubber Company: Through the years with Goodyear 1898–1977*, published by the company.
2. The quotation is from the Chairman's statement to the shareholders in the Annual Report, 1979.
3. This section draws particularly on 'Goodyear's solo strategy', *Business Week*, 28 August 1978.
4. 'Goodyear's bold move to broaden its tire base', *Business Week*, 6 August 1979.
5. *Glasgow Herald*, 27 September 1957.
6. ibid. It is worth pointing out that there was a good deal of resentment among the residents in the area following the building of the plant. Not only did the factory replace green fields and a serene rural setting, but pollution – obnoxious smells and dirt in the atmosphere – was a continuing problem.
7. *Scotsman*, 29 May 1957.
8. *Financial Weekly*, 23 February 1979.
9. See 'The tyre industry rides the import-export roundabout', *Financial Times*, 13 June 1978; 'Union attacks secrecy on imports', *Engineering Today*, 30 October 1978.
10. *The Economist*, 17 April 1976.
11. *Glasgow Herald*, 3 October 1977.
12. For an examination of this issue, see 'Sweden: Goodyear thinks about leaving', *Business Week*, 8 March 1976.
13. *Glasgow Herald*, 22 March 1979.

14. *Glasgow Herald*, 29 December 1978.
15. *Financial Times*, 20 February 1979.
16. Among the proposals put forward to save the plant was one by the Provost of Clydebank who tried to persuade the unions to offer a three-year no-strike guarantee and a 17-shift per week working system.
17. *Glasgow Herald*, 20 March 1979.
18. *Glasgow Herald*, 8 March 1979.

CONCLUSIONS – THE CAUSES OF RETREAT

Because of the case-study approach to the question of multinational retreat in Scotland, it is not possible to provide a formal or comprehensive set of explanations for the large-scale job losses which have occurred in the recent past. But on the basis of the experience of the six multinationals studied, it is clear that there are different levels to the analysis of failure which may be identified, even if within these the variety of issues involved is wide and complex.

At the first level, the issue of technological innovation as regards the nature of production processes and the nature of products emerges very clearly. The introduction of radial tyres at Goodyear, the replacement of electro-mechanical by electronic machines at NCR, and applications of micro-electronics at Singer, Hoover and Honeywell go alongside more general developments in the automation of production. The problems created by such labour-replacing developments have been exacerbated by failure within the corporations studied both to predict the demand take-off for products incorporating new technology and pursue production automation actively enough. It was these factors rather than a technological lag which created the major difficulties during the 1970s. In the main, the failures at this level represent failures of corporate management, although where substantial local autonomy existed as, say, in the case of Hoover Ltd then the affiliate also takes a share of the responsibility.

At the second level, problems were more specifically European in nature, focusing chiefly on European production and marketing strategies. The circumstances of the 1970s – especially the influence of growing European integration and the enlargement of the EEC, and the cost problems of suboptimal plant size within an increasingly competitive environment – were such as to push multinationals towards greater production and marketing integration. For companies such as NCR and Honeywell, in fact, such issues were handled at a global rather than at an exclusively European level. Problems of implementing such strategies as in Singer and Goodyear, or failure to pursue such a policy at all at Chrysler (both in terms of production and models) are major issues. Some companies were severely handicapped in their efforts to pursue a genuinely European policy by a historic

150

over-dependence on the UK. Furthermore, while the logic of integration is greater plant specialisation, following their 1974 strikes Hoover actually moved in the opposite direction, namely towards greater self-sufficiency at plant level. The additional problem for companies was that such policies were having to be planned and pursued within a more uncertain environment than had existed for over two decades: exchange rate instability, inflation and recession conditions and in some sectors government support for indigenous industries meant a frequent revision of planned volumes – commonly in a downwards direction.

The out-working of these various processes created enormous reorganisation and rationalisation pressures in Europe, with production switching (and the threat of production switching) and capacity reduction continuing as major issues throughout the period. At the third level of analysis, thus, are the factors which influence divestment and job rundown in particular affiliates within the multinationals' international networks. As the case material shows, Scotland as a manufacturing base was in competition with locations in England and Wales and Continental Europe. Usually, the choice was between established operations and only in one or two instances were there threats of moves to new sites in low-wage-cost Southern European or Third World locations. The experience illustrated by the cases was very diverse. On occasion Scottish operations were maintained, albeit much reduced in scale, at the expense of facilities elsewhere. So Hoover is to survive at Cambuslang while the company's oldest establishment factory at Perivale is to close; again NCR retained its Scottish and German facilities but shut other Continental European plants. In the other instances where, as in Hoover, attempts were being made to reduce capacity within the UK specifically, the Scottish factories were closed: this applied to both Talbot and Goodyear. At Honeywell, the Scottish complex suffered a more severe job rundown than some other factories, and the shutdown of Singer meant that the impact was more severe in Scotland than elsewhere.

Where the Scottish operations have suffered disproportionately, the reasons given normally related to low productivity, overmanning, restrictive practices or poor labour relations. Within a multinational system comparative plant performance may be closely monitored, and poor performers are highly vulnerable. If a plant is fairly small, does not represent a unique source for a particular product or component or has no research and development unit, then once again closure is a strong possibility when multinationals are taking restructuring or rationalisation decisions.

Low productivity can result from management countenancing inefficient working practices, but it also relates to investment levels. There are instances in the cases – Singer and Hoover in particular – where low investment made closure almost inevitable, although in Singer this cannot be disassociated from the first-level problem of corporate management failure.

Apart from the influence of the above factors in closure/rundown decisions, there are other variables which come into play when the choice relates to Scottish versus other UK facilities, including regional aids, distance from markets and so forth (see the Chrysler/Peugeot case). When the choice is British versus Continental European plants, factors such as the slow growth of demand in Britain, Government fiscal policies and the openness of the UK market to imports are to be set alongside the recognition by some of the sample firms that their investment is over-committed to Britain. In addition the unions have argued that some closures would not have occurred or would have occurred in a less extreme form if the Government had taken a stronger line on divestments. To quote the STUC: 'The Government's widely broadcast inaction in the field of industrial intervention has given the green light to multinational companies who are contracting their European operations and have plants in more than one country including Britain' (Annual Report, 1980, p.115). Whether this is true or not, the influence of Government involvement emerged clearly in the Honeywell case.

In total, the answer to the question, 'what were the factors leading to rundown and closure?' and the related question, 'how inevitable were the job losses?' is far from straightforward. Certainly jobs would have disappeared in Scotland, irrespective of plant performance or anything else. But equally, factory performance and corporate perceptions of this performance, especially in the labour area, did have a major impact on the closure decision in some instances. It is interesting to note a number of cases where a single event – particularly a long strike or a strike when management were fully occupied trying to meet demand or reorganising plant activities – seemingly had a decisive influence on divestment.

As a consequence of the recent pattern of events among multinationals in Scotland, there is no doubt that the benefit-cost balance relating to foreign direct investment has changed markedly. Net benefit would probably still be indicated, but the replacement of the large, well-established, highly self-sufficient affiliates studied here, by smaller units which, in the main, have fewer linkages with the local economy and have higher import propensities, has certainly reduced the favourable balance substantially. And this applies also to companies which are still in existence in Scotland such as NCR. The conclusion must be that in future much more scrutiny is required in considering the contribution multinationals make to the Scottish economy.

3

SOME POLICY ISSUES
AND FUTURE PROSPECTS FOR
FOREIGN DIRECT INVESTMENT
IN SCOTLAND

Public Policy and the MNE in Retreat

The foregoing evaluation of the case material has illustrated the complex variety of issues which emerge when the circumstances of individual corporations are examined in some detail. Many of these relate in some way to government policies in that corporate decisions do have an impact on the achievement of certain policy aims. But is there any material difference between the MNE and the domestically owned multi-plant firm in this regard? And does the MNE situation as observed in Scotland over recent years deserve any special comment, given the general decline in manufacturing employment? The analysis in the first part of this section is directed towards distinguishing between policy issues which are independent of ownership considerations ('ownership neutral') and those which take on somewhat different dimensions by dint of MNE involvement ('ownership specific'). This distinction is increasingly important in Scotland in view both of the adverse comment directed towards multinationals and of the need to arrive at a clear picture of the contribution of foreign direct investment in the future. As was already noted earlier, some of the reasons for regarding MNE decline as substantially different from other forms of industrial decline in Scotland, surround the long-established expectations historically associated with 'higher' technology, more dynamic management, international corporate strength, higher investment levels and so on. A number of these aspects have been debunked in this book. There are varieties of multinationals as there are varieties of domestic enterprises. At the same time the issue of whether this recent MNE experience in Scotland poses different policy problems still requires to be addressed, and this is the subject of the first part of this section. Consideration is given thereafter to the broad ways in which policy in these areas is developing in the UK and Europe and whether these trends have any bearing on problems such as are discussed in this study.

Retreating Multinationals and Major Policy Areas. In order to provide a framework for this discussion, table 1 denotes the principal policy areas upon which the retreating MNE impinges. For each of these areas, a distinction has been drawn between those policy issues which are, and those

153

Table 1. Public Policy and the MNE in Retreat

Policy Areas*	Principal Policy Issues	
	(A) Ownership Neutral	(B) Ownership Specific
Industrial Policy	i) Corporate dependence on UK markets ii) Effects of European industrial restructuring on UK capacity iii) Failure in managerial adaptation to change	i) Strategic flexibility in location and investment alternatives ii) Impact of MNE corporate integration policies in key UK sectors iii) National industrial policy v. global corporate policies
Trade and Balance of Payments	i) Impact of foreign competition and trade liberalisation on competitiveness of UK manufacture ii) Intra-group trading linkages iii) Long run effects of EEC entry on business investment strategy	i) Plant product and market franchise allocation criteria ii) Effect of integration in international plant networks on UK imports and exports
Regional Development	i) Local employment impact ii) Local plant performance v. other UK/European assisted areas iii) Branch plant characteristics iv) Responsiveness of corporate policies to Government incentives	i) High area dependence on strategies of multinationals ii) Role of fdi in industrial development in long run in view of 'footloose' industries iii) Competitive bidding for mobile international investment
Inward and Outward fdi	n.a.	i) Ineffectiveness of existing monitoring mechanisms ii) Relative use of market power as a bargaining tool by Government iii) Absence of national framework for fdi policy

* One policy area not discussed here relates to Government fiscal policies and credit controls (see the Hoover case). Arguably, there is a better understanding of the adverse impact frequent changes in such measures have upon specific industry sectors and a greater continuity of approach is perhaps likely in future.

which are not, related to multinationality. In some areas this is a rather arbitrary division, and both sets of policy issues are present in most cases. For example, the impact of trade liberalisation and foreign competition on the competitiveness of a Scottish plant, while 'ownership neutral', may be more (or less) severe depending on the product allocation policies of the MNE parent. A product range at or near maturity may be much more vulnerable than one where market growth is high and margins more secure. Bearing these limitations of definition in mind, table 1 is a useful point of reference for the next few paragraphs. In order to use it effectively, it is necessary to examine the origins and broad characteristics of recent UK policy in each of the key areas and thereafter consider the extent to which it is able to handle the MNE in decline.

The first area for consideration is *industrial policy*. For these purposes a distinction is drawn between industrial and regional policy in that the former includes the overall incentives to industry; public procurement policies; sectoral policies and other programmes intended to influence industrial structures. Specifically regional measures to foster industrial development are distinguished both by their nature and by their special role over a long period in a region such as Scotland.

The one thing that can be said with confidence of UK industrial policy over the last two decades is that it has been incoherent. Innovations, reappraisals and policy reversals there have been in abundance, not all of which can be attributed to differing political philosophies. It is interesting to note that in the 1960s and early 1970s when fdi was expanding at a rapid pace in Scotland, a number of these policy u-turns were visible. So selective employment tax (SET) provided a general incentive to manufacturing industry from 1966 to 1967, then a regional incentive from 1967 until its abolotion in 1973. Similarly the regional employment premium (REP) introduced in 1966, was phased out in the mid-1970s. During much of this period industrial policy has been set on one side, with priority being given to other policies which were deemed to be indirectly beneficial to industry. Industrial policy has, however, had its moments in Britain.[1] When the Labour Government took office in 1964, it did so with the intention of increasing the role of industrial policy, such measures being regarded as an important supplement to conventional fiscal and monetary measures. Selective investment measures, the Industrial Reorganisation Corporation with its aim of promoting industrial efficiency through further industrial concentration; and measures to assist certain technologically advanced projects under the Industrial Expansion Act, were all parts of that policy surge. For a variety of reasons this could not be regarded as a successful period, not least because the policies were being implemented in very difficult economic circumstances, where the pressing needs for shorter term measures became clear and where a number of the policy initiatives failed to offset the problems emerging from chronic balance of payments imbalance.

Although the new Conservative Government of 1970 stated a commitment to reduce intervention, the pressures of growing unemployment, especially in the development areas, led to marked shifts of direction by 1972. The rescues of Rolls-Royce and Upper Clyde Shipbuilders were harbingers of this change, much of which was consolidated in the measures under the Industry Act of 1972 with its provision for higher general investment incentives, and more regional and selective financial assistance to industry.

The 1974 Government change saw these directions reinforced and developed in a revived approach to industrial strategy. The years 1974–9 certainly represented the most coherent approach to industrial policy in the UK since World War II. The establishment, for example, of Sector Working Parties recognised a need to tailor analysis and policy to the complexities of individual industries and substantially improved our understanding of the links between business and government strategy. Not all of the measures introduced in this period were positive, in that much of the activity under the 1975 Industry Act was less selective than originally intended and often more directed to 'employment-sustaining' than to investment projects. This is classically illustrated in the activity of the National Enterprise Board where both financial constraints and the inheritance of some major problem cases in its portfolio (such as British Leyland) dulled its effectiveness in industrial strategy. Of particular interest in the context of this study was the much criticised measure of Planning Agreements. These were introduced in an environment of much controversy and implicit threat to companies refusing to sign. It was stated that enterprises in the latter category could forfeit discretionary government financial support or perhaps be faced with unfair competition from the signatories. The resistance to these agreements was substantial – both in active and passive forms. As has been noted earlier, the first agreement was with Chrysler UK and even in these very straitened circumstances it took some 15 months to complete. In the event it was wholly ineffective.

In what will almost certainly be recorded as one of the most extensive policy reversals for many decades, numerous initiatives in industrial policy ceased in 1979. So, while measures under the 1975 Industry Act continued, selective concepts rapidly emerged in an endeavour to facilitate disengagement by the new Conservative Government. Gone was any attempt to take an overall view of sectors, whether for expansion or phased contraction; gone too were Planning Agreements and soon to go were most differential aid schemes directed towards key sectors. By far the most positive initiatives were those designed to stimulate small firms via a bewildering array of measures. While the latter were undoubtedly desirable, this era has almost totally ignored the broader structural and transitional problems of large-scale private industry in the UK and hence has little bearing on the theme of this book.

What then has UK industrial policy to say to the MNE in retreat? In the early 1980s, the answer must be, very little. However, for both foreign and indigenous companies the inconsistencies outlined above are of profound importance, in that they have posed enduring problems for long-run

156

planning.[2] The major and distinctive option open to the MNE in such circumstances is that of being able to balance long-term investment in a variety of industrial climates. The weight of evidence points to international companies being more sensitive to changes in policy than to stable policies, even if these are somewhat restrictive. Provided market opportunities are deemed to exist, the latter can readily be managed. It would, therefore, be reasonable to assume that vagaries in UK industrial policy have played some role in shaping the European investment policies of multinationals. At the same time, many of the selective policies introduced to encourage invest-ment in higher technology sectors have been of considerable benefit to multinationals in Scotland and elsewhere. Turning to the specific question of retreating multinationals, the only UK industrial policy initiatives of recent years which might have had something to say about the issues in table 1 are sector-specific programmes and Planning Agreements. Both had the potential to be adapted to examine the effects of changes in MNE networks in key UK sectors, but neither was. On the sector programmes side, elements of this have continued and this approach has been used to good effect in attraction by, among others, the SDA. As yet, little has been done on the management of sectoral rundown where the MNE is involved. As regards Planning Agreements, while the concept was adaptable to straddle interna-tional boundaries and handle the multinational enterprise, there are considerable problems in so doing. Not least of these are differing disclosure requirements and modern versions of 'beggar thy neighbour' policies among our European partners. In effect, few governments object to structural change in multinationals or any other corporation, provided their own structure is not the one to change.

Before leaving this question it is worth remembering that somewhat unlike the pattern for UK industry as a whole, retreating multinationals have hit particular sectors within Scotland. In the UK, a recent study has noted that divestment appears to be as widely distributed across industries as acquisition and is not restricted to declining sectors.[3] It is readily accepted that the sale of second-hand assets is an essential part of the process by which an industrial structure does adapt to changing markets and technology. In the cases under consideration in this book, however, the reciprocal element of buying and selling assets is absent, since many total closures are involved. In Scotland any comprehensive industrial policy would have to be directed to the generation of replacement assets.

Following the format outlined in table 1, some limited comment is necessary on the diffuse subject of UK *trade and balance-of-payments policy*. As the table implies, all UK industry is open to certain pressures through international trading mechanisms. In the case of the MNE, of whatever origin, the 'ownership specific' issues noted simply serve as a further dimension. As regards UK policy in this area, various measures of trade protection for declining industries have been introduced in the recent past. But in a number of cases these have been brought in after earlier UK policy decisions had increased these adaptive pressures. Textile imports from low-income countries are a good example of this, in that UK policy has generally been more favourable than that of our EEC partners to such imports. Again the UK has been noted for its openness to imports from non-market economies under open general licence, thus giving away bargaining power when import volume and price considerations became pressing in certain areas. The background to this liberal British position is long and complex but the truth of the matter is that overall, little real protection has been afforded to problem sectors, let alone problem multinationals. This is in marked contrast to several of our competitors, notably France and Japan, who have administered their trade policy more actively.

Another important aspect of this question lies in the relationship between exchange rate policy and economic strategy.[4] On almost every measure, British manufacturing industry has been rapidly losing competitiveness over the last decade. This position was exacerbated by the strength of sterling in 1979/80 particularly, pushing a variety of indicators in precisely the opposite direction to that desired to improve competitiveness. It was foreseen a long time ago that North Sea oil through its effect on the exchange rate might well damage UK manufacturing industry. Earlier Dutch experience with natural gas pointed in that direction. From the UK position, it is not only the trade effect which has proved serious, large quantities of international hot money (especially from OPEC) attracted to the UK have provided the second effect. Obviously governments can control these flows, but the UK Government chose not to. In fact the Government, by removing exchange controls in 1979, may have thought that substantial rises in capital outflows would help to keep the exchange rate down. This did not happen because interest rate policy was working in the opposite direction.[5]

The extent to which these aspects of trade and balance-of-payments policy have contributed to the MNE in retreat is open to debate. On the one hand, the very existence of liberal trade policies in the UK has been an important factor in attracting and maintaining foreign direct investment, in view of the options for sourcing supplies and reallocating production. Similarly the British commitment to such policies reduces the risk of retaliation by other nations against a foreign investor exporting from the UK base. Viewed from these angles, the benefits are obvious. However, these same processes may have acted to aid the adjustment strategies of the MNE in the period under review. Clearly, low productivity and a strong £ are formidable disadvantages for an export base, especially where the corporation's technical comparative advantage is diminishing, as in a number of the cases examined. Again, the openness of the UK economy and the non-interventionist approach of the Conservative Government from 1979 posed few problems for the MNE undergoing major changes in its sourcing, to take account of relative factor costs, tariff variations and so on. It is an open question how the MNE sector would actually look in Scotland without these environmental 'aids' to strategic change.

Regional development is the third distinct policy strand noted in table 1.

Again a variety of issues arise from corporate retreat. In the 'ownership neutral' classification several factors affect regional imbalance in the short and long term. The effects emerge from the outworking of the policies of single- and multi-plant indigenous corporations and have no immediate connection with multinationality. This is an issue only in circumstances where there is a high area dependence on external investment decisions, or where regional development is able to be knocked completely off course by the departure of 'footloose' firms or industries.

Some brief comment on the nature of UK regional policies is pertinent to this discussion. Regional policies have operated, in varying forms and degrees, intermittently over the past half century, and continuously over the past 20 years or so. At the time of the last revisions to policy in July 1979, for example, 40 per cent of the UK population lived in areas eligible for some form of regional industrial aid; on the same date and at the upper extremes, Scotland, Wales and the Northern Region had some 95 per cent of their manufacturing employment in Development Areas or Special Development Areas. The two most recent decades have witnessed 14 different policy changes. Most of these were in redefinition of areas and in adjusted levels of support. Among items of major significance were the introduction of Office Development Permits, initially for London and Birmingham, in 1965; the advent of Regional Employment Premiums as an employment subsidy for manufacturing industry in Assisted Areas in 1967, with rates doubled in 1974 – phased out in 1977; and the continued use of Industrial Development Certificates throughout the period, until the easing of their limits from 1976 onwards. On the institutional side, the foundation of multi-purpose area development authorities is of considerable importance, with the Highlands and Islands Development Board being set up in 1965 and the Scottish and Welsh Development Agencies being established in 1975. The most recent trends since 1979 have been towards a marked reduction in the geographical coverage of regional assistance and an attempted rundown of more discretionary assistance.[6]

How then have these policy developments affected the MNE in Scotland, either in expansion or retreat? Some comment was made in the first part of the book about their role in attraction and expansion. This was difficult to determine empirically, but it was none the less positive.[7] Most multi-nationals stress the importance of predictability of incentives, and while not always true of other areas in UK, regional assistance measures have been reasonably predictable in Scotland and the other main Assisted Areas over the period. The abrupt phasing out of Regional Employment Premium so soon after the rates had increased was one exception to this. Another expansion theme concerns the relevance of selective schemes of aid. Here the activity of multinationals in higher technology sectors has been positively encouraged in the Scottish context. In the last five years, the competitive environment would appear to have laid more stress on the design of specific, tailor-made 'regional' packages in order to attract the new investor. And while there has been too much stress on the apparent willingness of the MNE to change potential locations solely on grounds of local financial packages, these are obviously vital in certain marginal cases. In short, no-one seriously suggests that long-standing regional policy measures and MNE investment levels in Scotland are not connected in some way.

With regard to the more negative side of corporate withdrawal, it has to be acknowledged that UK regional policy was never designed to take such eventualities into account. Neither are the regional policies of most developed countries. Of course, a variety of preconditions and performance requirements are written into most assistance schemes, to be adhered to by all recipient firms independent of ownership. Most of these in the UK concern the achievement of stated job targets by an agreed date, but they are neither onerous nor are they rigorously applied. Attempts to enforce the agreed preconditions would be strongly resisted by most corporations, and especially by the MNE as an offence to corporate autonomy. In effect, provided loan, grant and other broad conditions attached to the receipt of regional assistance are met, there are no sanctions when the system goes into reverse. Moreover, it is almost impossible to conceive of such a policy development on a unilateral basis, given the competition for investment. With the advantage of hindsight, it would have been possible to avoid in Scotland some of the more serious local impacts of decline at Linwood, Clydebank and Cunninghame. But a more discerning attraction policy was needed much earlier; haggling over the bones of a dead plant after the parent company had lost interest in its future would achieve nothing.

In all the policy areas considered to date in this section, the MNE as such has been a secondary consideration. It becomes central in the subsequent brief look at UK *policy towards inward and outward investing corporations*, and it is to this area that attention should be directed for most of the potential policy developments which might alleviate the effects of the MNE in retreat.[8] Britain as a major importer and exporter of capital for direct investment, has consistently taken a 'low profile' in this general area, although changed circumstances may require a reappraisal. There are two parts of existing UK policy towards inward investing multinationals which need special consideration, namely attraction and regulation.

As far as attraction is concerned the UK pattern of promotion agencies is bewilderingly complex, and there are at least four distinct tiers of activity. These range from the Invest in Britain Bureau (IBB) at the national level to local district councils at the most micro level. The trend since 1979 has been to attempt to coordinate this effort and direct it to best effect. This is reflected in Scotland by the establishment of Locate in Scotland (LIS) and in Northern Ireland by the formation of an Industrial Development Board. In different ways these bodies are intended to focus and coordinate the work of the variety of agencies within the regions concerned who have statutory responsibilities for industrial attraction. There is little doubt that the UK policy on attraction has been slow to develop, most of the important initiatives having had a strong regional bias. As a result it is pointless to look for a national strategy since it has never existed. Moreover, there is a real danger that a policy of ill-considered centralisation would damage the existing system by failing to achieve the correct balance between functions which are properly undertaken at national level and those best handled regionally.

On the question of regulations, a number of mechanisms for evaluating inward foreign investment do exist. They are implemented by a variety of Government departments, whose powers often overlap and apply with equal force to domestic companies. Among the many uncoordinated instruments there are a number worth noting. First, until 1979 all inward investment required permission from the Bank of England, working closely with the Treasury. Policy was apparently determined with regard to the effect of the transaction on U K reserves, the need for self-financing, and the payment of a 'fair price' in takeover cases. The speed with which approvals were given made this process largely a formality. Secondly, powers have existed under the Industry Act 1975 to prevent certain takeovers of 'important manufacturing undertakings' by foreign owners, with at least 30 per cent ownership being the measure of control adopted. This is really a reserve power and could not in any event be applicable to companies based in E E C countries. A third strand of policy arises from the initiative taken by the Inland Revenue in 1976 to establish a special unit to deal with the transfer pricing policies of multinationals. Little is known of this since its activities are not published. A final area of U K initiative lies in the role of the Monopolies and Mergers Commission (M M C), although of course its activities pertain to anti-competitive activity irrespective of company nationality. To that extent the nationality of the referred company might appear to be irrelevant. Although the M M C has had relatively few major references dealing with foreign companies (and only two since 1975 where takeover bids involving foreign firms were rejected), questions of strategic change and interplant roles after a merger do frequently come up in their reports. The U K approach has, quite properly, not been one of discriminating against foreign takeovers, and in the absence of broader policies on industrial strategy it is unreasonable to expect the M M C to look at the wider issues posed by M N E involvement.

While it will be apparent from the above that there is no unified or consistent approach to the evaluation of multinationals operating in the U K, policy does not stand still. Over the recent past there have been a number of cases where a more interventionist position has been taken by the U K Government, two examples of which are worth brief comment. The whole area of government purchasing and international companies is a sensitive one. During 1981 the Prime Minister intervened to ensure that the loss-making and state-backed International Computers Limited (I C L) would obtain the order for new computers at the Vehicle Licensing Centre in Swansea. Apparently going against official and legal advice, the contract was only to be negotiated with I C L. I B M, in the light of new rules on open tendering to be operated under G A T T and the E E C, and in the knowledge that the UK Government had been 'steering' earlier contracts to ICL, threatened to lodge formal international complaints about this practice. Moreover, IBM claimed that not only would their price be substantially lower than ICL, but also over 50 per cent of the value of the order would be supplied from UK plants. This case has to be seen against the background of government vascillation on open tendering; their belief in the market mechanism; and above all, perhaps, the fact that both France and Ireland have recently been reported to the European Court of Justice for infringing the rules of open international tendering for public contracts. Commenting on the confusion surrounding UK thinking in this case, one leading source made the appropriate observation that 'Britain's industrial policy is too often decided by an odd scribble in the margin of Government papers as they go through 10 Downing Street'.[9] This dispute between IBM and the British Government is very reminiscent of similar complaints raised by Honeywell on several occasions during the 1970s.

The fdi case which attracted most attention in 1981 was the Nissan-Datsun proposal to manufacture cars in Britain. From the outset Nissan anticipated opposition from European car and component producers, and the Japanese company's presumption proved correct, for within weeks of the announcement that they had decided in principle to set up in UK and were examining alternative sites, there was a powerful backlash. This came from the European CCMC (Comité des Constructeurs d'Automobiles du Marché Commun) who called for a change in the EEC rules on 'source of origin' so that a minimum of 80 per cent of a car had to be made in Europe. Among a wide variety of other demands was much good advice for the UK Government about the project. These included teeth being put in the 80 per cent clause, agreed means of monitoring Nissan performance, an agreed timescale to reach the 80 per cent level, and a clearer indication of Nissan's export and import intentions. The car producers, for obvious reasons, had some considerable difficulty in agreeing on a formula. Fears were expressed, including the possibility of the UK Government 'trundling in a Trojan horse which could open us up to a flood of cheap components from Japan'.[10] In the middle of this fracas, the UK Government was coy and somewhat embarrassed. While welcoming the investment, the Government view on the undertakings it wished to extract from Nissan was far from clear on many of the parameters identified by CCMC. Most of the initiative seemed to come from the Japanese. For example, they offered, assuming a 1984 plant start-up, 60 per cent EEC components' content at that date, rising to 80 per cent by 1986. In general, the Japanese attempted a conciliatory approach, which may well have been influenced by the opposition directed towards Hitachi, when in 1977 they tried to set up a plant in the North East of England.[11] Opposition on that occasion from unions and competitors was so severe that the proposal was withdrawn. Given the desire to require the Japanese to add value in Europe and the need for job replacement, this incident does draw attention to the need for a coherent UK approach.

The foregoing paragraphs have drawn attention to the absence of UK policy on inward fdi. The whole thrust of this book seems to show that a continuation of favourable impact cannot be guaranteed. Moreover, the maintenance of rates of growth of fdi is proving difficult. All of this points to the need for UK policy initiatives. Bearing in mind the need to comply with external commitments to international organisations and the internal constraints arising from the scale of foreign involvement in certain sectors and regions, there is scope for progress. It would clearly not be in the interests of the UK to pursue strong regulatory policies. At the same time there is a need for a strategy for inward direct investment, with consideration of the desired contribution from this sector. Even within a permissive policy, there is now ample evidence that there are still unresolved problems with reference to some desired goals. The present authors have consistently argued that monitoring should be a more important function at both affiliate and corporate level. Its objectives would include identifying possible changes in corporate strategy which have a bearing on UK affiliates, the identification of needs for new investment projects at an early stage, the identification of needs for new products and processes in UK plants, and so on. Such in-depth monitoring would only be required of a relatively small proportion of the foreign companies operating in the UK, but would declare the government's interest in corporate developments within the foreign investment stock.

The Lessons from Other Developed Countries. Within the vast scope of the topic, this section simply draws attention to a number of policy developments which might offer guidance to the handling of the MNE, especially in retreat. At the outset it should be noted that just as this phenomenon is not confined to Scotland, inexperience in handling it is widespread and few have directly tackled it.

It has been suggested throughout the previous section that almost all measures directed towards the MNE would be enhanced by a more sound industrial policy. While such a policy would be no substitute for higher UK economic growth, it might provide a framework within which a selective policy of 'interventionism' of various types could be pursued. It is in this setting perhaps that parallels with other countries should be drawn, rather than suggest that the institutions of other countries are in themselves transferable. Japan is often recognised as a model, through the work of the Ministry of International Trade and Industry (MITI).[12] Indeed, in a variety of rather half-hearted ways, various UK bodies such as the IRC and the NEDC have tried some of these initiatives – such as those towards key industries. Computers, machine tools, aerospace, shipbuilding and textiles are in this category. However, these policies have never been pursued with consistency in the UK nor has there been the same perception of strategy in policy formulation as in other countries such as Japan. This position has been well summarised for the UK: 'Industrial policies seem limited to a peripheral role of tidying up the edges of the economy rather than providing any central thrust to alter and improve industry's performance and that of the economy as a whole.'[13] As long as this approach is adopted it will be impossible to take a clear view of the desired role of foreign direct investment in the U K and, by extension, of the implications of decline in fdi in this country. Comparisons are often drawn between French and British experience in this area.[14] This is in many ways an easier comparison than with Japan, not least because attempts were made in Britain to emulate French experience in the 1960s. The French approach to indicative planning clearly did not travel well, for a variety of reasons. In France the plans adopted might well be used as a framework for some highly interventionist policies. Since the widespread recognition of the practice of planning in Britain in the early 1970s, the U K has lacked just such a point of reference. Beyond that it should be recognised that in France, industrial policy was pursued against a background of selected barriers to trade in order to aid restructuring. The British over-commitment to free trade has inhibited such supporting activities.[15].

Not everyone would regard industrial policy as the foundation of more specific policies towards foreign direct investment. For example, national industrial policy measures are sometimes criticised for not adjusting to changes in the international economy. Further the view is often expressed that many of the structural changes taking place in the world economy in, say, the 1950s took place despite industrial policies which resisted them. There is some validity in these views.[16] The real issue is whether the events of the 1970s and 1980s in Western Europe require materially different policies in order to manage, rather than resist, adjustment. This view has been succinctly expressed as 'events have made the need for industrial policy apparent with a persuasiveness that more general arguments lack'.[17] One small, but locally substantial, manifestation of these events is the subject of this book. For Scotland, the position is well summarised in an observation initially made about fdi in Belgium: 'Such small states are in a position of trying to manage both the speed at which they become intertwined with the international economy and the impact of the dependencies which result.'[18] This is precisely the problem which U K industrial policy does not address and why it offers no assistance on how to deal with the M N E in decline. The limited Scottish initiatives have focused on the adaptive and innovative, rather than on the defensive or stabilisation-centred approaches.

The scope for policy transfer in the regional sphere is limited by the E E C constraints placed upon financial packages for investment from all sources and by regional measures designed for expansion not contraction. E E C efforts towards transparency in aid schemes and differential aid ceilings are a welcome first step in limiting competitive bidding for mobile firms. The path towards commonality of approach, avoiding operational aids and hidden subsidies, is not, however, a smooth one, with everyone proceeding in the same direction at the same pace.[19] In various ways the French and Irish have put pressure on the bounds of the possible in order to preserve competitive advantages – the latter in their replacement in 1979 of their export profits tax relief system by a new low rate of corporation tax for all manufacturing firms. Britain has often given up too much too quickly in this international chess game.

Looking specifically at regional measures and the MNE in retreat, arguably the best assistance would come from more emphasis being placed on discretionary financial assistance which enabled all the facets of different cases to be taken into account. There is clearly no case for blanket financial support for units on grounds of threatened closure alone. There may be a case for supporting an affiliate in transition at a slightly higher aid level, provided the parent corporation has some demonstrable commitment to maintaining and developing that unit. To find this out requires a real understanding of, and close involvement with, the parent company. Such an approach is consistent with that taken, for example, in the reorganisation of the Industrial Development Authority (IDA) in Ireland in 1979 along sectoral lines and the abandonment of the distinction between home and overseas operations. In principle this could form the basis for the type of specialist response to corporate policies which is desirable at both UK and regional level. Such initiatives go beyond the scope of regional policy and merely draw attention to the need to coordinate all strands of policy, since no single measure in itself can cope with the MNE, or any other large-scale private corporation, when in retreat.

Turning to the lessons which the UK could learn from other industrialised nations on policy towards inward investment, these probably exist at a number of different levels. It is interesting to note that the United States, which is committed to general policies of non-interference with fdi, reacted strongly to the prospect of substantial inflows of capital from OPEC countries in 1974–5. After the hysteria died down, the more considered response was the establishment in 1975 of an inter-agency Committee on Foreign Investment in the United States (CFIUS). Among its functions are 'monitoring' foreign investment trends, reviewing investment which it deems would have major implications for US national interests, considering proposals for new legislation or regulation of fdi, and so on. To date CFIUS has generally been non-interventionist in its operations and indeed has reacted negatively to several proposals to expand the US Government's powers – for example, as regards restricting foreign investment in energy resources (1976) and farmland (1978). Even the emergence of such a body in the UK to consider and recommend policy on the many dimensions of fdi would be a major step forward, simply because it would provide a much needed focus.

Like the US, Germany is essentially non-interventionist where fdi is concerned. Nevertheless, there were informal responses to the perceived OPEC threat, including a notification system whereby banks and large corporations reported impending large foreign acquisitions to government. A number of such cases has led to German rather than foreign investment. Perhaps of greatest interest to the UK are some of the decisions over the years of the Federal Cartel Office which has tended to define the limits of fdi expansion in some parts of the economy more clearly than has ever happened in Britain.

Within Europe, French policy has been the most consistent and the most interventionist. For the UK lessons can be learned on both counts. A review process is operated for fdi, although investments from the EEC members can only really be blocked on grounds of balance-of-payments difficulties. Among the most notable aspects of this policy has been that directed to resisting foreign domination in particular sectors by subsidising indigenous companies and/or requiring joint foreign and domestic ventures in order to restrict or reduce the role played by powerful multinationals. The Honeywell case has already provided an illustration of this approach and its operation in an area where industrial and fdi policies are effectively synchronised. It would not be desirable for the UK to emulate directly the French approach to economic chauvinism. At the same time the events discussed in this book could well encourage a new look at where 'national interest' lies in the UK. If that were ever to happen, however cautiously, France would be a useful comparator.

The two other major industrialised nations with more active fdi policies are Canada and Japan, although the lines taken by the two have been quite different. The immediate lessons for the UK from both of these cases are limited by the distinctive circumstances out of which they emerged. The belated Canadian enactment of the Foreign Investment Review Act (FIRA) in 1973, requires careful consideration; and while the spirit of FIRA is relevant to the UK, it would be difficult to introduce a similar organisation as a unilateral barrier to entry, given the historic position of the UK on this subject, the existing pattern of foreign interest and the strength of UK outward investment. Analogies between the Japanese and UK experience are not easy to draw. Japan, after an extensive period of fdi restrictions, only moved towards a liberal attitude in the 1970s.[20] During the most restricted period, the government was consistently liberal in the importation of technology – a trend reflected in Japanese payments of patent royalties running at a level three times higher than all foreigners' earnings (dividends, etc.) from direct investment in Japan for much of the decade. It was not until the mid-1970s that liberalisation progressed sufficiently to allow 100 per cent foreign ownership in most Japanese industries and even then limitations remained in industries such as mining, forestry and petroleum. Validation is still required and in the case of takeovers, there remains a deep-seated reluctance to approve these – hence the emphasis in many cases on joint-ventures or strong minority foreign holdings. Even allowing for the different backgrounds of the two countries, there is little doubt that the studied Japanese policy of pursuing MNE benefits and minimising specific sovereignty costs provides some lessons for the UK. The recognition in Japan (and elsewhere) that different industries require different ownership formulae at different times is interesting. In contrast, the UK Government of the day took a very laissez-faire attitude to MNE investment in North Sea oil exploration, within a setting where many international precedents would have suggested that this was an obvious area for maximising national benefit with reduced foreign ownership. Technology was, of course, required but it could have been acquired under more favourable terms. The lessons from many of these countries would call for a more discerning policy framework in the UK, where specific developments can be handled by specific policies, established and developed over the long term.

Future Prospects for Foreign Direct Investment in Scotland

As a prelude to the consideration of policy in Scotland specifically, this section looks to the future. Prospects over the next 10 years for fdi in Scotland will, in all probability, be largely determined by the operation of two sets of factors. The first relates to global trends in foreign direct investment, and, in particular, the prospects for investment from non-US sources. The second dimension lies in what is likely to be happening as regards MNE corporate strategy within Europe, since this has particular implications for reinvestment decisions made by (or on behalf of) existing affiliates.

Global Fdi Trends and Scottish Expectations. As has been shown, Scotland has traditionally been dependent on US foreign direct investment rather than fdi from other sources. While this relative dominance has diminished, US trends remain important. Although the stock of US investment accounts for over 40 per cent of the worldwide fdi total, the US share of world flows has fallen from its peak of around three-fifths between 1961–7 to around one-third by 1980. In sharp contrast, West Germany's share of investment flows rose from around 7 to 18 per cent over that period; while the corresponding Japanese figures are 2 per cent and 14 per cent. From the viewpoint of the recipients of these investment flows, the European share of the world total has remained largely stable at slightly above 60 per cent. But this figure masks some very significant shifts within Europe since the mid-1960s, with large rises being recorded in Belgium, France and Norway and substantial falls in West Germany, Italy, Sweden and the UK. Neither of these two trends in the pattern of flows acts in Scotland's favour.

There are other problems moreover. It would appear that the competitive pressures in the second part of the 1970s substantially affected Scotland. The contrast is often made between the Scottish performance in attracting fdi and that of Eire. The two are by no means directly comparable for many reasons, including the rudimentary Irish industrial base, the level of grant assistance and the nature of many of the enterprises. What is of interest is the ability of Eire to attack certain sectors of the MNE market in which Scotland was once very strong. For example, around one-third of the US companies in Scotland first started overseas manufacture in Scotland. A considerable number of the US companies in Eire appear to be new or relatively new entrants into international production, apparently attracted by the high fiscal incentives. Again, contrary to expectations the Irish have generated around 10,000 jobs over the past 5–7 years in electronics and allied activity from a standing start. Other things being equal, the relative advantages of agglomeration, skilled labour pools, subcontracting possibilities and sourcing points, would appear to have been in favour of areas such as Scotland. Similarly, the attractiveness of the Irish package and the vigour and skill

167

with which it has been marketed, has tapped another market, namely that of being able to prise off a subsidiary from within an established European MNE network and have a plant established in Eire. Paradoxically, the relative success of Eire has coincided with the events studied in this book, although the two are not directly related. In many senses Eire has much of the dynamism of a new entrant to the fdi market in Europe and one whose track record has yet to be established. That this can happen is a salutary lesson for a more established MNE base like Scotland.

The character of direct investment is also changing in a number of important ways. Foreign direct investment is now much more varied in respect of industrial sector, size of parent company, methods of entry and financing than it was in the 1960s. Wholly-owned subsidiaries are not as common as they once were. Among the many possible reasons for this are those associated with technology. Where an investing company has no significant technological lead or its technology is mature, joint ventures or acquisitions are often preferable to greenfield operations. In the recession prevailing in the world economy over recent years, the acquisition of existing facilities does not immediately change market supply, and the presence of established market connections reduces some of the risks involved in new foreign ventures. The very inexperience of many European and Japanese firms now entering international production has led many of them to look for low-risk acquisitions, and US multinationals are not exempt from the same pressures. So the ratio of greenfield to acquisition investment for US multinationals in developed countries fell from 3 in 1976 to 0.2 in 1979 – measured in terms of value of investment. Moreover, in recent years only some 6 per cent of the growth in the stock of US investment abroad, has been the result of investment in new wholly-owned operations, the remainder is in the form of acquisitions and joint ventures. As a recipient of investment from all the major source nations, Scotland will not be exempt from these trends. They are already strongly reflected in the European-owned sector in Scotland.

In projecting the role of fdi in Scotland over the next decade, it is necessary to comment upon the prospects from each of the principal source nations. Taking the *United States* first, table 2 draws attention to the significant changes in the distribution of American investment in the EEC over the past two decades. The relative decline in the UK position is clear and a more detailed look at the figures would suggest that the formation and subsequent expansion of the EEC stimulated investment in the member states and diverted investment from the UK. It is too early to say whether the rise in the UK's share of US fdi in 1979 and 1980 represents the beginning of a reversal in this trend. The true nature of this change is not easily determined but some clues exist. The latest US Benchmark Study relates to the fdi position in 1977. This is in effect a census of all but the smallest US foreign affiliates and allows a more precise study of the UK/EEC relative position. The information collected related to 3,540 US parents and their 24,666 foreign affiliates. Table 3 provides a summary of the UK and EEC(9) position for that year on the basis of selected indicators. These comparisons are rather striking in some respects. In all countries (except Ireland) labour costs were at least 50 per cent above UK levels. Sales per employee were everywhere in excess of those in the UK, varying from figures of $72,900 and $73,800 in Ireland and France respectively to $169,000 in Denmark. Taking a broad look at the UK position, while this country accounted for almost 40 per cent of total employment in US affiliates in the EEC in 1977, it obtained only 25 per cent of compensation paid and accounted for less than 29 per cent of the sales.

Table 2. US Foreign Direct Investment Stock in Manufacturing Industries in EEC Countries

	1961	1971	1973	1975	1977	1978	1979	1980
Total ($m.)	3,964	19,318	18,501	22,907	27,747	32,180	35,739	41,476
				Percentage of EEC total				
Belgium and Luxembourg	4.3	7.3	8.1	8.8	9.4	8.7	9.4	8.6
France	11.6	15.615.9	16.8	14.9	14.4	14.3	14.3	
West Germany	18.8	23.7	24.0	23.4	25.3	25.9	24.0	23.3
Italy	4.7	7.3	7.6	7.5	7.1	7.4	7.9	8.0
Netherlands	2.4	6.3	6.5	7.4	7.4	7.8	8.3	7.5
Denmark	n.a.	0.5	0.4	0.5	0.5	0.5	0.5	0.5
Rep. of Ireland	n.a.	n.a.	1.7	2.5	3.4	4.0	3.6	3.9
UK	58.1	39.3	35.7	33.2	31.9	31.3	32.0	33.9

SOURCE: US Department of Commerce, *Survey of Current Business*, various issues.

Table 3. Benchmark Data for US Investment in EEC(9) and UK (1977)

	Assets per employee ($000)	Sales per employee ($000)	Compensa- tion per employee ($000)	Net income as % of sales	Net income as % of assets
EEC(9)	61.3	84.0	12.4	3.3	4.5
UK	51.2	60.5	7.7	3.5	4.1

SOURCE: US Department of Commerce, *Survey of Current Business*, April 1981.

Conversely, Germany accounted for 27 per cent of sales, 22 per cent of employment and around 30 per cent of employee remuneration. Caution is advocated in the interpretation of such figures as many factors underly the observed differences, a number of which have little to do with foreign direct investment. Among the disturbing aspects, however, is the possibility that low labour costs in Britain may encourage more semi-skilled labour intensive operations which could well be those which are most vulnerable to locational competition from the peripheral areas of Southern Europe and Third World nations over the next decade. Scotland is not exempt from these risks and such considerations must be at the forefront when relevant agencies are evaluating the longer-term prospects for the existing US stock, including investment in the electronics area.

One of the more encouraging features of the Benchmark Study was that over half of all imports shipped to the US from affiliates in the EEC(9) came from the UK. On the face of it this is short-term good news. It may not be in the longer term, depending on which of a variety of explanations of this pattern is accepted. If the product-cycle model of international investment is considered, it may mean that the UK is the main location for the manufacture of mature (rather than advanced) technology products for which the US has lost its comparative advantage. If this interpretation is valid, then Continental Europe locations might be expected to manufacture products with a higher technology input for the European market itself.

Before leaving US investment, some comment is necessary on the relevance of aggregate rate of return measures in influencing subsequent investment decisions. For many years the US Department of Commerce has published rate of return data on US foreign direct investment, the last decade of which is shown in figure 1. The measure of income as a percentage of end-year investment stock is a rather limited one. And it is bound, by definition, to inflate the figures in locations such as Eire where many of the US operations are relatively rudimentary, have lower investment levels and/or are subject to income gains from goods transferred into the country to take advantage of the fiscal régime (without much local value being added). As the data in figure 1 illustrate, the EEC(9) countries with high rates of return are Eire and West Germany. Whatever the true value of such comparisons they do provide valuable publicity for industrial attraction and may well be of importance in determining perceptions. On that count, it is interesting to note that the UK position improved between 1976 and 1979, and in the latter year the returns exceeded that of the EEC as a whole for the first time in the 1970s. Unfortunately, positive increases in this measure cannot be regarded as of unequivocal benefit to the UK or Scotland. Since the stock value of US investment in the UK has not been increasing as rapidly as that in the EEC(9) or in the other two countries in figure 1, the higher rate of return may just be a reflection of companies generating income out of declining investment stock and mature products. Another interpretation of figure 1 is that it indicates the effectiveness of the rationalisation and divestment measures undertaken by US companies since the mid-1970s. Alternative explanations of expanding export performance from US affiliates and/or dramatic improvements in productivity seem implausible in view of the strength of sterling, general investment levels and so on. The true

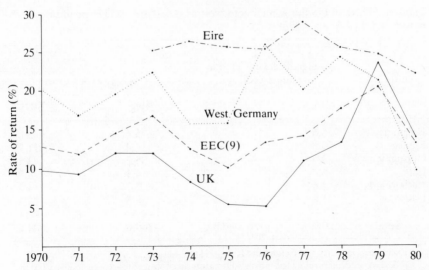

Figure 1. Rates of return (income as % of end-year investment stock) of u s direct investment in manufacturing industry in Europe. Source: u s Department of Commerce, *Survey of Current Business*, various issues.

position may have elements of a number of these explanations as well as the more obvious improvement in general performance which is implied.

A final important u s fdi trend should be noted, namely the shift in the geographical distribution of R & D activity relative to the changing patterns of foreign investment. During the decade covered in table 4, the overall growth of u s R & D expenditures in the e e c almost exactly matches the proportionate increase in the stock of fdi. In the case of the u k, there is a reasonably close relationship between declining shares of both items, although even in 1966 the u k was apparently less attractive as a location in which to undertake R & D than as a manufacturing base. West Germany stands out sharply in table 4, in that by 1975 it accounted for just under one-quarter of u s fdi in the e e c, but over two-fifths of R & D expenditures. Extrapolating the relevance of this trend for Scotland, the question of investment quality is again raised. While there is no reason to believe that the Scottish position differs markedly from that of the u k, generating higher quality activities based on local R & D will continue to be difficult and very much dependent on designated product roles and local affiliate perform-ance.

Data sources on *West German fdi* are relatively limited. From around 1975 German direct investment abroad began to exceed direct investment flowing into the country. This outward flow is clearly motivated by a variety of push and pull factors, including rising domestic labour costs and the sustained appreciation of the Deutsche Mark. As the data in table 5 indicate, the u k has not benefited greatly from this expansion; indeed Britain had by

Table 4. Shares of US Foreign Direct Investment and of R & D Expenditures in the EEC* (1966 and 1975)

Country	% of total Foreign direct investment in manufacturing		R & D expenditures†	
	1966	1975	1966	1975
Belgium‡	5.6	9.1	5.1	5.0
France	14.8	17.3	14.4	11.7
Germany	22.7	24.1	35.2	43.1
Italy	6.6	7.7	4.1	8.8
Netherlands	4.6	7.6	2.7	4.3
UK	45.8	34.2	38.5	27.1
Total	100.0	100.0	100.0	100.0

* Excluding Denmark and Ireland and R & D in Luxembourg.
† R & D expenditures relate to both manufacturing and non-manufacturing industry but the latter is very small.
‡ Includes Luxembourg for fdi.
SOURCE: D. Creamer, *Overseas Research & Development by United States Multinationals, 1966–1975*, The Conference Board (New York) 1976, p. 39 for R & D Expenditures;
N. Hood and S. Young, *European Development Strategies of US Owned Manufacturing Companies Located in Scotland*, HMSO (Edinburgh) 1980, p.21 for fdi data.

Table 5. Flows of West German Direct Investment Abroad (1966–77)

	1966		1970		1974		1975–7	
	Value (DM000)	%	Value (DM000)	%	Value (DM000)	%	Value (DM000)	%
Total EEC	410	35.0	886	35.3	1,611	32.6	4,733	27.0
UK	73	6.2	158	6.3	205	4.2	786	4.5
US	69	5.9	296	11.8	502	10.2	3,826	18.7
Total World	1,172	100.0	2,509	100.0	4,935	100.0	17,531	100.0

SOURCES: 'Feasibility Study on Investment from Other Countries in the Least Prosperous Regions of the Community', *Metra Consulting Group*, August 1975.
'Reversal in the Balance of Direct Investments', *Monthly Report of the Bundesbank*, vol.130, 1978.

1980 dropped out of the top 10 destinations for German fdi. From the Scottish perspective, it was noted earlier that the German interest was likely to be more biased towards acquisition than greenfield sites if recent trends are maintained. In short, there are few reasons for Scottish confidence in substantial direct investment expansion from this source; the focus of any growth perhaps lies in joint ventures, licensing or related involvement.

The prospects of an expansion of *Japanese* foreign direct investment in the UK have substantially improved over recent years in line with the general growth from that source. Some indications of the geographical distribution of the Japanese fdi stock are given in table 6. While the proportion in less developed countries remains high, there is some suggestion of a trend towards developed country locations. Of these the US dominates, taking around one-quarter of all Japanese investment. Although table 6 indicates some volatility in Europe's position as a recipient of Japanese fdi stock, the flows to both Europe and the UK have fallen considerably as a proportion of the total. For example, in 1970 Europe received some 37 per cent of the flow of total Japanese fdi while the 1978 figure was 7 per cent. Having said that, in the period 1951–78 the UK received by far the largest share of Japanese investment in Europe – in effect nearly one-half of the cumulative flow during these years or some six times that of its nearest European rival, West Germany.

What then of the prospects for the UK and Scotland? Before confronting that issue directly, it should be stressed that Japanese industry has traditionally relied on exports from the home country to service foreign markets. On the whole, direct investments overseas have been considered only when exports were no longer possible, either because of changes in comparative advantage or because of import restrictions. Normally such ventures have been in less technologically advanced areas in order to achieve vertical integration between the foreign and domestic operations of Japanese firms. The underlying objective of such policies has often been to extend the life cycle of existing products and labour intensive technology when the comparative advantage of producing in Japan has ended.

Times, however, are changing for Japanese companies. Japan is now outstanding in a number of high technology fields and it has therefore an incentive to produce overseas in developed nations, but the country is also facing growing protectionist pressures. These factors will increase Japanese fdi but often at a pace which does not match the aspirations of industrial developers in Europe. As suggested, few Japanese companies have experience of extensive overseas production in developed nations. Rarely do they have a cadre of international managers to compare with US and European firms of comparable size. While there is, therefore, the prospect of very large increases in Japanese fdi, if Japanese firms do move to adopt similar market sourcing ratios (foreign production as a percentage of exports + foreign production) to those of US and European companies, this is likely to develop cautiously. Japanese companies show every sign of being very sensitive on the question of whether their corporate, comparative advantage can be maintained by production in developed-country environments with different quality concepts, productivity norms and labour relations traditions. So avoidance of risk is predictable.

As at the end of 1981 some 28 Japanese manufacturing units were operating in the UK. Three of these were in Scotland with two others on the way (Polychrome; Daiwa Sports; No Fuse Circuit Breakers; Mitsubishi-

Table 6. The Stock of Japanese Outward Direct Investment by Major Regions (1957–77)

Region	1957 $m	1957 %	1965 $m	1965 %	1972 $m	1972 %	1977 $m	1977 %
N. America	26.7	34.0	240.7	25.4	1,550	22.9	5,360	24.3
Europe	1.3	1.7	24.8	2.6	1,660	24.5	3,070	13.9
Oceania	0.5	0.7	7.4	0.8	430	6.3	1,260	5.7
L. America*	26.0	33.1	277.0	29.3	990	14.6	3,750	17.0
Middle East	0.2	0.3	195.6	20.7	610	9.0	1,430	6.5
Other Africa	–	–	11.0	1.2	150	2.2	910	4.1
Other Asia	23.8	30.3	189.2	20.0	1,390	20.5	6,320	28.6
Total	78.6	100.0	957.0	100.0	6,780	100.0	22,100	100.0
Share of Developed Countries (%)	36.4		28.7		53.7		43.9	
Share of Less Developed Countries (%)	63.6		71.2		46.3		56.2	

* Includes West Indies
SOURCE: Japanese Ministry of International Trade and Industry.

Tandberg; and NEC Semiconductors); the earliest of these was set up in 1977. At least one-third of those operations established in UK are less than 100 per cent owned. The total Japanese investment in UK at the end of 1981 was estimated at $2 billion compared with $500 million in West Germany as the nearest European rival. From a Scottish perspective, there is some scope for optimism in attracting Japanese investment, as it would appear that a considerable proportion of Japanese expansion might be in the UK. Expectations should not be pitched too high. First, it should be borne in mind that the Japanese employment in Scotland is unlikely to reach the equivalent of even the depleted US figure for a very long time. Secondly, both the Japanese and US market motivations are European, but there the direct comparison ends. Almost all the Japanese entrants will have very well established sales and marketing networks in Europe, in view of their dominant exporting position. These are unquestionably not located in Assisted Areas, and this may tend to encourage companies to choose centralised locations. Thirdly, the pace of decision making, before substantial commitments are made to large-scale international production, is likely to be slow and dependent at least as much on Japanese governmental attitudes to protectionism as on corporate decisions. For Scotland, thus, expectations should be tempered with realism. Wales may be in the best position to benefit from Japanese fdi in Britain, especially if Nissan choose to locate their car plant there. It will then have the greatest concentration of Japanese firms and this may have an influence on the site selection processes of others.

This brief review of global fdi trends has suggested that the maintenance of around 80,000 MNE jobs in the manufacturing sector in Scotland will be a tough assignment. Prospects of investment from the most rapidly expanding fdi nations are at best fair and difficult to realise. The balance of ownership will change in the next decade and the maintenance of existing job levels in this sector should be deemed the priority and the main criteria of success.

Strategic Changes in MNE Corporate Networks in Europe. That developments within the strategies of existing multinationals with affiliates in Scotland will be an important determinant of future prosperity, is a proposition likely to commend itself to most observers. More difficult is the exercise of predicting with authority what directions change will take. Such forecasts will only be as robust as the assumptions made at the time. It is possible to set the specific company experience within a general framework and it is probable that the forces under discussion will continue to play a part in shaping corporate change in the MNE sector for the next five or seven years. In order to give some perspective on the type of changes which may continue to occur, two different approaches have been selected in this section. The first, based on some earlier published empirical work undertaken by the authors, sets the six cases into a wider corporate context. The second, derived from an extensive programme of work by a team initially based at Harvard, takes a complementary look at the strategies of similar groups of companies and provides an interesting typology by which strategic change can be examined.

Strategic Change in 30 US MNEs in Europe. The interview results which are briefly discussed in this section were undertaken by the authors as part of a larger study.[21] By reporting the findings here it is possible to illustrate the more general effects of the out-working of the specific pressures for change which were examined in detail in the cases. Moreover, it draws attention to the fact that the arena of adjustment is not Scotland, but Europe, and, on occasion, beyond. The 30 us parent corporations in the sample include the six examined in the case section. They are very large on average, with mean 1978 sales of over $5 billion and employment of 81,000 worldwide. Some characteristics of the specifically European operations of the sample are shown in table 7. Four-fifths of the firms started foreign direct investment in Europe from a base in the United Kingdom. Since the primary factor in choosing the sample was the existence of a Scottish plant within the European network, the sample is overrepresented in terms of uk plants. As regards the period of entry, more than one-quarter of the sample established their first operations in Europe prior to World War II, with a similar proportion commencing European manufacture from 1945 to 1954. This distribution is probably rather different from that for all us multinationals in the uk and is certainly dissimilar to that for all American firms in Europe where the years post-1955 are particularly significant.

The predominant motivation for entry identified in interviews was the desire to exploit European (and particularly EFTA) markets for a well-developed line of us products. Manufacture in situ was often considered necessary in order to obtain an adequate share of the market. In this sense local manufacture was regarded as an important marketing tool, in some cases reinforced by nationalism among Government purchasers in Europe. Many of the European facilities were set up to parallel us operations using existing management and technology and gradually adopting the American product range. Aside from marketing considerations, some corporations were drawn into direct investment in Europe by the nature of their product, and the impact of transport costs and duties. Cost factors were frequently cited as an initial motivating force, especially when skilled manpower was (at time of entry) regarded as both cheap and efficient. The speed with which technology changes and the volatility of markets were both important entry determinants among the electronics companies. Finally, an interesting sub-group of motivations was identified related to the need to have facilities in Europe as part of the international servicing of major us companies.

While most of this sample began manufacture in the uk, only a few have confined their manufacturing to that location. uk operations were often seen as a forward base for mainland Europe, and on average (table 7) the sample corporations had manufacturing facilities in four different European countries at the end of the 1970s. As regards sectoral distribution the sample (being Scottish-related) is significantly over-concentrated in sic VII (Mechanical Engineering), a factor of some relevance in explaining certain of the

Table 7. Characteristics of 30 Sample US Corporations

1. Location of first European manufacturing operations

	No. of corporations
France	2
Germany	3
Netherlands	1
UK	24

2. Period of first establishment or takeover in Europe

	No. of corporations
Pre-1945	8
1945–54	8
1955–64	9
1965–74	5

3. Present no. of manufacturing plants in Europe*

	No. of corporations
1 or 2	9
3 or 4	11
5 or 6	5
7 or more	5

4. Present locations and numbers of manufacturing plants of sample corporations*

	No. of manufacturing plants
Belgium/Lux.	11
France	19
Germany	22
Italy	5
Netherlands	7
UK	49
Spain	4
Other†	8
Total	125

5. Industry group (Standard industrial classification)

Order no.	Industry	No. of corporations
V	Chemicals and allied industries	3
VII	Mechanical engineering	13
VIII	Instrument engineering	3
IX	Electrical engineering	6
XI	Other metal goods	1
XIII	Textiles	1
XV	Clothing and footwear	1
XVI	Bricks, pottery, glass	1
XIX	Other manufacturing industries	1

* Different locations within the same country are counted separately. But, for example, two units operated in the same town are included as only one operation.

† Other as follows: Denmark–2; Greece–1; Ireland–1; Portugal–1; Sweden–2; Switzerland–1.

effects of the loss in technological advantage during the 1970s. Having set the broad scene, the emphasis hereafter is on the way in which the sample corporations have reacted to the variety of external stimuli identified earlier in this book. For these purposes three policy areas are chosen for illustration, namely, changing product roles, market allocations, and locational networks.

Product Roles: The circumstances prevailing in the 1970s might have been expected to lead certain types of multinationals to change product alloca- tions to their affiliates. Such reallocations would be expected to lead to greater interdependence in affiliate manufacturing activities, especially where economies of scale were potentially significant but were not being fully exploited under earlier plant/product allocation systems. Looking at the sample and bearing in mind the considerable difficulties in making accurate distinctions between the various categories, table 8 suggests that some two-thirds of the companies had gone at least part of the way in the direction of product or component specialisation. In the main, such specialisation was related to European rather than to worldwide operations, although this latter extension was expected in a number of cases. In sharp contrast to the integrating companies, one-third of the sample was found to be still producing competitive product lines in different European locations. There were clearly a number of reasons for this, including the production of goods where economies of scale were of relatively little importance or where substantial product adaptation was necessary for national markets within Europe; the avoidance of over-dependence on one location and so on. If anything, another set of reasons dominated, namely, delays in response to the changing environmental circumstances, owing to managerial inefficiency, recent date of entry, and so forth.

The factors which influenced product strategies during the 1970s are very recent in origin and many of the patterns suggested in table 8 are unstable. The general direction of change in half of this sample was towards greater specialisation, the most active reorganisation being in the longer established firms. The greater homogeneity of the European market in the last 20 years, the breakdown of linguistic, cultural and marketing barriers as well as a learning process among US multinationals were all factors influencing this pattern. Again those reorganising product strategy were mainly companies with larger affiliate networks. This may be a reflection of European experience, but it also reflects a higher minimum efficient scale of production with newer technology. Some of these suggestions were supported by the industry pattern shown in table 8, where a high proportion of the mechanical engineering firms had been involved in plant/product reallocations. These were not only generally long established in Europe, they were also operating in a sector with mature technology and thus facing pressures to reduce capacity. At the other end of that spectrum were the electronics and allied companies which tended to go for globally integrated product-allocation systems from the outset.

Market Allocations: Closely linked to the issue of the manufacturing

Table 8. Changes in Product Roles of European Affiliates since Establishment

Classification Variables	No change*	Fundamental changes in products manufactured†	Plant/product specialisation for European markets	Plant/product specialisation for world markets
Period of first establishment or takeover in Europe				
Pre-1945	1	1	5	1
1945–54	2	–	4	2
1955–64	5	1	1	2
1965–74	5	–	–	–
All corporations	13	2	10	5
Present number of manufacturing plants in Europe				
1 or 2	6	2	–	1
3 or 4	5	–	4	2
5 or 6	2	–	2	1
7 or more	–	–	4	1
All corporations	13	2	10	5
Industry group				
Mechanical engineering	3	1	8	1
Instrument and electrical engineering	4	1	–	4
Other	6	–	2	–
All corporations	13	2	10	5

* 8 of the 13 operated with European plants manufacturing similar products and with no product or component links. In other cases more integrated product roles were allocated from the outset.
† In these cases changes were made without any increased integration between European affiliates.

responsibility assigned to the plant, is the designation of the market areas to be supplied out of European plants. It was not always possible to match changing product roles with changing market roles, simply because different corporations adopt different policies. Moreover, where the product role became one of component manufacture as part of a global plant specialisation within a corporation, it was no longer possible to designate a geographical market area to the plant. In such situations plants are frequently ranked as first-, second- or third-sourcing points for the whole corporate system.

The broad directions of change in market allocations emerging in this study are shown in table 9, although the patterns existing at any one time were often complicated. For example, some affiliates may on the one hand have worldwide market remits for a part of the product range for which that affiliate had developmental responsibility, while being a second- or third-sourcing point for Europe in a variety of other corporate products. The general trend was seen to be away from serving specific national markets towards wider European responsibility.

Table 9. Changes in Market Allocations for Affiliates of Sample Corporations since Establishment

		No. of corporations
1.	No change*	13
2.	Suppliers of specific national markets† to suppliers of European market (assoc. with plant/product specialisation)	6
3.	Suppliers of specific national markets† to suppliers of European market plus selected other areas (assoc. with plant/product specialisation)	2
4.	Suppliers of European market to suppliers of Europe plus selected other areas (assoc. with plant/product specialisation)	3
5.	Abandonment of plant/market allocations in moves towards worldwide sourcing	4
6.	Other‡	2
		30

* Basically the same corporations which reported 'no change' in product role. Actual market allocations vary widely.

† Typically, former product allocation would involve the UK affiliate supplying EFTA (and often the Commonwealth) and Continental European affiliates supplying the EEC.

‡ One company had begun to establish plants in Continental Europe to reduce dependence on UK; in the process the company was moving back towards a situation in which EEC affiliates supply Continental Europe and UK affiliates supply the UK and Commonwealth.

In the other corporation the changes in market allocations depend on the product line concerned.

Locational Networks: The final consideration in this brief review was to link the evidence on product and market reorganisation to the impact on locational networks in Europe. In order to categorise the nature of the changes, table 10 distinguishes three groups with respect to the dynamics of their location networks in Europe during the late 1970s. The largest single group was characterised by rationalisation and divestment, the latter involving complete disengagement from a particular location. It is interesting to note that at a maximum the 30 sample companies owned and controlled 145 manufacturing operations throughout Europe. This figure

Table 10. Characteristics of the Locational Networks of the Sample Corporations

Classification Variables	Locational Networks characterised by:			
	Stability/ expansion	Rationalisation†	Rationalisation and divestment‡	Total
Period of first establishment or takeover in Europe				
Pre-1945	1	1	6	8
1945–54	3	3	2	8
1955–64	5	2	2	9
1965–1974	2	–	3	5
All corporations	11	6	13	30
*Maximum number of manufacturing plants in Europe**				
1 or 2	3	–	3	6
3 or 4	6	2	2	10
5 or 6	–	4	4	8
7 or more	2	–	4	6
All corporations	11	6	13	30
Industry group				
Mechanical engineering	2	3	8	13
Instrument and electrical engineering	4	1	4	9
Other	5	2	1	8
All corporations	11	6	13	30

(contd. p.182)

* Note this refers to the maximum number of manufacturing plants operated, *not* the present operations.
† Rationalising companies were those reducing capacity and levels of employment in Europe. In some cases plant closures were involved, but these are not counted as divestments so long as the firm concerned still retains a manufacturing presence at a particular location.
‡ Refers only to complete cessation of manufacturing in certain locations. Includes instances where manufacturing ceases but a firm retains a selling, servicing or general headquarters operation. In total the 13 firms undertook 20 divestments, although in one case the company retained a 30% stake and in another instance the divestment was subject to legal proceedings at time of interview. Of the 20 divestments, 16 involved closures and 4 took the form of sale of all or part of the operations.

Table 10 (contd.)

Characteristics of divestments undertaken:
1. *Divestments classified by country in which divestment occurred*

No. of	Belgium/Lux.	France	Germany	Netherlands	Switzerland	UK	Total no. of divestments
divestments	1	2	10	1	2	4	20
No. of divestments as % of present no. of European plants	9.1	10.5	43.5	16.7	—	8.2	16.0

2. *Divestments classified by timing of divestments undertaken*

	Pre-1965	1965–70	1970–5	1976–9
No. of divestments	1	1	9	9

only included facilities at different geographical locations and thus under-states the number of individual manufacturing units. At the time of the study in 1978–9 only 125 manufacturing units remained. The notes to table 10 draw attention to the distribution of these 20 closures and stress that the vast majority occurred during the 1970s, even before the forces of the latest recession gathered momentum. In addition, a great deal of rationalisation had occurred without plant closure as there were invariably many reasons for maintaining a presence (albeit much reduced) in a market, especially one where the corporation had long-established marketing connections.

The study reported here is fairly recent in date. While adjustment has in some cases taken place more rapidly as a result of the economic recession in the early 1980s, the evidence points to a differential pattern of development along a similar path. Technologies, sites, products, markets and organisa-tions are all involved in this particular iterative process. Of course, the observations here are only one small aspect of a continuing process of organic adjustment for all firms of whatever origin. There is no reason to believe that this process has been completed in the MNE sector in Scotland or even that it will ever be wholly completed. What is distinctive about these events is the coincidence of similar problems in a once dynamic sector and the scale of the localised effects of adjustment. As this interview series has shown, the ripple effects of such changes are continuing on a European and not just a Scottish scale.

Harvard Study. The study described in previous paragraphs is by no means the only one to consider these adjustment problems. For a number of years a Harvard originated group has been examining empirical evidence on strategic management in multinationals.[22] This work has been extensive, but the aim of this section is to draw attention to the way in which some of the analysis reinforces many aspects of this book.

One of the central premises of the Harvard Study is that the evolution of multinationals is characterised by a growing conflict between the require-ments for economic survival and success (the economic imperative) and the adjustments made necessary by the demands of host governments (the political imperative). The reduction of trade barriers and the substantial economies of scale which are still available in many industries, together with the extensive competition from low-cost exporters are among the forces pushing towards rationalisation and integration.[23] Conversely, the level of international interdependence arising from free trade and MNE rationalisation makes individual countries more vulnerable to external factors and renders their traditional domestic economic policies much less effective. The work of this group has, *inter alia*, been directed to analysing the strategies and administrative processes used by multinationals to reconcile these two sets of imperatives.

Faced with such conflicts, three principal strategies may emerge.[24] First, a worldwide integration strategy may be pursued in response to the economic imperative and in a desire to improve international competitiveness. This approach has, of course, been described previously. Secondly, it is suggested that certain multinationals forego some of the economic benefits of integration and allow subsidiaries to adjust to the demands of their host government – pursuing a 'national responsiveness' strategy. Such parent companies exercise relatively little strategic influence over their subsidiaries and, normally, manufacture on a local market basis with few inter-subsidiary transfers. The third approach rejects both of these clear-cut decisions and attempts to search for structural and administrative adjustments rather than strategic solutions. In that sense the strategy is to have no strategy, but rather to balance the costs and benefits of both of the former two approaches as appropriate. Thus 'strategy is not a search for an overall optimum fit, but a series of limited adjustments made in response to specific developments, without an attempt to integrate these adjustments into a consistent comprehensive strategy'.[25]

The basic premise is that the type of strategy to suit a particular MNE will be a function of market structure, competition and technology. In order to illustrate the operation of these effects, figure 2 is presented. This reports the results of a study of six industries where the economic and political imperatives are seen to be in conflict. The patterns shown represent no more than the preferred strategy of the parent company, whereas in practice most companies will have deviant subsidiaries. Figure 2 pertains to data collected in Western Europe and assumes that in a given industry, trade restrictions are similar. Examining this data, the researchers evoke a number of interesting hypotheses which are of some relevance in interpreting future trends. For example, looking at the relationship between market structure, competition and strategy, they conclude that smaller firms, such as Honeywell (relative to IBM) are likely to find administrative coordination more suitable and will enlist host governments' support and subsidies to enable them to compete against the leading multinationals. The Honeywell-CII arrangements discussed earlier in the case section are cited by the authors as indicative of this point. It will be noted in figure 2 that the nature of the strategies varies substantially across the industries concerned. For example, the economic imperative strongly directs car producers towards worldwide integration since they operate in markets with low-government sales participation. At the other end of the scale, is the influence exerted by interested governments in the strategies of the electrical power companies.

The present conclusions must be regarded as only indicative of some of the ways in which multinationals operating within Scotland might be influenced. The drawing together of technological and market structure components is of importance. It is clearly useful to determine the direction in which strategic change is moving as well as noting the different types of regional activity which are represented by each of these strategies.

Policy Initiatives at Scottish Level

The opening pages of this chapter served to illustrate the real difficulties faced when trying to determine whether various U K policy measures had a contribution to make in coping with the problems of the M N E in retreat. In truth, they have little to offer in relation to most of the problems of industrial restructuring, whoever owns the assets. From the Scottish perspective, therefore, expectations of national policy developments should remain low. For that reason, it is necessary to turn to second-best solutions at regional level. There can be no substitute for national policy measures, but given the level of delegated authority on certain economic matters which exists in Scotland, there is scope for making some independent progress on policy matters. In the light of the problems discussed in this book, these powers have to be directed towards the expansion and replacement of the foreign-owned investment stock and towards indigenous industrial development. (While the emphasis is on the former in the context of this book, the latter must inevitably receive top priority.)

The previous two sections of this chapter have been largely concerned with the operation of forces which are external to Scotland. Their influence might readily appear to be global, remote and not subject to pressure at national, let alone regional, level. In many respects that is true, so that policy cannot have a great influence either on the flow of fdi or on the behaviour of multinationals. The key variables influencing foreign direct investors are well recognised as market size and growth, productivity, labour costs and so on, none of which will be affected by changing policy responses. At the same time, the nature of such responses will be of crucial importance in determining the share of foreign investment achieved by Scotland and the level and quality of jobs created from these sources.

Every sign points to the end of the era of the gifted amateur in the attraction of fdi. The European market for mobile investment is now one of the toughest in the world. It is a market with few barriers to entry and thus one which can readily be attacked by public authorities of all shapes and sizes. Its pricing structure, in spite of E E C regulations, is fiercely competitive – especially in the large projects' area. It is subject to intense promotion, both above and below the line, and attempts made to differentiate one location from another are frequently fraught with difficulty, because there are always many genuinely attractive locations for the M N E. Moreover, the increased information available to multinationals on both the availability of

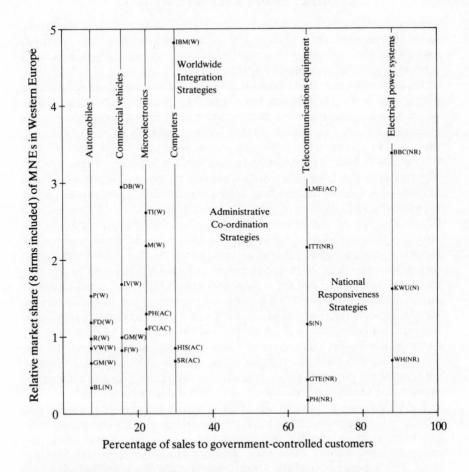

Figure legend (axes, as printed on the chart):

- Y-axis: Relative market share (8 firms included) of MNEs in Western Europe
- X-axis: Percentage of sales to government-controlled customers

Vertical column labels: Automobiles · Commercial vehicles · Microelectronics · Computers · Telecommunications equipment · Electrical power systems

Strategy zones: Worldwide Integration Strategies · Administrative Co-ordination Strategies · National Responsiveness Strategies

Data points:
IBM(W), DB(W), TI(W), M(W), IV(W), P(W), PH(AC), FD(W), FC(AC), R(W), GM(W), VW(W), F(W), GM(W), BL(N), HIS(AC), SR(AC), BBC(NR), LME(AC), ITT(NR), KWU(N), S(N), WH(NR), GTE(NR), PH(NR)

Types of Strategies are indicated next to company initials:
w = Worldwide (or regional) integration; AC = Administrative co-ordination;
NR = National responsiveness; N = National company.

Company names are represented by initials:

P = Peugeot S.A.	M = Motorola	ITT = International Telegraph & Telephone
FD = Ford of Europe	PH = Philips	
R = Renault	FC = Fairchild	S = Siemens
VW = Volkswagen	IBM = International Business Machines	GTE = General Telephone & Electronics
GM = General Motors		
BL = British Leyland	HIS = Honeywell Information Systems	BBC = Brown Boveri
DB = Daimler Benz		KWU = Kraftwerk Union
IV = IVECO	SR = Sperry Rand	WH = Westinghouse
F = Ford	LME = LM Ericsson	TI = Texas Instruments

Figure 2. Customers, market shares and multinational strategies. Source: Y. Doz, 'Strategic management in multinational companies', *Sloan Management Review*, vol.21, no.2, Winter 1980, p.34.

locations and on the performance experience of others in these locations, has made the market much less imperfect than it was in the 1960s. For these and many other reasons a thoroughly professional and efficient industrial attraction machine is essential for Scotland during the 1980s.

To date only some of these trends have been recognised and reflected at operational level. Deficiencies have been long recognised but the pace at which Scotland has travelled to its present institutional arrangements for attracting fdi has been painfully slow. The conditions of the 1960s were presumed to prevail in the 1980s – clearly they did not. This whole question was initially debated by the Committee on Scottish Affairs in August 1980.[26] The report of this Committee drew attention to the need for progress in a number of areas, not least in more effective information generation, and in the planning and targeting of the Scottish attraction efforts. In addition, the Committee argued that priority should be given to the coordination of the efforts of the variety of authorities involved in 'selling Scotland' to potential foreign investors. While presenting some sound analysis of the problems, this report was lean both on coherent recommendations to tackle the problems it diagnosed and in the prescription of credible action which would alleviate these difficulties.[27] The Government response to these recommendations was published in March 1981 and, fortunately, avoided much of the most damaging advice given to it by the Committee. The document led to the establishment of Locate in Scotland (LIS), and was designed to lay the basis for Scottish fdi attraction activity in the early 1980s.[28] Established to coordinate the Scottish effort and take a strong lead, LIS presented an opportunity to tackle the new conditions. But did it go far enough?

The Government's perceptions of the activities of LIS were apparently of a body whose responsibilities for inward investment were concerned with two main issues – namely promotion and negotiation. While these are necessary, they are not sufficient as functions to be performed at Scottish level. The presumption of the Government in March 1981 appeared to be that all the more strategic functions relating to the attraction of inward investment namely, information on fdi flows by country, sector, etc.; planning and targeting; monitoring and evaluation would ultimately reside at national level. While it is highly desirable that some of these do have a national focus (in that, for example, monitoring over a multi-plant network needs many resources), such developments are in effect unlikely. The second-best solution, therefore, is for more widespread regional initiatives which extend into planning and targeting on a truly Scottish scale and into the monitoring of the developments in European strategy at least within the major corporations. It is in this area arguably that the existence of the Scottish Development Agency and of LIS, operating from within the Agency, offers a distinctive opportunity for some consistent sectoral policy. The juxtaposition of major sectoral analysis and the planning, promotion and monitoring of fdi would, if effectively coordinated, provide considerable competitive advantages for Scotland. The two have, however, to be strongly linked and extended to examine the activities of the existing companies as well as potential investors. Thus even while at UK level there may be little interest in the matching of industrial and fdi policies, LIS and the SDA do offer the possibilities that this could be achieved in Scotland.

The possibilities are indeed there, but there are real barriers to their realisation. First, some of these concern the short-term credibility of the LIS effort. A clear plan is required from LIS if the appropriate leadership is to be given to other organisations and authorities concerned with industrial development in Scotland. Coordinating random efforts will not in itself be enough. Aggregating much unplanned activity will not constitute a plan for action. Closely allied to this point is the second potential barrier, namely the local authorities and New Towns, both of whom are charged with industrial attraction responsibilities. They can be coerced into cooperation but it would be better if this was not necessary. They have skills and experience which are vital to the success of the LIS project. The third barrier is whether those directing LIS will extend its operations into information, monitoring and evaluative activity. There is much to be gained from systematic back-room activity in these areas, which is directed to identifying expansion opportunities and leading to more effective field work. The temptation for LIS is to indulge in too many missions in order to be seen to be active. Back-up activity of the highest quality is required as part of the development of the Scottish product. LIS has to be a strategic and planning-centred activity which is built on the premise that achieving inward investment is now a difficult and a long-term exercise. It requires systematic segmentation of the various markets concerned and a dogged pursuit of all opportunities. The fourth set of barriers concerns the level of consistency of political support for this effort. There have already been signs that a number of UK departments are wholly convinced that much inward investment activity could be readily centralised without any deterioration in the net UK results. There is a case for this with respect to certain, but by no means all, functions. Conversely, there is plenty of evidence that an effective balance of regional and national effort provides both the focus and commitment so necessary for effective industrial promotion. In the case of Scotland there are no grounds for believing that (as some would advocate) the Foreign and Common-wealth Office is unilaterally capable of promoting industrial development overseas and that all LIS offices abroad should be closed. The general skills of diplomacy, however commercialised, are not those required to mount this effort in the 1980s. The various functions are clearly outside of the expertise of such staff. Simply because of the costs involved, the sensitivity of these issues and the problems of monitoring such effort at a distance, the LIS overseas offices are likely to be before the public eye on many occasions. The moral for LIS and the SDA is to coordinate their effectiveness and make the Scottish fdi effort as efficient as possible. There are formidable, but not impossible, problems for LIS to solve before it can be an effective promotional body. Promotion is, nevertheless, but one of its desired functions. As this book has shown so clearly, at least as much attention must be paid to stemming the multinational retreat and, more optimistically, to encouraging existing companies to locate expansions in Scotland.

It was noted in the previous paragraph that strategy and planning were essential for a modern LIS-type activity. This requires a build-up of knowledge about the developments in key sectors and in key companies. The latter implies monitoring of the strategies of the existing foreign companies within Scotland; and it involves understanding the threats and opportunities to their Scottish and European operations. There are both positive and negative reasons for undertaking such exercises. Early warning of problems is obviously desirable, but equally desirable is the advanced warning of new projects and expansion plans. In the case of the defensive aspects of monitoring, what this book has revealed is that many foreign-owned companies are as vulnerable as any other type of firm to misreading market trends and failing to invest in new products, to management failures and so forth. Nor are all multinationals sophisticated companies by international standards. Some of their problems could be alleviated by regular discussions and, most importantly, positive initiatives by LIS; and, on occasions, by pooling UK private and public sector resources at the correct time. In order to make this type of activity effective, it has to be paralleled by good sectoral support work. Information, monitoring and evaluative work are thus inseparable parts of an effective inward investment agency and every effort should be made to bring these together as part of LIS. This implies LIS operating at the boundaries of its remit and at the edge of its relationship with UK Government departments. The demands of flexibility and authority make this necessary, if an effective Scottish-based operation is to be maintained, but there is ample scope for many of these recommendations to be implemented without adjusting the LIS remit.

It should be clear from the issues examined in this book that it would be futile to expect any policy initiatives to insulate Scotland from the processes of change in the MNE sector. Faced, therefore, with substantially diminished expectations from multinationals, the policy focus in Scotland has at least to be balanced by increased efforts in other industrial sectors. In formulating such a strategy, the following are important and are ranked in order of priority:

1) Much more emphasis will have to be placed on the development of indigenous industry. It would be simplistic to suggest that this is easy, given the evidence that as such companies expand so their ownership changes. Nor can such policies of development be insular; they must encourage a greater level of internationalisation on the part of such companies, involving exporting, licensing, joint ventures and total ownership of overseas production capacity. Nor should such policies over-emphasise the micro firm, where, if anything, too many resources have been directed in recent years. In looking to the expansion and development of middle ranking indigenous enterprises, there is considerable scope for greater mobilisation of the Scottish international investment and financial expertise which exists

in the private sector. Above all, what is required is a climate for the encouragement of indigenous entrepreneurial activity and the adoption of contemporary technology. It is fairly clear that the recent levels of profitability in many indigenous companies will preclude high levels of investment unless significant corporate financial restructuring takes place first. Many are already far behind in the field of technology; fortunately others are at the forefront.

2) At all levels and in all sectors, the encouragement of good performance is crucial. There is little question that investment flows, from whatever source, are influenced by performance records, especially in multi-plant companies. Most industry located in Scotland is in this category. Corporate experience in this area ranges across the spectrum, from the superb to the appalling. There are many shades of grey in this area, with management, innovation, product mix and investment levels being among the variables playing a part in determining performance. However, perhaps the single most significant contribution to the industrial health of Scotland would be to improve the relative performance of all Scottish plants within multi-plant networks. If this is accepted, there are lessons for the thrust of effort from the S D A and other government agencies.

3) It remains important to have a healthy and more stable M N E sector in Scotland, especially one which is fuelled by new entrants in greenfield sites and has a wide industrial mix within it. Unrealistic job targets should not be set for it either in terms of absolute numbers or annual job creation. To do so is, and has been, diversionary. On this basis it must be acknowledged that a high level of organisational efficiency will be required even to maintain the foreign-owned sector at its reduced 1981 size; indeed the prescriptions earlier in this section should be regarded as the minimum necessary for such a strategy.

NOTES AND REFERENCES

1. A useful summary of these in the earlier period is provided in Chapter 2 of G. Denton, S.O. Cleireacain and S. Ash, *Trade Effects of Public Subsidies to Private Enterprise*, published for Trade Policy Research Centre, Macmillan (London) 1975.
2. A matter which has invoked comment from many quarters. See, for example, A. Knight, 'Government intervention: its impact on the textile industry', *Journal of General Management*, vol.3, no.1, Autumn 1975; M. Edwardes, 'A new industrial strategy for the United Kingdom', *Long Range Planning*, vol.10, no.3, June 1977.
3. B. Chiplin and M. Wright, 'Divestment and structural change in U K industry', *National Westminster Quarterly Review*, February 1980.
4. For an interesting summary of these issues, see F. Blackaby, 'Exchange-rate policy and economic strategy', *Three Banks Review*, no.126, June 1980.
5. Of course, high exchange rates in themselves are not the only issue. For a useful review of this matter, see D. Higham, 'Strong currencies and

economic performance: lessons from Germany, Japan and Switzerland', *Three Banks Review*, no.130, June 1981.

6. For a much fuller examination of this issue, see J. Marquand, *Measuring the Effects and Costs of Regional Incentives*, Government Economic Service Working Paper no.32, February 1980.

7. As recently reviewed in *The Effects of Investment Incentives and Disincentives on the International Investment Process*, Committee on International Investment and Multinational Enterprises, OECD (Paris), 1981

8. A more exhaustive coverage of the setting in which UK policy has operated is provided in N. Hood & S. Young, 'British policy and inward direct investment', *Journal of World Trade Law*, vol.15, no.3, 1981.

9. 'Mrs Thatcher v. IBM', *The Economist*, 21 November 1981, p.34.

10. *Financial Times*, 21 April 1981.

11. 'Hitachi was chased away', *The Economist*, 19 December 1977.

12. Recently considered in I.C. Magaziner & T.M. Hont, *Japanese Industrial Policy*, Policy Studies Institute, no.585, January 1980.

13. P. Mottershead, 'Industrial policy' in F. Blackaby (ed.), *Deindustrialisation*, Heinemann (London) 1979, p.483.

14. This is usefully presented in C.J.F. Brown, 'Industrial policy and economic planning in Japan and France', *National Institute Economic Review*, no.93, August 1980.

15. A. Singh, 'UK industry and the world economy – a case of deindustrialisation', *Cambridge Journal of Economics*, no.1, 1977.

16. A number of which are expounded in J. Pinder, T. Hosomi, W. Diebold, *Industrial Policy and the International Economy*, The Triangle Papers no.19, The Trilateral Commission (New York) 1979, pp.8–11.

17. W. Diebold, Jr, *Industrial Policy as an International Issue*, McGraw-Hill (New York) 1980, p.250.

18. S.J. Warnecke and E.N. Suleiman, *Industrial Policies in Western Europe*, Praeger (New York) 1975, p.7.

19. This is, of course, not always obvious when the formal provisions of various national schemes are evaluated. For the most comprehensive exercise of this kind, see D. Yuill and K. Allen (eds), *European Regional Incentives: 1981*, Centre for the Study of Public Policy, University of Strathclyde (Glasgow) 1981.

20. For an interesting review of Japanese policy, see R.S. Ozaki, *Control of Imports and Foreign Capital in Japan*, Praeger (New York) 1972.

21. The Hood & Young study for the Scottish Economic Planning Department was extended to look in more depth at a smaller sample of 30 of the largest US multinationals. The findings were published in S. Young & N. Hood, 'The strategies of US multinationals in Europe', *Multinational Business*, no.2, 1980.

22. The work undertaken by Doz, Prahalad & Bartlett has been widely published. Some of the directly relevant pieces are referred to below.

23. This is by no means confined to US multinationals. See, for example, L.G. Franko, *The European Multinationals*, Greylock (Stamford, Conn.) 1976.

24. Y.L. Doz, 'Strategic management in multinational companies', *Sloan Management Review*, Winter 1980. See also Y.L. Doz, C.A. Bartlett & C.K. Prahalad, 'Global competitive pressures and host country demands', *Californian Management Review*, vol.XXIII, no.3, 1981.

25. Doz, op. cit., p.29.

26. Second Report from the Committee on Scottish Affairs, Session 1979–80, *Inward Investment*, vol.2, HC769-I, HMSO (London) 1980.

27. The present authors expressed these views to the Government in a memorandum published as, *Inward Direct Investment in Scotland After the Select Committee: A Critique and A Way Ahead*, Strathclyde Business School, Working Paper Series, no.8005, November 1980.
28. First Special Report from the Committee on Scottish Affairs, Session 1980–81, *Inward Investment: The Government's Reply to the Committee's Second Report of Session 1979–80*, HC205, HMSO (London) 1981.

INDEX